GPU Pro⁷

Advanced Rendering Techniques

GPU Pro⁷

Advanced Rendering Techniques

Edited by Wolfgang Engel

CRC Press
Taylor & Francis Group
Boca Raton London New York

CRC Press is an imprint of the
Taylor & Francis Group, an **informa** business

AN A K PETERS BOOK

CRC Press
Taylor & Francis Group
6000 Broken Sound Parkway NW, Suite 300
Boca Raton, FL 33487-2742

First issued in hardback 2019

© 2016 by Taylor & Francis Group, LLC
CRC Press is an imprint of Taylor & Francis Group, an Informa business

No claim to original U.S. Government works

ISBN-13: 978-1-4987-4253-5 (hbk)

Library of Congress Cataloging-in-Publication Data

Names: Engel, Wolfgang.
Title: GPU pro 7 : advanced rendering techniques / edited by Wolfgang Engel.
Description: Boca Raton : CRC Press, Taylor & Francis Group, [2016] |
Includes bibliographical references and index.
Identifiers: LCCN 2016000447 | ISBN 9781498742535 (alk. paper)
Subjects: LCSH: Computer graphics. | Rendering (Computer graphics) |
Real-time data processing. | Digital video. | Graphics processing
units--Programming.
Classification: LCC T385 .G68876 2016 | DDC 006.6/6--dc23
    LC record available at http://lccn.loc.gov/2016000447

Visit the Taylor & Francis Web site at
http://www.taylorandfrancis.com

and the CRC Press Web site at
http://www.crcpress.com

Contents

III   Rendering   129
Christopher Oat

IV   Mobile Devices   173
Marius Bjørge

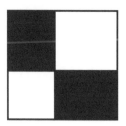

Acknowledgments

The *GPU Pro: Advanced Rendering Techniques* book series covers ready-to-use ideas and procedures that can help to solve many of your daily graphics programming challenges.

The seventh book in the series wouldn't have been possible without the help of many people. First, I would like to thank the section editors for the fantastic job they did. The work of Wessam Bahnassi, Marius Bjørge, Michal Valient, and Christopher Oat ensured that the quality of the series meets the expectations of our readers.

The great cover screenshots were contributed by Wade Brainerd and Christer Ericson from Activision. They are from *Call of Duty: Advanced Warfare* and are courtesy Activision, Sledgehammer Games.

The team at CRC Press made the whole project happen. I want to thank Rick Adams, Charlotte Byrnes, Kari Budyk, and the entire production team, who took the articles and made them into a book.

Special thanks goes out to our families and friends, who spent many evenings and weekends without us during the long book production cycle.

I hope you have as much fun reading the book as we had creating it.

—Wolfgang Engel

P.S. Plans for an upcoming *GPU Pro 8* are already in progress. Any comments, proposals, and suggestions are highly welcome (wolfgang.engel@gmail.com).

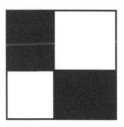

Web Materials

Example programs and source code to accompany some of the chapters are available on the CRC Press website: go to http://www.crcpress.com/product/isbn/9781498742535 and click on the "Downloads" tab.

The directory structure closely follows the book structure by using the chapter numbers as the name of the subdirectory.

General System Requirements

- The DirectX June 2010 SDK (the latest SDK is installed with Visual Studio 2012).

- DirectX 11 or DirectX 12 capable GPU are required to run the examples. The article will mention the exact requirement.

- The OS should be Microsoft Windows 10, following the requirement of DirectX 11 or 12 capable GPUs.

- Visual Studio C++ 2012 (some examples might require older versions).

- 2GB RAM or more.

- The latest GPU driver.

Updates

Updates of the example programs will be posted on the website.

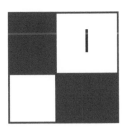

Geometry Manipulation

This section of *GPU Pro* contains two chapters that describe rendering techniques used in recent games to enrich the environment and increase the visual quality.

The section begins with a chapter by Anton Kai Michels and Peter Sikachev, who describe the procedural snow deformation rendering in *Rise of the Tomb Raider*. Their deferred deformation is used to render trails with depression at the center and elevation on the edges, allowing gradual refilling of the snow tracks, but it can also easily be extended to handle other procedural interactions with the environment. The technique is scalable and memory friendly and provides centimeter-accurate deformations. It decouples the deformation logic from the geometry that is actually affected and thus can handle dozens of NPCs and works on any type of terrain.

The second chapter in this section deals with Catmull-Clark subdivision surfaces widely used in film production and more recently also in video games because of their intuitive authoring and surfaces with nice properties. They are defined by bicubic B-spline patches obtained from a recursively subdivided control mesh of arbitrary topology. Wade Brainerd describes a real-time method for rendering such subdivision surfaces, which has been used for the key assets in *Call of Duty* on the Playstation 4 and runs at FullHD at 60 frames per second.

—Carsten Dachsbacher

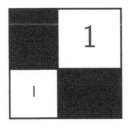

Deferred Snow Deformation in *Rise of the Tomb Raider*

Anton Kai Michels and Peter Sikachev

1.1 Introduction

Procedural snow deformation is one of the defining graphical features in the *Rise of the Tomb Raider*. (See Figure 1.1.) It creates a discernable connection between Lara and her environment while serving as a key gameplay element, allowing the titular Tomb Raider to track her targets while remaining hidden from sight. At

Figure 1.1. Deformable snow in *Rise of the Tomb Raider*. [Image courtesy of Square Enix Ltd.]

the core of this technology is a novel technique called *deferred deformation*, which decouples the deformation logic from the geometry it affects. This approach can scale with dozens of NPCs, has a low memory footprint of 4 MB, and can be easily altered to handle a vast variety of procedural interactions with the environment. This chapter aims to provide the reader with sufficient theoretical and practical knowledge to implement deferred deformation in a real-time 3D application.

Procedural terrain deformation has remained an open problem in real-time rendering applications, with past solutions failing to provide a convincing level of detail or doing so with a very rigid set of constraints. Deferred deformation delivers a scalable, low-memory, centimeter-accurate solution that works on any type of terrain and with any number of deformable meshes. It renders not only the depression in the trail center but also elevation on the trail edges and allows for gradual refilling of snow tracks to emulate blizzard-like conditions.

Some terminology used in this publication with regards to snow trails and deformation will be outlined in Section 1.2. Section 1.3 then takes a look at past approaches, where they succeeded and why they were ultimately not suitable for *Rise of the Tomb Raider*. Section 1.4 outlines a simple, straightforward algorithm for rendering snow deformation that will serve as a prelude to deferred deformation in Section 1.5, which elaborates on the core ideas behind the technique and the use of compute shaders to achieve it. Section 1.6 details the deformation heightmap used in our algorithm and how it behaves like a sliding window around the player. Section 1.7 explains how the snow tracks fill over time to emulate blizzard-like conditions. Section 1.8 covers the use of adaptive hardware tessellation and the performance benefits gained from it. Finally, Section 1.9 discusses alternate applications of this technique and its future potential.

1.2   Terminology

Here is a collection of terms used throughout the article (see Figure 1.2):

- Snow height: The vertical coordinate (in our case `vertex.z`) of the snow prior to any deformation.

- Deformation points: 3D points estimating Lara's feet and other objects that cause deformation.

- Foot height: The vertical height of a deformation point (`point.z`).

- Trail depression: The part of the trail that is stomped down and is lower than the original snow height.

- Trail elevation: The small bump along the edges of the trail caused from pushing snow out of the way.

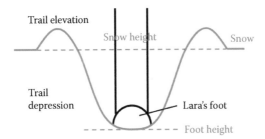

Figure 1.2. The various components of a snow trail.

- Deformation heightmap: Single 32-bit texture, 1024×1024 pixels, that stores the deformation.

- Depression depth: abs(snow height − foot height).

- Deformation shader: Compute shader used to output the deformation to the heightmap.

- Fill shader: Compute shader used to fill snow tracks during a blizzard.

- Snow shader: The shader used for objects with deformable snow material.

1.3 Related Work

Deformation from dynamic objects is a key component in making snow look believable in 3D applications. The following two titles took very different approaches in this regard, each with its own advantages and disadvantages.

1.3.1 Assassin's Creed III

As a Playstation 3 and Xbox 360 title, *Assassin's Creed III* could not make use of Shader Model 5.0 features like compute shaders and hardware tessellation for the console version of the game. Instead, a render-to-vertex-buffer trick was used to create tessellated triangles at runtime using the GPU, with the limitation that all triangles created this way must have the same tessellation factor. These tessellated triangles are then pushed down using a geometrical approximation of the character's movement [St-Amour 13].

Advantages of this technique include the creation of persistent tracks on a large scale and support of various terrain (forests, slopes, etc.). The disadvantages are a lack of support for filling the trails in snowy conditions and not producing an elevation along the trail edges. This technique also requires encoding the maximum possible deformation in snow mesh vertices to avoid pushing the snow below the terrain, a further drawback.

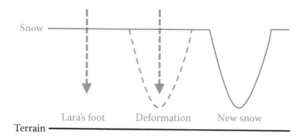

Figure 1.3. Basic snow deformation uses the snow and the terrain height to clamp the deformation height when it is rendered.

1.3.2 Batman: Arkham Origins

The most recent AAA title using procedural snow deformation, *Batman: Arkham Origins*, takes place in an urban environment devoid of slopes and terrain and thus uses rectangular rooftop meshes for its deformable snow. These rectangular boxes form orthogonal view frustums into which dynamic objects affecting the snow are rendered. The resulting render target is used as a heightmap to displace the vertices of the snow mesh [Barré-Brisebois 14].

   This technique leverages the rendering pipeline to create very accurate snow deformation, which is enhanced by GPU tessellation on DirectX 11–compatible hardware. Filling tracks during a snowstorm is also supported. The disadvantage is that this technique is unusable for anything other than flat rectangular surfaces. And like *Assassin's Creed III*, it does not produce elevation along the trail edges.

1.4   Snow Deformation: The Basic Approach

Consider a terrain mesh, a snow mesh on top of it, and a number of dynamic objects deforming the snow. One approach to rendering the snow deformation is to first render the terrain and snow meshes from a bird's-eye view into two separate heightmaps, then render the dynamic objects or some approximation of these objects into a deformation heightmap and clamp the rendered values between the terrain and snow height. Finally, the deformation heightmap is sampled when rendering the snow to displace vertices and calculate normals (Figure 1.3).

   The simplicity of this approach has several drawbacks. First is the need to gather all necessary terrain and snow meshes and render them from a bird's-eye view. Second is that each dynamic object affecting the snow requires its own draw call. Both of these problems are solved with deferred deformation, as shown in the next section.

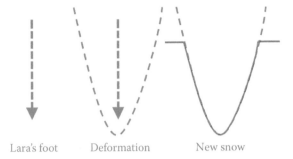

Figure 1.4. Deferred deformation forgoes the initial use of the snow and terrain height and instead clamps the deformation height during the snow rendering.

1.5   Deferred Deformation

The idea behind deferred deformation is as follows: during the snow render pass, the snow height is already provided by the vertices of the snow mesh. There is therefore no need to pre-render the snow mesh into a heightmap, and the deformation height can be clamped when it is sampled instead of when it is rendered. This allows the heightmap to be rendered with an approximate deformation using the dynamic objects only. The exact deformation is calculated later during the actual rendering of the snow, hence the term *deferred deformation* (Figure 1.4). Note that it is important to pass the original snow height from the snow vertex shader to the snow pixel shader for per-pixel normals. (See Listing 1.1 for an overview of the deferred deformation algorithm.)

```
Deformation Shader (compute shader)
  affected_pixels = calculate_deformation(dynamic_object)
Fill Shader (compute shader)
  all_pixels += snow_fill_rate
Snow Shader
  Snow Vertex Shader
    snow_height = vertex.Z
    deformation_height = sample_deformation_heightmap()
    vertex.Z = min(snow_height, deformation_heightmap)
    pixel_input.snow_height = snow_height
  Snow Pixel Shader
    snow_height = pixel_input.snow_height
    deformation_height = sample_deformation_heightmap()
    calculate_deformed_normal()
```

Listing 1.1. Deferred deformation algorithm overview.

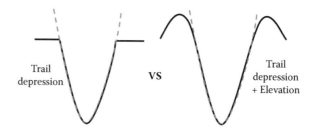

Figure 1.5. It is desirable to add an elevation along the edges of the trail to enhance the overall look.

1.5.1 Rendering the Deformation Heightmap

A key insight during the development of the deferred deformation algorithm was observing that the desired trail shape closely resembles a quadratic curve. By approximating dynamic objects with points, the deformation height around these points can be calculated as follows:

$$\text{deformation height} = \text{point height} + (\text{distance to point})^2 \times \text{artist's scale}.$$

These deformation points are accumulated into a global buffer, and the deformation shader is dispatched with one group for each point. The groups write in a 32^2 pixel area ($1.64\ \text{m}^2$) around the deformation points and output the deformation height of the affected pixels using an atomic minimum. This atomic minimum is necessary as several deformation points can affect overlapping pixels in the heightmap. Since the only unordered access view (UAV) types that allow atomic operations in DirectX 11 are 32-bit integer types, our deformation heightmap UAV is an `R32_UINT`.

1.5.2 Trail Elevation

What has been described thus far is sufficient to render snow trails with depression, but not trails with both depression and elevation (Figure 1.5). Elevation can occur when the deformation height exceeds the snow height, though using this difference alone is not enough. The foot height must also be taken into account, as a foot height greater than the snow height signifies no depression, and therefore no trail and no elevation (Figure 1.6). For this reason the foot height is also stored in the deformation texture using the least significant 16 bits (Figure 1.7). It is important that the deformation height remain in the most significant 16 bits for the atomic minimum used in the deformation shader. Should the snow shader sample a foot height that is above the vertex height, it early outs of the deformation and renders the snow untouched.

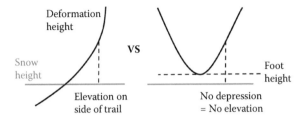

Figure 1.6. The deformation height alone is not enough to know if there is elevation. The foot height is also needed.

Figure 1.7. Bit allocation scheme used for the deformation heightmap.

1.5.3 Calculating the Elevation

Constructing the elevation first requires the elevation distance, i.e., the distance between the start of the elevation and the point being rendered (Figure 1.8). To calculate the elevation distance, the following variables are introduced (see Figure 1.9 for a detailed illustration):

- Depression distance: the distance between the center of the deformation and the end of the depression.

- Distance from foot: the distance between the center of the deformation and the point being rendered. Note that this is the sum of the depression distance and the elevation distance.

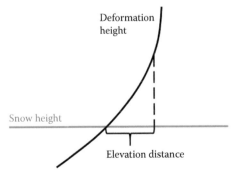

Figure 1.8. The elevation distance at a given point is the distance between that point and the start of the elevation.

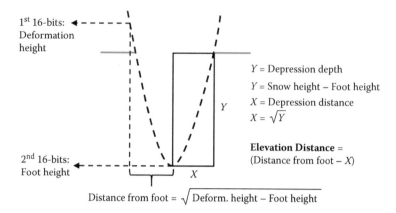

Figure 1.9. Illustration of the various calculations involved in rendering the elevation.

The above values are calculated as follows:

$$\text{depression distance} = \sqrt{\text{snow height} - \text{foot height}},$$

$$\text{distance from foot} = \sqrt{\text{deformation height} - \text{foot height}},$$

$$\text{distance from foot} = \text{depression distance} + \text{elevation distance},$$

$$\text{elevation distance} = \text{distance from foot} - \text{depression distance}.$$

The elevation should scale with the depth of the trail—deeper trails produce greater elevation along the trail edges because more snow is being displaced. The depression depth is therefore used to calculate a maximum elevation distance using a linear function with an artist-driven scale. Knowing the elevation distance and the maximum elevation distance, we can compute an elevation ratio and pass this ratio into a quadratic function to get a smooth, round elevation on the edges of the trail:.

$$\text{ratio} = \frac{\text{elevation distance}}{\text{max. elevation distance}},$$

$$\text{height} = \text{max. elevation distance} \times \text{artist's scale},$$

$$\text{elevation} = ((0.5 - 2 \times \text{ratio})^2 + 1) \times \text{height}.$$

1.5.4   Texture Selection

To give deformed snow a more disorderly and chaotic look, different snow textures are applied to different parts of the deformation. A smooth texture selection value between 0 and 2 is generated to choose between the textures. (See Figure 1.10.) The value 0 corresponds to the center of the trail, the value 1 corresponds to the

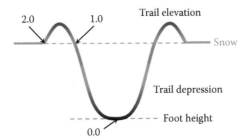

Figure 1.10. Different textures are used for the trail using a generated selection value between 0 and 2.

end of the depression and start of the elevation, and the value 2 corresponds to undeformed snow after the elevation. Artists fetch this value in *Rise of the Tomb Raider*'s shader node system and use it to dynamically select the desired textures. The texture selection variable is calculated using the depression distance, maximum elevation distance, and distance from foot variables.

1.6 Deformation Heightmap

The deformation heightmap is a 32-bit 1024×1024 texture (4 MB) with a resolution of 4 cm per pixel, covering an area of 40.96 m^2 centered on Lara. The texture holds two 16-bit values (deformation height and foot height). It is created as an R16G16_TYPELESS texture and given an R16G16_UNORM shader resource view (SRV) and an R32_UINT UAV (needed for the atomic minimum in the compute shader).

1.6.1 Sliding Window Heightmap

In order to keep the area of deformation centered on Lara, the deformation heightmap acts as a sliding window around her position. As Lara moves, the pixels of the heightmap that fall out of range are repurposed as the new pixels that have fallen into range. The implementation of this feature falls into two parts: reading and writing. In both cases, points out of range of the deformation area centered on Lara cause an early out for the shader to prevent tiling. (See also Figure 1.11.)

- Reading: In order to read from a sliding window texture, it is sufficient to scale world-space coordinates to match the texture resolution and then use them as UVs with a wrap sampler. Tiling is prevented with the early out mentioned above.

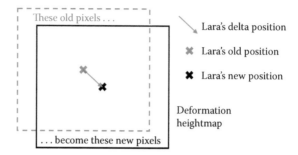

Figure 1.11. The deformation heightmap acts as a sliding window to keep the snow deformation area centered on Lara.

```
float2 Modulus(float2 WorldPos, float2 TexSize) {
  return WorldPos - (TexSize * floor(WorldPos/TexSize));
}
```

Listing 1.2. Modulus function for the compute shader.

- Writing: Writing to a sliding window heightmap is possible with the use of compute shaders and unordered access views. The deformation shader writes in 32×32 pixel areas around the deformation points, with the output pixels calculated at runtime. In order for the deformation shader to work with a sliding window texture, the calculations of these output pixels use the modulus function in Listing 1.2, which acts in the same way a wrap sampler would.

1.6.2   Overlapping Deformable Meshes

Despite the use of a single heightmap, deferred deformation allows for vertically overlapping snow meshes, i.e., deformable snow on a bridge and deformable snow under a bridge. This is accomplished by overriding the heightmap deformation in the deformation shader if the newly calculated deformation differs by more than a certain amount (in our case, 2 m), regardless of whether it is higher or lower than the existing deformation. The snow shader then early outs if the sampled foot height differs too greatly from the snow height (again 2 m in our case). Thus, snow deformation on a bridge will be ignored by snow under the bridge because the foot height is too high, and deformation under the bridge will be ignored by the snow on the bridge because the foot height is too low.

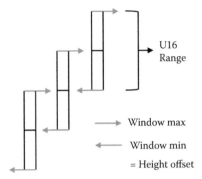

Figure 1.12. The vertical range of the snow deformation dynamically adjusts with Lara's position. This allows us to increase the precision of the deformation height and foot height stored in the deformation heightmap.

1.6.3   Vertical Sliding Window

Working with 16-bit values and extracting a sufficient level of precision from them means limiting their effective range. To overcome this problem, deferred deformation employs a vertical sliding window technique for the deformation heightmap (Figure 1.12). At any given time, the snow deformation has a minimum global height. This is used as an offset when the deformation heightmap is rendered and sampled. Whenever Lara goes below this height offset, the sliding window shifts down by half the window frame. Whenever she climbs above the window's maximum height, the sliding window shifts up by half a frame. The reason half a frame is used as the increment/decrement value is to avoid cases where minor changes in Lara's position will cause the window to switch back and forth. Whenever the sliding window shifts up or down, half the range is also added/subtracted to the global fill rate (Section 1.7) for that frame, bringing the heightmap values in accordance with the new height offset.

1.7   Filling the Trail over Time

Snow deformation in *Rise of the Tomb Raider* emulates blizzard-like conditions by filling the snow tracks over time. For this, a second compute shader called the *fill shader* is dispatched with 1024^2 threads to cover the entire heightmap. This fill shader increases the value of each pixel by a global fill rate. It is not sufficient, however, to only increase the deformation height, as this will cause the elevations on the trail edges to move inward, giving a weird and unnatural result. Separate fill rates for both the deformation height and the foot height are required to remedy this, with manual adjustments needed to attain convincing results.

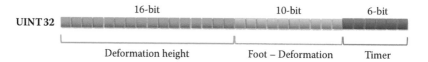

Figure 1.13. Exponential edge erase provides a much smoother finish to the trails over a more simple approach.

Figure 1.14. New bit allocation scheme used for the deformation heightmap.

1.7.1   Erasing the Edges of the Sliding Window

A key component in the sliding window functionality is erasing the pixels along the edge of the sliding window. A straightforward way to do this is by resetting the values of the pixels to `UINT32_MAX` along the row and the column of the pixels farthest away from Lara's position (use the `Modulus` function in Listing 1.2 to calculate this row and column). The downside to this approach is that it will create very abrupt lines in the snow trails along the edges of the sliding window, something the player will notice if they decide to backtrack.

Instead of erasing one row and one column, a better solution is to take eight rows and eight columns along the sliding window border and apply a function that exponentially increases the snow fill rate for these pixels. This will end the trails with a nice upward curve that looks far more natural (Figure 1.13).

1.7.2   Reset Timer

Filling trails over time conflicts with the ability to have vertically overlapping snow meshes. If a trail under a bridge fills over time, it will eventually create a trail on top of the bridge. However, this will only happen if the initial trail is filled for a long time. A per-pixel timer was therefore implemented to reset deformation after a set period. This period is long enough to allow for the deep tracks to fill completely and short enough to prevent overlapping snow meshes from interfering with each other. Once the timer reaches its maximum value, the pixel is reset to `UINT32_MAX`.

The implementation of this timer uses the least significant 6 bits of the foot height in the deformation heightmap (Figure 1.13). This leaves the foot height with only 10 bits (Figure 1.14). To compensate for the lost precision, the heightmap does not store the foot height but rather the deformation height minus the foot height. The foot height is then reconstructed in the snow shader.

Figure 1.15. High-poly snow mesh without tessellation. Normal pass: 3.07 ms. Composite pass: 2.55 ms.

1.8 Hardware Tessellation and Performance

With deferred deformation, the cost shifts from rendering the deformation heightmap to reconstructing the depression and elevation during the snow render pass. Because these calculations involve multiple square roots and divisions, the snow vertex shader's performance takes a significant hit. This makes statically tessellated, high-poly snow meshes prohibitively expensive (offscreen triangles and detail far from the camera are a big part of this cost). (See Figure 1.15.)

Much of this cost is alleviated with adaptive tessellation and a reduced vertex count on the snow meshes. The tessellation factors are computed in image space, with a maximum factor of 10. Frustum culling is done in the hull shader, though back-face culling is left out because the snow is mostly flat. Derivative maps [Mikkelsen 11] are used to calculate the normals in order to reduce the vertex memory footprint, which is crucial for fast tessellation. Further performance is gained by using Michał Drobot's ShaderFastMathLib [Drobot 14], without any noticeable decrease in quality or precision. (See Figure 1.16.)

The timings for the fill shader and deformation shader are 0.175 ms and 0.011 ms, respectively, on Xbox One.

1.9 Future Applications

Given that our deferred deformation technique does not care about the geometry it deforms, the same deformation heightmap can be repurposed for a wide variety of uses (for example, mud, sand, dust, grass, etc.). Moreover, if the desired deformation does not require any kind of elevation, the technique becomes all the more simple to integrate. We therefore hope to see this technique adopted, adapted, and improved in future AAA titles.

Figure 1.16. High-poly snow mesh with tessellation. Normal pass: 1.60 ms. Composite pass: 1.14 ms.

1.10   Acknowledgments

We would like to thank the guys from the Labs team at Eidos Montreal, Nixxes Software, and Crystal Dynamics for their help in implementing this feature in *Rise of the Tomb Raider*.

Bibliography

[Barré-Brisebois 14] Colin Barré-Brisebois. "Deformable Snow Rendering in *Batman: Arkham Origins*." Presented at Game Developers Conference 2014, San Francisco, CA, March 17–21, 2014.

[Drobot 14] Michał Drobot. "ShaderFastMathLib." *GitHub*, https://github.com/michaldrobot/ShaderFastLibs/blob/master/ShaderFastMathLib.h, 2014.

[Mikkelsen 11] Morten Mikkelsen. "Derivative Maps." *Mikkelsen and 3D Graphics*, http://mmikkelsen3d.blogspot.com/2011/07/derivative-maps.html, 2011.

[St-Amour 13] Jean-François St-Amour. "Rendering Assassin's Creed III." Presented at Game Developers Conference 2013, San Francisco, CA, March 25–29, 2013.

2

Catmull-Clark
Subdivision Surfaces
Wade Brainerd

2.1 Introduction

Catmull-Clark subdivision surfaces, or SubDs, are smooth surfaces defined by bicubic B-spline patches extracted from a recursively subdivided control mesh of arbitrary topology [Catmull and Clark 78]. SubDs are widely used in animated film production and have recently been used in games [Brainerd 14]. They are valued for their intuitive authoring tools and the quality of the resultant surface (Figure 2.1).

In recent years, research has advanced rapidly with respect to rendering subdivision surfaces on modern GPUs. Stanford University's survey [Nießner et al. ar] gives a comprehensive picture of the state of the art.

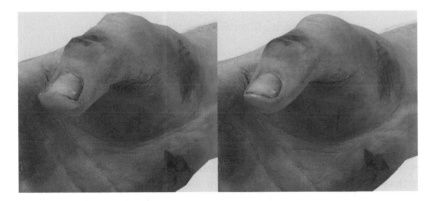

Figure 2.1. A hand modeled as a Catmull-Clark subdivision surface (right), with its corresponding control mesh on the left.

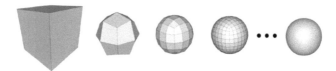

Figure 2.2. Several iterations of Catmull-Clark subdivision applied to a cube, with the eventual limit surface on the far right. Note that each corner is an extraordinary vertex.

In this chapter, we describe a real-time method for rendering subdivision surfaces that is utilized for key assets in *Call of Duty* titles, running in 1920×1080 resolution at 60 frames per second on Playstation 4 hardware. As long as the topology remains constant, our implementation allows the control mesh to deform and animate while being subdivided in real time and dynamically adapts the subdivision amount to the geometry curvature and the view.

2.1.1 Terminology

We provide definitions for a few basic and important terms. For a thorough survey of quad mesh terminology, refer to the 2013 survey by Bommes et al. [Bommes et al. 13].

control point A vertex that is used as a B-spline support.

control mesh A mesh consisting of control points, which defines a surface.

valence The number of edges around a face, or incident to a vertex.

regular vertex A vertex with valence 4.

extraordinary vertex A vertex with valence other than 4.

regular quad A quad in which all vertices are regular.

manifold mesh A mesh in which each edge is connected to either one or two faces, and the faces connected to each vertex form a continuous fan.

limit surface A smooth surface resulting from a Catmull-Clark subdivision.

2.1.2 Catmull-Clark Subdivision Surfaces

Catmull-Clark subdivision surfaces are a generalization of bicubic B-spline surfaces to arbitrary topology. Standard bicubic B-spline and NURBS surfaces require that control meshes be constructed from regular grids without extraordinary vertices. Careful stitching between grids is necessary to maintain smoothness. This can be inconvenient for artists, and the stitching does not always hold up well under animation.

Figure 2.3. A model rendered using feature adaptive subdivision. Red patches are regular in the control mesh, green patches after one subdivision, and so on. Tiny purple faces at the centers of rings are connected to the extraordinary vertices.

The method of Catmull and Clark solves this problem by finely subdividing the control mesh and extracting regular B-spline grids from the subdivided result. The subdivision rules are chosen to preserve the base B-spline surface for regular topology and to produce a smooth, aesthetically pleasing surface near extraordinary vertices. (See Figure 2.2.)

In theory, infinite subdivisions are required to produce a surface without holes at the extraordinary vertices. The result of infinite subdivisions is called the *limit surface*. In practice, the limit surface may be evaluated directly from the control mesh by exploiting the eigenstructure of the subdivision rules [Stam 98] or approximated by halting subdivision after some number of steps.

2.1.3 Feature Adaptive Subdivision

Feature adaptive subdivision [Nießner et al. 12] is the basis for many real-time subdivision surface renderers, such as OpenSubdiv [Pixar 15]. It is efficient, is numerically stable, and produces the exact limit surface.

In feature adaptive subdivision, a preprocessing step extracts bicubic B-spline patches from the control mesh where possible, and the remaining faces are subdivided. Extraction and subdivision are repeated until the desired subdivision level is reached. To weld T-junctions that cause surface discontinuities between subdivision levels, triangular *transition patches* are inserted along the boundaries. Finally, all the extracted patch primitives are rendered using hardware tessellation. With repeated subdivision, extraordinary vertices become isolated but are never eliminated, and after enough subdivision and extraction steps to reach the desired level of smoothness, the remaining faces are rendered as triangles. (See Figure 2.3.)

2.1.4 Dynamic Feature Adaptive Subdivision

In dynamic feature adaptive subdivision, Schäfer et al. extend feature adaptive subdivision to dynamically control the number of subdivisions around each extraordinary vertex [Schäfer et al. 15].

The subdivided topology surrounding each extraordinary vertex is extracted into a *characteristic map* of n subdivision levels. To render, a compute shader determines the required subdivision level $l \leq n$ for the patches incident to each extraordinary vertex and then uses the characteristic map as a guide to emit control points and index buffers for the patches around the vertex.

Dynamic feature adaptive subdivision reduces the number of subdivisions and patches required for many scenes and is a significant performance improvement over feature adaptive subdivision, but it does add runtime compute and storage costs.

2.2 The Call of Duty Method

Our method is a subset of feature adaptive subdivision; we diverge in one important regard: B-spline patches are only extracted from the first subdivision level, and the remaining faces are rendered as triangles. The reason is that patches that result from subdivision are small and require low tessellation factors, and patches with low tessellation factors are less efficient to render than triangles.

We render the surface using a mixture of hardware-tessellated patch geometry and compute-assisted triangle mesh geometry (Figure 2.4). Where the control mesh topology is regular, the surface is rendered as bicubic B-spline patches using hardware tessellation. Where the control mesh topology is irregular, vertices which approach the limit surface are derived from the control mesh by a compute shader and the surface is rendered as triangles.

Because we accept a surface quality loss by not adaptively tessellating irregular patches, and because small triangles are much cheaper than small patches, we also forgo the overhead of dynamic feature adaptive subdivision.

2.3 Regular Patches

A *regular patch* is a control mesh face that is a regular quad embedded in a quad lattice. More specifically, the face must be regular, and the faces in its *one ring neighborhood* (Figure 2.5) must all be quads. The control points of neighboring faces are assembled into a 4×4 grid, and the limit surface is evaluated using the bicubic B-spline basis functions in the tessellation evaluation shader.

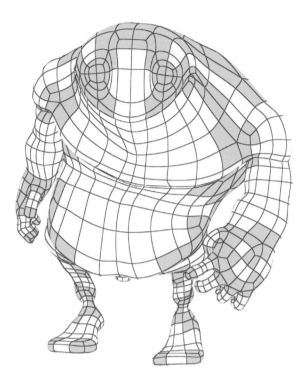

Figure 2.4. Bigguy model with regular patches in white and irregular patches in red.

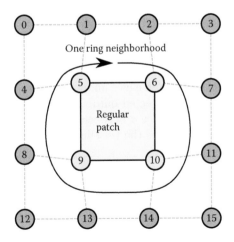

Figure 2.5. A regular patch with its one ring neighborhood faces and numbered control points.

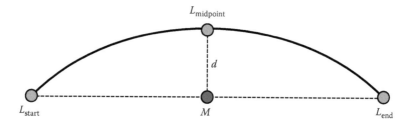

Figure 2.6. An edge with elements labeled related to the adaptive tessellation metric.

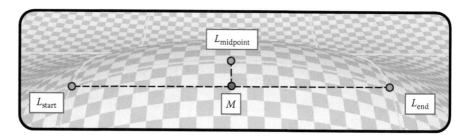

Figure 2.7. An edge with elements labeled related to the adaptive tessellation metric.

2.3.1   Adaptive Tessellation

A principal feature of the hardware tessellation pipeline is the ability to vary tessellation dynamically along each edge and in the interior of the patch. We utilize dynamic tessellation adaptively, to increase tessellation as needed to represent curvature and to decrease tessellation in flatter areas to reduce costs. Savings include vertex evaluation costs and also overshading costs caused by small or thin triangles being submitted to the rasterizer.

Our adaptive tessellation metric (Figures 2.6 and 2.7) requires evaluation of three limit surface points per patch edge: midpoint L_{midpoint} and endpoints L_{start} and L_{end}. Point L_{midpoint} is projected onto the line through L_{start} and L_{end} as M, and the square root of distance a between L_{midpoint} and M, multiplied by a constant quality factor k, becomes the tessellation factor f:

$$f \leftarrow k\sqrt{\left\|\texttt{bspline}(t{=}.5) - \frac{\texttt{bspline}(t{=}0) + \texttt{bspline}(t{=}1)}{2}\right\|}. \qquad (2.1)$$

The quality factor k is the reciprocal of the target distance between the limit surface and the rendered edge segments, in screen coordinates. The points are then projected to the screen space, to control tessellation in a view-dependent manner. After projection, depth should be clamped to $\epsilon \leq z$, and screen coordinates should be clamped to a guard band outside the view frustum $|x| \leq g$,

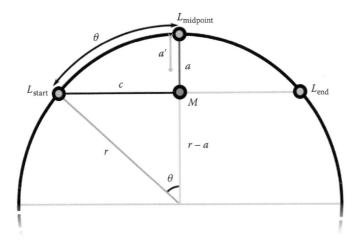

Figure 2.8. Curve segment approximated as an arc of a circle.

$|y| \leq g$, $g \approx 2.0$, to avoid over-tessellation of edges connected to vertices that cross outside near the view and develop large magnitudes.

Rationale We begin by approximating the curvature of the patch edge as a circular arc from L_{start} to L_{end}, intersecting L_{midpoint}, with radius r and angle 2θ. (See Figure 2.8.) Given half-segment $\vec{C}$ and distance a between midpoint M and L_{midpoint}, we can determine the radius r and angle θ of the half-arc. For the triangle with edges r, c, and $r - a$, length r can be determined from a and c as follows:

$$(r - a)^2 + c^2 = r^2$$
$$r^2 - 2ra + a^2 + c^2 = r^2$$
$$-2ra + a^2 + c^2 = 0$$
$$a^2 + c^2 = 2ra \tag{2.2}$$
$$\frac{(a^2 + c^2)}{2a} = r.$$

For the angle θ between $\vec{A}$ and $\vec{R}$, note that $\angle CA$ is $90°$:

$$\theta = \arccos\left(\frac{r - a}{r}\right)$$
$$= \arccos\left(1 - \frac{a}{r}\right). \tag{2.3}$$

Consider an error threshold a' (similar to a) representing the maximum desired distance between segment $\vec{C}$ and the arc. If $a \leq a'$, no tessellation is needed.

Using a segment with length c' for the same curve ($r' = r$), given a' and r, without knowing c we can determine θ':

$$\theta' = \arccos\left(1 - \frac{a'}{r}\right). \tag{2.4}$$

If tessellation factor $f = 1$ represents the arc θ, we roughly need to subdivide θ into f segments of θ' that satisfy the error threshold. In terms of starting distance a, starting segment length c, and target distance a',

$$
\begin{aligned}
f &= \frac{\theta}{\theta'} \\
&= \frac{\arccos\left(1 - \frac{a}{r}\right)}{\arccos\left(1 - \frac{a'}{r}\right)}.
\end{aligned} \tag{2.5}
$$

For small values of x, we can approximate $\arccos x$:

$$
\begin{aligned}
\cos x &\approx 1 - \frac{x^2}{2} \\
\arccos\left(1 - \frac{x^2}{2}\right) &\approx x, \\
\text{let } y &= \frac{x^2}{2}, \\
\arccos\left(1 - y\right) &\approx \sqrt{2y}.
\end{aligned} \tag{2.6}
$$

Thus, we can reasonably approximate the tessellation factor f in terms of a and a':

$$
\begin{aligned}
f &= \frac{\arccos\left(1 - \frac{a}{r}\right)}{\arccos\left(1 - \frac{a'}{r}\right)} \\
&\approx \frac{\sqrt{\frac{2a}{r}}}{\sqrt{\frac{2a'}{r}}} \\
&\approx \sqrt{\frac{a}{a'}}.
\end{aligned} \tag{2.7}
$$

The constant factor k in Equation (2.1) corresponds to $\frac{1}{a'}$, where a' is the screen-space distance threshold.

Results Our adaptive metric is fast and high quality, compared with global subdivision. In Figure 2.9, note that adaptive subdivision disables tessellation on straight edges and flat patches and maintains or increases tessellation in areas of high curvature.

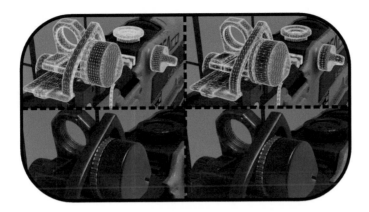

Figure 2.9. Our adaptive metric in practice; blue edges represent tessellated regular patches. Clockwise from top left: wireframe global subdivision, wireframe adaptive subdivision, shaded adaptive subdivision, and shaded global subdivision.

2.3.2 Rendering

Regular patches are rendered using the hardware tessellation pipeline. In OpenGL, this consists of the vertex shader, tessellation control shader, tessellation evaluation shader, and fragment shader stages. In Direct3D, it consists of the vertex shader, hull shader, domain shader, and fragment shader stages. For consistency with the sample code, we use OpenGL terms in this text.

The static index buffer contains the 16 control points per patch, and the vertex buffer holds the vertices of the control mesh (Algorithm 2.1).

Procedure setup()
$vertexBuffer_{control} \leftarrow controlMesh$;
$indexBuffer \leftarrow$ **extractControlPoints**($mesh$);
Procedure render()
setGpuControlPointsPerPatch(16);
drawPatches($vertexBuffer_{control}$, $indexBuffer$, $bsplineShaders$)

Algorithm 2.1. Render bicubic B-spline patches using hardware tessellation.

2.4 Irregular Patches

Control mesh faces that do not not meet the regular patch criteria are called *irregular patches*; these are recursively subdivided and rendered as triangles. To subdivide irregular patches, for each subdivision level, the following steps are taken (follow along with Figure 2.10):

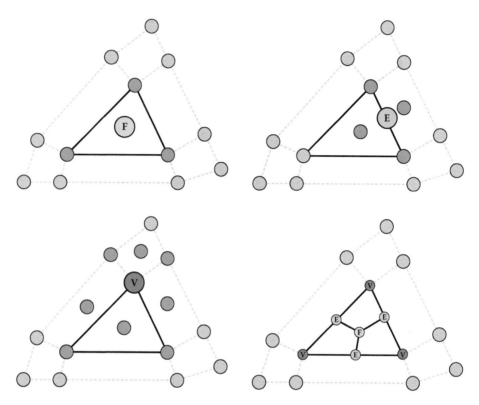

Figure 2.10. A triangle with its subdivided face point, edge point, and vertex point influences highlighted, followed by the subdivided quads.

- A new *face point* is added at the center of each control mesh face.

- A new *edge point* is added along each control mesh edge.

- A new *vertex point* replaces each control mesh vertex.

To subdivide each face, the face point is connected to an edge point, vertex point, and subsequent edge point to form a new quad. The process is repeated for every edge on the face. For a face of valence n, n quads are introduced. Note that after a single step of subdivision, only quads remain in the mesh. These quads are typically not planar.

Each Catmull-Clark subdivision produces a new, denser control mesh of the same subdivision surface. The face, edge, and vertex points of one control mesh become the vertex points of the next. With repeated subdivison, the control mesh becomes closer to the limit surface. In our experience with video game models, we have found it sufficient to stop after two subdivisions of irregular patches.

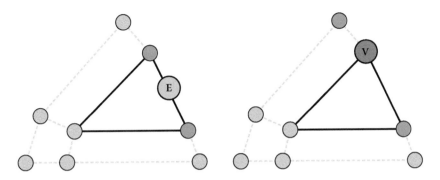

Figure 2.11. Influences for edge points and vertex points with border edges.

2.4.1 Face, Edge, and Vertex Point Rules

For a closed mesh, the Catmull-Clark rules for subdividing vertices are as follows (the influences are illustrated in Figure 2.10):

face point Average of the face's vertices: e.g., the centroid.

edge point Average of the edge's endpoints and its adjacent face points.

vertex point Weighted average of the vertex and its adjacent face and edge endpoints. The vertex weight is $\frac{n-2}{n}$, and the face and edge point weights are $\frac{1}{n^2}$, where n is the vertex valence.

Note that the edge point and vertex point calculations depend on the results of face point calculations; this has implications for parallel evaluation.

2.4.2 Borders and Corners

In the absence of neighboring faces and vertices, the weighted averages are altered. An edge connected to only one face is called a *border edge*. A vertex connected to two border edges is called a *border vertex* (Figure 2.11).

border edge point Average of the edge endpoints: e.g., the midpoint.

border vertex point Weighted average of the vertex and its two border edge endpoints. The vertex weight is $\frac{3}{4}$, the endpoint weights are $\frac{1}{8}$.

Rules are not given for non-manifold, double-sided, bowtie, degenerate, and other problematic topology cases. Their subdivision surfaces are not well defined, and they should typically be rejected by the asset pipeline.

Corners and creases Extensions to the subdivision rules allow edges to be tagged as sharp creases [Hoppe et al. 94], and as semi-sharp creases with a fractional *sharpness* value [DeRose et al. 98]. Our pipeline does not explicitly support creases. Instead, we represent sharp creases by splitting vertices and relying on boundary rules. Semi-sharp creases may be emulated in smooth meshes by manually inserting edge loops and bevels. SubD implementations may also elevate border vertex points to *corner vertex points* based on their valence (see [Pixar 15]).

corner vertex point Remains pinned to its location.

Consistency There are several variations of the subdivision rules to choose from, each having subjective qualities with respect to the behavior of the limit surface. Ultimately, models need to be rendered consistently with how they were built, so these decisions need to take into account the behavior of the modeling software being used.

In our pipeline, we follow the default behavior of Autodesk Maya, which, although undocumented, is straightforward to reverse-engineer by construction of test cases.

2.4.3   Subdivision Tables

To render irregular patches using the GPU, we must first factor the subdivision rules into a form that can be processed by a compute shader. As the Catmull-Clark subdivision rules can all be defined as weighted averages of neighboring vertices, we generalize them into a table of weights and vertex indices, called a *subdivision table* (Figure 2.12)

The subdivision table is stored in a GPU buffer, which is processed by a *subdivision table compute shader* (Listing 2.1). For each table row, the compute shader accumulates the weighted influences from the control mesh vertices and writes the result to the vertex buffer. To allow a single index buffer to reference control mesh vertices and subdivision table outputs, the control mesh vertices C are prepended to the subdivision table output. Table row k therefore stores its weighted average at vertex buffer location $||C|| + k$.

2.4.4   Subdivision Table Factorizing

Each subdivision table row is a weighted average of the face, edge, and vertex points from the same or prior subdivision. These points are in turn weighted averages of face, edge, and vertex points from the prior subdivision. At the first subdivision, all influences are weighted averages of vertices in the control mesh.

To account for dependencies between table rows, the subdivision table evaluation must be partitioned into separate face, edge, and vertex dispatches per subdivision level, with GPU read/write fences in between. However, as every

kind	id	label	influences	weights
control mesh verts	0	c0		
	1	c1		
	2	c2		
	3	c3		
face points	4	f0	0 1 2 3	0.25...
edge points	5	e0	0 1 4 ?	0.25...
	6	e1	1 2 4 ?	0.25...
	7	e2	3 2 4 ?	0.25...
	8	e3	2 0 4 ?	0.25...
vertex points	9	v0	0 1 3 4 ? ? ? ?	0.5 0.625...
	10	v1	1 0 2 4 ? ? ? ?	0.5 0.625...
	11	v2	2 1 3 4 ? ? ? ?	0.5 0.625...
	12	v3	3 0 2 4 ? ? ? ?	0.5 0.625...

Figure 2.12. A subset of subdivision tables generated for the vertices connected to one quad. Each row of the table represents one subdivided vertex. Note that "?" is used to depict vertices that are present but not shown in the drawing. The control mesh vertices c_n are implicitly prepended to the table.

weighted average is a linear combination of its inputs, *all* subdivision tables may be factorized to depend only on the vertices of the control mesh.

Factorizing is accomplished by recursively replacing each weighted influence that is not from the control mesh with its own influences, appropriately weighted. Though this increases the average number of influences per table row, it eliminates dependencies between tables and therefore allows all subdivision tables to be evaluated in a single compute dispatch.

2.4.5 Rendering

Irregular patches are rendered using the standard triangle pipeline consisting of vertex shader and fragment shader. The static index buffer contains the triangulated subdivided quads, and the vertex buffer is filled by the subdivision table compute shader.

As the control mesh vertices are typically prepended to the subdivision table output vertex buffer, this is typically the same vertex buffer that is used to render regular patches. If any control mesh vertices have changed, the subdivision table compute shader is dispatched before rendering to update the subdivided vertex buffer (Algorithm 2.2).

2.5 Filling Cracks

2.5.1 Transition Points

While the B-spline evaluation performed by the tessellation hardware evaluates points on the limit surface, recursive subdivision evaluates points that merely

```
layout( local_size_x = 32, local_size_y = 1) in;

uniform uint baseVertCount;

layout( std430, binding = 0 ) buffer TablesBuffer {
    uint tables[];
};

layout( std430, binding = 1 ) buffer InfluencesBuffer {
    uint influences[];
};

layout( std430, binding = 2 ) buffer VertsBuffer {
    float verts[];
};

void main()
{
  uint index = gl_GlobalInvocationID.x;

  uint data = tables[index];

  uint first = data & 0xffffff;
  uint count = data >> 24;

  vec3 result = vec3( 0 );

  for ( uint i = first; i < first + count; i++ )
  {
    uint vertIn = influences[i * 2 + 0];

    float weight = uintBitsToFloat( influences[i * 2 + 1] );

    vec3 p = vec3(
      verts[vertIn * 3 + 0],
      verts[vertIn * 3 + 1],
      verts[vertIn * 3 + 2] );

    result += p * weight;
  }

  uint vertOut = baseVertCount + index;

  verts[vertOut * 3 + 0] = result.x;
  verts[vertOut * 3 + 1] = result.y;
  verts[vertOut * 3 + 2] = result.z;
}
```

Listing 2.1. Subdivision table compute shader.

approach the limit surface. Where a regular patch and an irregular patch share an edge, this manifests as a crack in the rendered surface.

The discrepancy can be resolved by using the B-spline basis functions in the subdivision table evaluation compute shader to evaluate the limit surface position for the irregular vertices along the edge. We call these limit surface points

Procedure setup()
> $mesh \leftarrow controlMesh;$
> $vertexBuffer_{control} \leftarrow controlMesh;$
> **foreach** i *in subdivisions* **do**
> > $facePoints \leftarrow$ **extractFacePoints**$(mesh);$
> > $edgePoints \leftarrow$ **extractEdgePoints**$(mesh);$
> > $vertexPoints \leftarrow$ **extractVertexPoints**$(mesh);$
> > $faces \leftarrow$ **subdivideFaces**$(mesh);$
> > $shaderBuffer_i \leftarrow$
> > **factorizeTables**$(facePoints,\ edgePoints,\ vertexPoints);$
> > $indexBuffer_i \leftarrow$ **triangulate**$(faces);$
> > $mesh \leftarrow (facePoints, edgePoints, vertexPoints, faces);$
>
> **end**

Procedure render()
> $i \leftarrow$ **chooseSubdivisionLevel**$(camera);$
> **if** *control mesh vertices changed* **then**
> > $vertexBuffer \leftarrow$
> > **dispatchCompute**$(vertexBuffer_{control},\ shaderBuffer_i,\ tableShader);$
> > **waitForCompute**$();$
>
> **end**
> **drawTriangles**$(vertexBuffer,\ indexBuffer_i,\ standardShaders)$

Algorithm 2.2. Render irregular patches as triangles.

transition points, and they are written to the vertex buffer by an alternate code path within the subdivision table evaluation compute shader.

Transition point tables are appended to the subdivision table and use largely the same data format. In place of influences, transition points store the 16 control points of the regular patch, and in place of weights, they store the domain location to be evaluated (Figure 2.13).

2.5.2   Tessellation Factor Synchronization

While hardware-tessellated regular patches can be divided into any number of segments, recursively subdivided irregular patches are limited to power-of-two divisions.

We resolve this inconsistency by flagging edges of regular patches that are shared with irregular patches. When a regular patch edge is flagged, it forgoes its adaptive metric and snaps to the global tessellation factor, which corresponds to the level of recursive subdivision (Figure 2.14). In the hardware tessellation pipeline, patch flags are stored in a static shader buffer that is bound to the tessellation control shader.

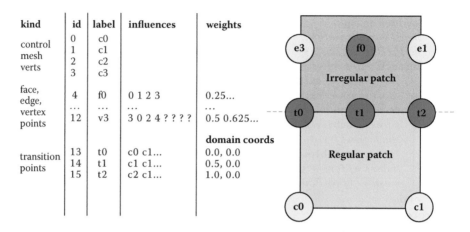

kind	id	label	influences	weights
control mesh verts	0 1 2 3	c0 c1 c2 c3		
face, edge, vertex points	4 ... 12	f0 ... v3	0 1 2 3 ... 3 0 2 4 ? ? ? ?	0.25... ... 0.5 0.625...
				domain coords
transition points	13 14 15	t0 t1 t2	c0 c1... c1 c1... c2 c1...	0.0, 0.0 0.5, 0.0 1.0, 0.0

Figure 2.13. A regular and irregular patch sharing an edge, with crack-welding transition points along the boundary.

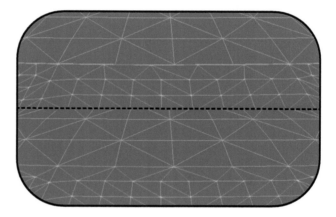

Figure 2.14. An edge shared by regular patches (blue) and irregular patches (red), shown with tessellation factors desynchronized (top) and synchronized (bottom).

2.5.3 Bireversal Invariant B-Spline Basis

When two regular patches share an edge, control mesh topology may dictate that they parameterize the edge in opposite directions. That is, the edge may interpolate A to B from 0 to 1 in one patch, and B to A from 0 to 1 in the other (Figure 2.15). Along these edges, numeric precision errors can introduce slight cracks at high tessellation factors.

To avoid cracking, we use a direction-invariant version of the B-spline basis from [Nießner et al. 12] that is mathematically equivalent when interpolating from

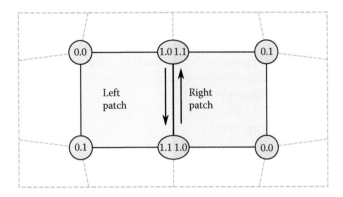

Figure 2.15. Two clockwise-oriented regular patches with opposite parameterization along the shared edge.

```
void EvaluateBSplineBasis (float u, out vec4 b)
{
  float s = 1.0 - u;
  float t = u;

  b.x = (s*s*s                                    ) * 1.0/6.0;
  b.y = (4*s*s*s + t*t*t + 12*s*t*s + 6*t*s*t) * 1.0/6.0;
  b.z = (4*t*t*t + s*s*s + 12*t*s*t + 6*s*t*s) * 1.0/6.0;
  b.w = (t*t*t                                    ) * 1.0/6.0;
}

void EvaluateBSpline (vec3 cp[16], vec2 uv,
                      out vec3 position)
{
  vec4 uBasis, vBasis;
  EvaluateBSplineBasis (uv.x, uBasis);
  EvaluateBSplineBasis (uv.y, vBasis);

  position = vec3(0);
  for (int i = 0; i < 4; i++)
  {
    position += vBasis[i] * (cp[i*4 + 0] * uBasis.x +
                             cp[i*4 + 1] * uBasis.y +
                             cp[i*4 + 2] * uBasis.z +
                             cp[i*4 + 3] * uBasis.w);
  }
}
```

Listing 2.2. Evaluating a B-spline patch using the bireversal invariant method from feature adaptive subdivision [Nießner et al. 12].

A to B by u, and when interpolating from B to A by $1 - u$. Listing 2.2 gives an implementation of bireversal invariant bicubic B-spline evaluation.

2.6   Going Further

We have thus far given an introduction to implementing Catmull-Clark subdivision surfaces in a game engine, but more work remains to complete the pipeline.

This section describes extensions that may be implemented or not, depending on individual game requirements.

2.6.1   Secondary Components

A vertex may have different values for secondary components, such as colors, texture coordinates, tangent basis, etc., for each incident face. With the exception of texture coordinates (see Section 2.6.3), it is usually acceptable to linearly interpolate secondary components across subdivided patches. When extracting control points and subdivision tables from the mesh topology, a *render vertex* must be generated that is a unique combination of the vertex and secondary components from the correct faces.

For regular patch control points that are strictly *supports* (not one of the interior four), render vertices may be generated without regard to the values of the secondary components. To avoid introducing extra render vertices, these components may be drawn from any face that is connected to the supporting control point.

2.6.2   Normals and Tangents

Normals and tangents may be evaluated directly by the shader, giving the true limit surface normal, or they may be treated as secondary components and interpolated. The choice is a tradeoff between quality and performance: limit normals and tangents give better shading but add calculation cost (Listing 2.3).

Note that if the same tangent-space normal map is applied to a SubD mesh and traditional LOD meshes, limit normals and tangents must be transferred to the LOD meshes to avoid using an inconsistent tangent basis. Additionally, normal map baking tools must render to a mesh with limit normals and tangents, to ensure that the normal map is encoded in the proper basis.

For regular patches, the limit surface normal is evaluated by the cross product of the patch tangent vectors. Irregular patches use the same method, but tangents are evaluated using *limit stencils* (see [Halstead et al. 93], Appendix A).

2.6.3   Texture Coordinate Smoothing

Because the subdivision rules weight a vertex by its neighbors without regard for their endpoints, the relative length of incident edges affects the subdivided position. For example, if a regular vertex is connected to three short edges and one long edge, the subdivided vertex will move toward the endpoint of the long edge. This can cause control mesh faces to change size and shape in the subdivided

```
void EvaluateBSplineBasis(float u, out vec4 b, out vec4 d)
{
  float s = 1.0 - u;
  float t = u;

  b.x = (s*s*s                                   ) * 1.0/6.0;
  b.y = (4*s*s*s + t*t*t + 12*s*t*s + 6*t*s*t) * 1.0/6.0;
  b.z = (4*t*t*t + s*s*s + 12*t*s*t + 6*s*t*s) * 1.0/6.0;
  b.w = (t*t*t                                   ) * 1.0/6.0;

  d.x = -s*s;
  d.y = -t*t - 4*s*t;
  d.z =  s*s + 4*s*t;
  d.w =  t*t;
}

void EvaluateBSpline( vec3 cp[16], float u, float v,
                      out vec3 position, out vec3 normal )
{
  vec4 uBasis, vBasis, uDeriv, vDeriv;
  EvaluateBSplineBasis(uv.x, uBasis, uDeriv);
  EvaluateBSplineBasis(vv.x, vBasis, vDeriv);

  position         = vec3(0);
  vec3 tangent     = vec3(0);
  vec3 bitangent = vec3(0);

  for (int i = 0; i < 4; i++)
  {
    vec3 positionBasis = (cp[i*4 + 0] * uBasis.x +
                          cp[i*4 + 1] * uBasis.y +
                          cp[i*4 + 2] * uBasis.z +
                          cp[i*4 + 3] * uBasis.w);

    vec3 positionDeriv = (cp[i*4 + 0] * uDeriv.x +
                          cp[i*4 + 1] * uDeriv.y +
                          cp[i*4 + 2] * uDeriv.z +
                          cp[i*4 + 3] * uDeriv.w);

    position  += vBasis[i] * positionBasis;
    tangent   += vBasis[i] * positionDeriv;
    bitangent += vDeriv[i] * positionBasis;
  }

  normal = normalize( cross( bitangent, tangent ) );
}
```

Listing 2.3. Bicubic B-spline evaluation shader extended to return normals.

mesh. If texture coordinates are linearly interpolated across the face, the texture parameterization will be distorted (Figure 2.16).

The solution employed by modeling packages such as Autodesk Maya is to construct a second topology from the *texture coordinates* of the control mesh and to smooth it in two dimensions using the Catmull-Clark subdivision rules. Smoothing the texture coordinates effectively inverts the distortion caused by smoothing the vertices.

Figure 2.16. From left to right: A textured cube control mesh with beveled caps, the surface with linearly interpolated texture coordinates, and the surface with smoothed texture coordinates.

To implement texture coordinate smoothing efficiently, we utilize *vertex-dominant topology*. Intuitively, texture-coordinate topology follows position topology but may introduce texture-only boundary edges where discontinuous parameterizations meet. More formally, the topology of secondary coordinates is embedded in the vertex topology with limitations: An edge that is a boundary in vertex topology must be a boundary in secondary topology, and an edge that is smooth in vertex topology either is a boundary in secondary topology or else connects the same two faces as in vertex topology.

When extracting regular patches from vertex-dominant topology, the texture-coordinate topology must be checked to ensure that it is also regular. If it is not, the entire patch is directed to recursive subdivision. Secondary component smoothing need not be specific to texture coordinates, but it is expensive and should be limited to where it has the greatest impact.

2.6.4 Regular Patch Extrapolation

To extract the 16 control points required to make a regular patch from a control mesh face, the face, its vertices, and its one ring neighborhood faces must all have valence 4. For some boundary and corner patches, it is possible to *extrapolate* missing control points and construct a B-spline boundary patch that evaluates to the Catmull-Clark limit surface (Figure 2.17).

We begin by defining some special cases of boundary vertices.

non-corner boundary vertex Vertex of valence 3 with two boundary edges.

convex corner boundary vertex Vertex of valence 2 with two boundary edges.

concave corner boundary vertex Vertex of valence 4 or more with two boundary edges.

Non-corner and convex corner boundary vertices may have their supporting control points extrapolated to form a valid B-spline patch:

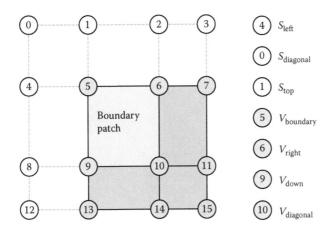

Figure 2.17. Extrapolated supporting control points for a convex corner boundary vertex.

- Non-corner boundary vertices require one extrapolated support:

$$S_{\text{edge}} = 2V_{\text{boundary}} - V_{\text{opposite}}. \tag{2.8}$$

- Convex corner boundary vertices require three extrapolated supports:

$$\begin{aligned} S_{\text{left}} &= 2V_{\text{boundary}} - V_{\text{right}}, \\ S_{\text{diagonal}} &= 4V_{\text{boundary}} - 2V_{\text{right}} - 2V_{\text{down}} + V_{\text{diagonal}}, \\ S_{\text{top}} &= 2V_{\text{boundary}} - V_{\text{down}}. \end{aligned} \tag{2.9}$$

- Concave corner boundary vertices may not be extrapolated and require recursive subdivision.

If all vertices of a control mesh face are regular or are borders that support extrapolation, the needed supports may be added as rows to the subdivision tables and the patch may be treated as regular. If texture coordinates are smoothed (Section 2.6.3), regular patch extrapolation may be applied to texture coordinates as well. Note that the extrapolation formulae are linear combinations of control mesh vertices and are therefore compatible with the subdivision table compute shader.

Causing more faces to render as regular patches in this manner improves image quality and reduces subdivision table size (Figure 2.18).

2.6.5 View Frustum Culling

In the hardware tessellation pipeline, it is possible to cheaply discard patches by setting the tessellation factor to 0. Additionally, the convex hull of the control points of a B-spline patch is a convex hull of the surface.

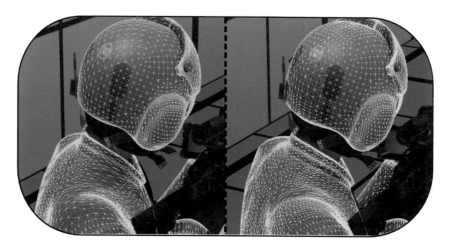

Figure 2.18. Comparison of models with (right) and without (left) regular patch extrapolation for texture coordinates. Blue wireframe represents regular patches, and yellow edges are extrapolated borders.

We can utilize these properties to add coarse view frustum culling of patches, saving surface evaluation and triangle setup costs. In the tessellation control shader, we transform each control point to clip space and test against the unit cube:

$$
\begin{aligned}
x_\text{clip} &> w_\text{clip}, \\
y_\text{clip} &> w_\text{clip}, \\
x_\text{clip} &< -w_\text{clip}, \\
y_\text{clip} &< -w_\text{clip}, \\
w_\text{clip} &\leq 0.
\end{aligned}
\tag{2.10}
$$

If all control points pass one of the tests, the patch is discarded.

2.6.6 Back Patch Culling

Shirman and Abi-Ezzi describe a *cone of normals*: a region of space from which no part of a corresponding Bézier patch may be seen front facing [Shirmun and Abi-Ezzi 93].

Using the cone of normals, we can implement *back patch culling*, discarding entire patches without evaluating the surface or submitting triangles for rasterization. Once calculated, the cone test is extremely fast, consisting of a single dot product and comparison:

$$
\hat{v} \cdot \hat{a} \leq \sin(\alpha).
\tag{2.11}
$$

The calculation of the cone is expensive, however, and requires converting the B-spline patch control points to the Bézier basis. Therefore, this test is reserved for control meshes that do not animate.

It is also possible to consider occlusion in the culling calculation. "Patch-Based Occlusion Culling for Hardware Tessellation" by Nießner and Loop [Nießner and Loop 12] describes a method for building and testing a hierarchal depth buffer in the tessellation control shader.

2.7 Conclusion

In this chapter, we have described a practical real-time implementation of Catmull-Clark subdivision surfaces that has been utilized in multiple AAA console games. It is hoped that the reader will come away with an appreciation for the opportunities presented by the tessellation hardware in modern GPUs and the knowledge that it is practical to implement SubDs in games today.

2.8 Acknowledgments

The author would like to thank Paul Allen Edelstein for improvements to the quality of the adaptive tessellation metric and for deriving its mathematical basis, and the reviewers for their feedback.

Bibliography

[Bommes et al. 13] David Bommes, Bruno Lévy, Nico Pietroni, Enrico Puppo, Claudio Silva, Marco Tarini, and Denis Zorin. "Quad-Mesh Generation and Processing: A Survey." *Computer Graphics Forum* 32:6 (2013), 51–76. Article first published online, March 4, 2013, DOI: 10.1111/cgf.12014, http://vcg.isti.cnr.it/Publications/2013/BLPPSTZ13a.

[Brainerd 14] Wade Brainerd. "Tessellation in Call of Duty: Ghosts." http://wadeb.com/siggraph_2014_tessellation_in_call_of_duty_ghosts.zip, 2014.

[Catmull and Clark 78] E. Catmull and J. Clark. "Recursively Generated B-Spline Surfaces on Arbitrary Topological Meshes." *Computer-Aided Design* 10:6 (1978), 350–355.

[DeRose et al. 98] Tony DeRose, Michael Kass, and Tien Truong. "Subdivision Surfaces in Character Animation." In *SIGGRAPH '98: Proceedings of the 25th Annual Conference on Computer Graphics and Interactive Techniques*, pp. 85–94. New York: ACM, 1998. Available online (http://graphics.pixar.com/library/Geri/).

[Halstead et al. 93] Mark Halstead, Michael Kass, and Tony DeRose. "Efficient, Fair Interpolation Using Catmull-Clark Surfaces." In *SIGGRAPH '93: Proceedings of the 20th Annual Conference on Computer Graphics and Interactive Techniques*, pp. 35–44. New York: ACM, 1993.

[Hoppe et al. 94] H. Hoppe, T. DeRose, T Duchamp, M. Halstead, H. Jin, J. McDonald, J. Schweitzer, and W. Stuetzle. "Piecewise Smooth Surface Reconstruction." In *SIGGRAPH '94: Proceedings of the 25th Annual Conference on Computer Graphics and Interactive Techniques*, pp. 295–302. New York: ACM, 1994.

[Nießner and Loop 12] Matthias Nießner and Charles Loop. "Patch-Based Occlusion Culling for Hardware Tessellation." Paper presented at Computer Graphics International, Poole, UK, June 12–15, 2012.

[Nießner et al. 12] M. Nießner, C. Loop, M. Meyer, and T. DeRose. "Feature-Adaptive GPU Rendering of Catmull-Clark Subdivision Surfaces." *ACM Transactions on Graphics (TOG)* 31:1 (2012), 6.

[Nießner et al. ar] Matthias Nießner, Benjamin Keinert, Matthew Fisher, Marc Stamminger, Charles Loop, and Henry Schäfer. "Real-Time Rendering Techniques with Hardware Tessellation." *Computer Graphics Forum*. First published online DOI: 10.1111/cgf.12714, September 21, 2015.

[Pixar 15] Pixar. "Subdivision Surfaces." *OpenSubdiv Documentation*, http://graphics.pixar.com/opensubdiv/docs/subdivision_surfaces.html, 2015.

[Schäfer et al. 15] Henry Schäfer, Jens Raab, Benjamin Keinert, and Matthias Nießner. "Dynamic Feature-Adaptive Subdivision." In *Proceedings of the ACM SIGGRAPH Symposium on Interactive 3D Graphics and Games*, pp. 31–38. New York: ACM, 2015.

[Shirmun and Abi-Ezzi 93] Leon A. Shirmun and Salim S. Abi-Ezzi. "The Cone of Normals Technique for Fast Processing of Curved Patches." *Computer Graphics Forum* 12:3 (1993), 261–272.

[Stam 98] Jos Stam. "Exact Evaluation Of Catmull-Clark Subdivision Surfaces at Arbitrary Parameter Values." In *SIGGRAPH '98: Proceedings of the 25th Annual Conference on Computer Graphics and Interactive Techniques*, pp. 395–404. New York: ACM, 1998.

II

Lighting

We have four great chapters in the "Lighting" section this year. We present a great solution to art-driven volumetric cloud rendering, and we have three chapters focused on improving the lighting and shading pipelines.

Modern engines and AAA games are running into limitations of the commonly used deferred rendering. Ever-increasing resolutions and desire to have proper antialiasing drive the bandwidth costs very high, fixed G-buffer setup usually allows engineers to implement only a handful of shading models, and, of course, most engines still have to implement full forward rendering paths to support transparencies.

Various forward rendering implementations, which aim to solve the aforementioned problems, became very popular in recent years. Tiled rendering techniques map particularly well to modern hardware but are not without limitations.

Three chapters presented in this section try to solve a particular set of performance or quality issues in tiled forward or deferred rendering techniques. The fourth chapter brings new ideas to cloud rendering and lighting and goes beyond the usual ray marching through several layers of Perlin noise.

The first chapter, "Clustered Shading: Assigning Lights Using Conservative Rasterization in DirectX 12" by Kevin Örtegren and Emil Persson, discusses an interesting improvement and simplification of clustered shading by utilizing conservative rasterization available in DirectX 12. Tiled shading partitions screen into a set of 2D tiles and for each tile finds all lights that intersect it. Geometry rendering then reads the light information from the corresponding tile and performs actual shading. Clustered shading uses 3D cells instead of 2D tiles and reduces the amount of lights that can potentially affect a given pixel.

"Fine Pruned Tiled Light Lists" by Morten S. Mikkelsen describes a novel tiled rendering optimization used in *Rise of the Tomb Raider*. Assignment of lights to tiles happens in two steps. The first step computes a simple bounding volume intersection with the 2D tile. The second step actually determines whether any pixel in the tile intersects with the light shape in three dimensions and excludes all lights that do not affect the visible pixels. The second step is more costly but greatly reduces the amount of lights per tile. This chapter also utilizes asynchronous compute to utilize spare GPU cycles during shadow map rendering, effectively making this computation almost free.

The third chapter is "Deferred Attribute Interpolation Shading" by Christoph Schied and Carsten Dachsbacher and presents an exciting take on classical deferred shading. Instead of storing material properties in the G-buffer, the authors chose to store triangle information for each pixel and evaluate the material at a later stage of the rendering. This approach greatly reduces the bandwidth requirements of deferred rendering and allows for much easier support of multi-sample antialiasing techniques.

The last chapter of the "Lighting" section, "Real-Time Volumetric Cloudscapes" by Andrew Schneider, describes the cloud rendering solution used in *Horizon: Zero Dawn* by Guerrilla Games. the author focuses on two important aspects of cloud rendering. First, he describes a novel way of combining Worley and Perlin noises and flow maps to approximate shapes of various cloud types. Second, the chapter focuses on challenges of correct approximation of various lighting phenomena in the clouds.

I would like to thank all authors for sharing their ideas and for the effort they put into the chapters.

—Michal Valient

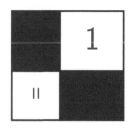

Clustered Shading: Assigning Lights Using Conservative Rasterization in DirectX 12

Kevin Örtegren and Emil Persson

1.1 Introduction

Dynamic lights are a crucial part of making a virtual scene seem realistic and alive. Accurate lighting calculations are expensive and have been a major restriction in real-time applications. In recent years, many new lighting pipelines have been explored and used in games to increase the number of dynamic light sources per scene. This article presents a GPU-based variation of *practical clustered shading* [Persson and Olsson 13], which is a technique that improves on the currently popular *tiled shading* [Olsson and Assarsson 11, Swoboda 09, Balestra and Engstad 08, Andersson 09] by utilizing higher-dimensional tiles. The view frustum is divided into three-dimensional clusters instead of two-dimensional tiles and addresses the depth discontinuity problem present in the tiled shading technique. The main goal we aimed for was to explore the use of conservative rasterization to efficiently assign convex light shapes to clusters.

Clustered shading is a technique similar to tiled shading that performs a light culling step before the lighting stage when rendering a scene. The view frustum is divided into sub-frustums, which we call *clusters*, in three dimensions. The purpose of the light culling step is to insert all visible lights into the clusters that they intersect. When the light culling is done, the clusters contain information of which lights intersect them. It is then easy to fetch the light data from a cluster when shading a pixel by using the pixel's view-space position. The goal of the technique is to minimize the number of lighting calculations per pixel and to address some of the problems present in tiled shading. Tiled shading uses two-dimensional tiles and relies on a depth prepass to reduce the tiles in the z-dimension, whereas clustered shading has a fixed cluster structure in view space at all times.

(a) Conservative rasterization.   (b) Normal rasterization.

Figure 1.1. Difference between rasterization modes. Red cells represent the pixel shader invocations for the triangle.

Previous work on clustered shading first surfaced in 2012 [Olsson et al. 12] and have since spawned a few presentations and demos on the subject: Intel demo on forward clustered shading [Fauconneau 14], GDC15 presentation from AMD on tiled and clustered shading [Thomas 15], and a practical solution to clustered shading from Avalanche [Persson and Olsson 13]. As of writing this, there is one released game using clustered shading, namely *Forza Horizon 2* [Leadbetter 14].

1.2 Conservative Rasterization

The use of the rasterizer has traditionally been to generate pixels from primitives for drawing to the screen, but with programmable shaders there is nothing stopping the user from using it in other ways. The normal rasterization mode will rasterize a pixel if the pixel center is covered by a primitive. *Conservative rasterization* is an alternative rasterization mode where if any part of a primitive overlaps a pixel, that pixel is considered covered and is then rasterized. The difference between these modes is illustrated in Figure 1.1.

1.3 Implementation

This section will go through the different steps included in the light assignment algorithm as well as explain how the main data structure used for storing light and cluster data is created and managed, as it is an intricate part of the technique. An overview of the algorithm is listed below:

For each light type:

1. Shell pass: Find minimum and maximum depths in every tile for every light.

2. Fill pass: Use the minimum and maximum depths and fill indices into the light linked list.

The light assignment is complete when all light types have been processed and the light linked list can be used when shading geometry.

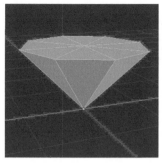
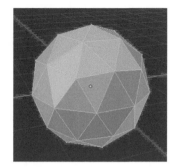

(a) A unit cone mesh with 10 vertices.   (b) A unit sphere mesh with 42 vertices.

Figure 1.2. Two example unit shapes created in Blender.

1.3.1 Light Shape Representation

Lights must have a shape representation to be able to be inserted into clusters. Approximating every light shape as an analytical sphere is the easiest and computationally cheapest approach, but it will be inaccurate for light shapes that are not sphere shaped. An analytic shape representation is suitable when performing general intersection calculations on the CPU or in, for example, a compute shader. Some shapes will, however, have a very complex analytical representation, which is why many techniques resort to using spheres.

The technique presented here uses the rasterizer and the traditional rendering shader pipeline, which is well suited to deal with high amounts of vertices. Shapes represented as vertex meshes are very simple and provide general representation models for all light shapes. The level of flexibility when working with vertex meshes is very high because the meshes can be created with variable detail.

Meshes are created as unit shapes, where vertices are constrained to -1 to 1 in the x-, y-, and z-directions. This is done to allow arbitrary scaling of the shape depending on the actual light size. Some light shapes may need to be altered at runtime to allow for more precise representations: for example, the unit cone will fit around a sphere-capped cone for a spot light, and thus the cap must be calculated in the vertex shader before light assignment. In the case of using low amounts of vertices for light shapes, the shapes could easily be created in code and also use very small vertex formats: for example, R8G8B8 is enough for the shapes in Figure 1.2.

1.3.2 Shell Pass

The *shell pass* is responsible for finding the clusters for a light shape that encompasses it in cluster space. The pass finds the near and far clusters for each tile for each light and stores them in an R8G8 render target for the following

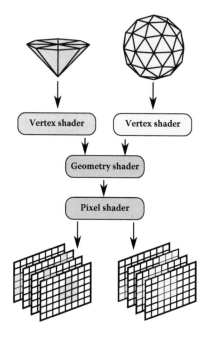

Figure 1.3. Illustration of the entire shell pass.

pass to fill the shell. The number of render targets for the shell pass correspond
to the maximum number of visible lights for each light type. All render targets
have the same size and format and are set up in a `Texture2DArray` for each light
type. The sizes of the render targets are the same as the x- and y-dimensions
of the cluster structure, otherwise known as the *tile dimension*. An overview
illustration of the shell pass can be seen in Figure 1.3. The shell pass uses the
traditional shader pipeline with conservative rasterization to ensure that the light
meshes invoke all the pixels they touch. To activate conservative rasterization
in DirectX 12, it is simply a matter of setting the `ConservativeRaster` flag to
`D3D12_CONSERVATIVE_RASTERIZATION_MODE_ON` when creating a pipeline state object
for the shader pipeline.

Vertex shader Each light type has its own custom vertex shader for translating,
rotating, and scaling the light mesh to fit the actual light. This and the mesh
are the only two things that have to be introduced when adding a new light type
for the light assignment. The algorithm starts by issuing a `DrawIndexedInstanced`
with the number of lights as the instance count. Also fed to the vertex shader is
the actual light data containing position, color, and other light properties. The
shader semantic `SV_InstanceID` is used in the vertex shader to extract the position,
scale, and other properties to transform each vertex to the correct location in
world space. Each vertex is sent to the geometry shader containing the view-

space position and its light ID, which is the same as the previously mentioned SV_InstanceID.

Geometry shader The vertices will simply pass through the geometry shader where packed view positions for each vertex in the triangle primitive are appended to every vertex. The vertex view positions are flagged with nointerpolation as they have to remain correctly in the view space through the rasterizer. The most important task of the geometry shader is to select the correct render target as output for the pixel shader. This is done by writing a render target index to the SV_RenderTargetArrayIndex semantic in each vertex. SV_RenderTargetArrayIndex is only available through the geometry shader; this is a restriction of the current shading model and makes the use of the geometry shader a requirement. The geometry shader is unfortunately not an optimal path to take in the shader pipeline because it, besides selecting the render target index, adds unnecessary overhead.

Pixel shader The pixel shader performs most of the mathematics and does so for every triangle in every tile. Each pixel shader invocation corresponds to a tile, and in that tile the nearest or farthest cluster must be calculated and written for every light. When a pixel shader is run for a tile, it means that part of a triangle from a light shape mesh is inside that tile, and from that triangle part the minimum and maximum depths must be found. Depth can be directly translated into a Z-cluster using a depth distribution function, which is discussed in more detail in the next section.

All calculations are performed in view space because vertices outside a tile must be correctly represented; if calculations were performed in screen space, the vertices behind the near plane would be incorrectly transformed and become unusable. Tile boundaries are represented as four side planes that go through the camera origin $(0, 0, 0)$. Each pixel shader invocation handles one triangle at a time. To find the minimum and maximum depths for a triangle in a tile, three cases are used; see Figure 1.4. The three points that can be the minimum or maximum depths in a tile are as follows:

(a) Where a vertex edge intersects the tile boundary planes: Listing 1.1 shows the intersection function for finding the intersection distance from a vertex to a tile boundary plane. The distance is along the edge from vertex p0. Note that both N and D can be 0, in which case N / D would return NaN or, in the case of only D being 0, would return +/-INF. It is an optimization to not check for these cases, as the IEEE 754-2008 floating point specification in HLSL [Microsoft] states that

 1. the comparison NE, when either or both operands is NaN, returns TRUE;

 2. comparisons of any non-NaN value against +/-INF return the correct result.

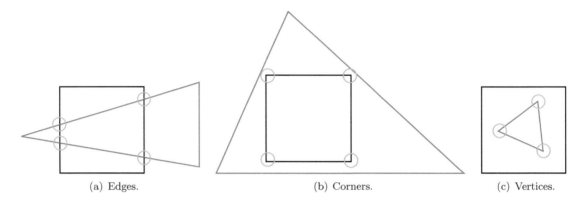

(a) Edges.   (b) Corners.   (c) Vertices.

Figure 1.4. The three cases of finding minimum and maximum depths on a triangle in a tile.

```
bool linesegment_vs_plane(float3 p0, float3 p1, float3 pn, out
                          float lerp_val)
{
    float3 u = p1 - p0;

    float D = dot(pn, u);
    float N = -dot(pn, p0);

    lerp_val = N / D;
    return !(lerp_val != saturate(lerp_val));
}
```

Listing 1.1. Vertex edge versus tile boundary plane intersection.

The second rule applies to the intrinsic function saturate. These two rules make sure that the function always returns the correct boolean.

(b) Where a triangle covers a tile corner: Finding the depth at a corner of a tile is simply a matter of performing four ray-versus-triangle intersections, one at each corner of the tile. The ray–triangle intersection function in Listing 1.2 is derived from [Möller and Trumbore 05].

(c) Where a vertex is completely inside a tile: The signed distance from a point to a plane in three dimensions is calculated by

$$D = \frac{ax_1 + by_1 + cz_1 + d}{\sqrt{a^2 + b^2 + c^2}},$$

where (a, b, c) is the normal vector of the plane and (x_1, y_1, z_1) is the point to which the distance is calculated. The variable d is defined as $d = -ax_0 -$

```
bool ray_vs_triangle(float3 ray_dir, float3 vert0, float3 vert1,
                     float3 vert2, out float z_pos)
{
  float3 e1 = vert1 - vert0;
  float3 e2 = vert2 - vert0;
  float3 q = cross(ray_dir, e2);
  float a = dot(e1, q);

  if(a > -0.000001f && a < 0.000001f)
    return false;

  float f = 1.0f / a;
  float u = f * dot(-vert0, q);

  if(u != saturate(u))
    return false;

  float3 r = cross(-vert0, e1);
  float v = f * dot(ray_dir, r);

  if(v < 0.0f || (u + v) > 1.0f)
    return false;

  z_pos = f * dot(e2, r) * ray_dir.z;

  return true;
}
```

Listing 1.2. Ray versus triangle intersection.

$by_0 - cz_0$, where (x_0, y_0, z_0) is a point on the plane. As all planes go through the origin in the view space, the variable d is eliminated; because the plane normals are length 1, the denominator is also eliminated. This leaves the function as $D = ax_1 + by_1 + cz_1$. Further simplification can be done by splitting the function into two separate functions: one for testing the side planes and one for testing the top and bottom planes. These functions are $D = ax_1 + cz_1$ and $D = by_1 + cz_1$, respectively, as the y-component of the plane normal is zero in the first case and the x-component is zero in the second case. By knowing the direction of the plane normals, the sign of the distance tells on which side of the plane the vertex is. See Listing 1.3 for HLSL code of these two functions.

When all three cases have been evaluated, the minimum and maximum depths for a tile have been determined and the result can be stored. The result is stored in a render target with the same size as the x- and y-dimensions of the cluster structure. When a triangle is run through a pixel shader, it can be either front facing or back facing. In the case of a triangle being front facing, the minimum depth will be stored, and in the back facing case, the maximum depth will be stored.

To save video memory, the depth values are first converted into Z-cluster space, which is what is used in the following pass. The render target uses the

```
bool is_in_xslice(float3 top_plane , float3 bottom_plane ,
                  float3 vert_point)
{
   return (top_plane.y * vert_point.y + top_plane.z * vert_point.z
           >= 0.0f && bottom_plane.y * vert_point.y +
           bottom_plane.z * vert_point.z >= 0.0f);
}

bool is_in_yslice(float3 left_plane , float3 right_plane ,
                  float3 vert_point)
{
   return (left_plane.x * vert_point.x + left_plane.z * vert_point↩
      .z
          >= 0.0f && right_plane.x * vert_point.x +
          right_plane.z * vert_point.z >= 0.0f );
}
```

Listing 1.3. Vertex point versus tile boundary planes intersection.

format `R8G8_UNORM`, which allows for the cluster structure to have up to 256 clusters in the z-dimension. As many triangles can be in the same tile for a light shape, it is important to find the minimum and maximum Z-clusters for all the triangles. This is done by writing the result to the render target using using a `MIN` rasterizer blend mode, which ensures that the smallest result is stored. To be able to use the same shader and the same blend mode for both front-facing and back-facing triangles, the HLSL system value `SV_IsFrontFace` is used to select in which color channel the result is stored. In the case of back-facing triangles, the result must be inverted to correctly blend using the MIN blend mode; the result is then inverted again in the next pass to retrieve the correct value. Figure 1.5 illustrates the found minimum and maximum depth points in a tile for a point light shape. A top-down illustration of the final result of the shell pass can be seen in Figure 1.6, where two point lights and a spot light have been processed, with the colored clusters representing the minimum and maximum Z-clusters for each tile and light.

1.3.3 Depth Distribution

The *depth distribution* determines how the Z-cluster planes are distributed along the z-axis in the view space. The depth distribution is represented as a function that takes a linear depth value as input and outputs the corresponding Z-cluster. Two functions have been evaluated in this implementation; one linear and one exponential. The linear distribution simply divides the z-axis into equally spaced slices while the exponential function is

$$Z = \log_2(d)\frac{1}{\log_2(f) - \log_2(n)}(c-1) + \left((1 - \log_2(n))\frac{1}{\log_2(f) - \log_2(n)}(c-1)\right),$$

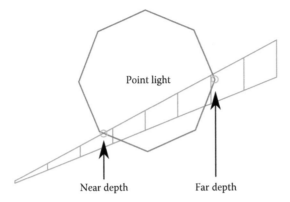

Figure 1.5. Top-down view of one tile and the found minimum and maximum depths for a point light mesh.

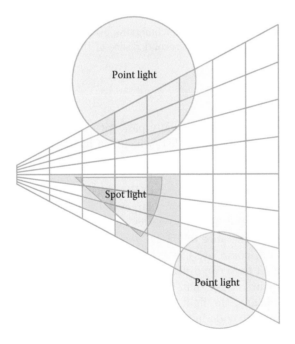

Figure 1.6. Two-dimensional top-down view of a shell pass.

where d is the view-space distance along the z-axis, f is the distance to the last z-plane, n is the distance to the second z-plane, and c is the number of clusters in the z-dimension. Note that most of these are constants and are not recalculated. Figure 1.7 shows the two functions in a graph with example values.

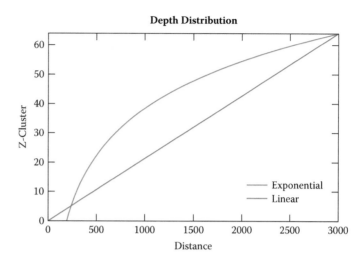

Figure 1.7. Graph of two distribution functions over an example depth of 3000 with 64 clusters in the z-dimension. The second z-slice of the exponential function is set to start at 200.

1.3.4 Fill Pass

The *fill pass* is a compute-shader-only pass with one purpose: to write the assigned lights into the light linked list, which is a linked list on the GPU derived from [Yang et al. 10].

Light linked list A light linked list is a GPU-friendly data structure for storing and managing many index pointers to larger data. In the case of this algorithm, a fixed number of unique lights are active each frame, and hundreds of clusters can contain the same instance of a light. It would be wasteful to store the actual light data (position, color, etc.) in every cluster; instead, an index to the light data is stored. Light data can differ between light types and implementation, but in most cases they are larger than 64 bit, which is the size of the light linked list node. More specifically, the light linked list node contains three pieces of data: the pointer to the next node in the list, the pointer to the actual light data, and the light type. These can fit into either 64 bits or 32 bits, depending on the maximum amount of lights needed in the game. Examples of the data in a node are shown in Table 1.1. The 64-bit node has support for more lights than modern hardware can manage in real time, but the 32-bit node is at the limit of what could be viable in a modern game engine. A tradeoff has to be made between memory savings and the maximum number of supported lights. Note that in Table 1.1 the 32-bit node uses 2 bits for the light type and 10 bits for the light ID, which results in 4096 total lights. This can be switched around to whatever

	(a)	
Data	**Size**	**Max. Value**
Light type	8 bits	256
LightID	24 bits	16777216
Link	32 bits	4294967296

	(b)	
Data	**Size**	**Max. Value**
Light type	2 bits	4
LightID	10 bits	1024
Link	20 bits	1048576

Table 1.1. Examples of (a) 64-bit and (b) 32-bit node layouts.

fits the implementation best; for example, if only point lights and spot lights are used, the light type would only need 1 bit.

The data structures used to build the light linked list consists of three parts and can be seen in Figure 1.8. The start offset buffer is a Direct3D `ByteAddress-Buffer` with cells corresponding to each cluster. The elements are `uint32` and act as pointers into the linked node light list. Each cell in the start offset buffer points to the head node for a cluster. Simply following the head node in the linked list will go through all nodes for a given cluster. The light linked list is a large one-dimensional structured buffer containing the previously mentioned nodes. Each used node points to actual light data that can be fetched and used for shading.

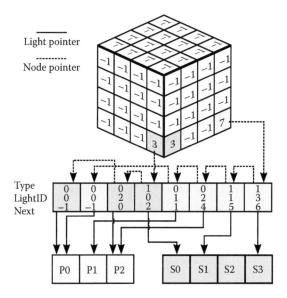

Figure 1.8. Illustration of the light linked list. The "Next" field is the index to the next node in the linked list; if a node is pointed to and has −1 as its next node, it means that it is the tail node and no more nodes are linked to that sequence. The three-dimensional structure contains a pointer from each cluster to the head node for that cluster. If a cluster is empty, there will be −1 in the corresponding cell. The types can be chosen per implementation, and in this case 0 stands for point lights and 1 stands for spot lights. For example, the cluster that points to node 7 touches lights P0, P1, P2, S1, and S3.

```
//This array has NUM_LIGHTS slices and contains the near and far
//Z-clusters for each tile.
Texture2DArray<float2> conservativeRTs : register(t0);

//Linked list of light IDs.
RWByteAddressBuffer StartOffsetBuffer : register(u0);
RWStructuredBuffer<LinkedLightID> LinkedLightList : register(u1);

[numthreads(TILESX, TILESY, 1)]
void main( uint3 thread_ID : SV_DispatchThreadID ){
  //Load near and far values (x is near and y is far).
  float2 near_and_far = conservativeRTs.Load(int4(thread_ID, 0));

  if(near_and_far.x == 1.0f && near_and_far.y == 1.0f)
    return;

  //Unpack to Z-cluster space ([0,1] to [0,255]). Also handle
  //cases where no near or far clusters were written.
  uint near = (near_and_far.x == 1.0f) ? 0 :
      uint(near_and_far.x * 255.0f + 0.5f);
  uint far  = (near_and_far.y == 1.0f) ? (CLUSTERSZ - 1) :
      uint(((CLUSTERSZ - 1.0f) / 255.0f - near_and_far.y)
          * 255.0f + 0.5f);

  //Loop through near to far and fill the light linked list.
  uint offset_index_base = 4 * (thread_ID.x + CLUSTERSX *
                                 thread_ID.y);
  uint offset_index_step = 4 * CLUSTERSX * CLUSTERSY;
  uint type = light_type;
  for(uint i = near; i <= far; ++i){
    uint index_count = LinkedLightList.IncrementCounter();
    uint start_offset_address = offset_index_base
                                 + offset_index_step * i;

    uint prev_offset;
    StartOffsetBuffer.InterlockedExchange(start_offset_address,
                                           index_count, prev_offset);

    LinkedLightID linked_node;
    linked_node.lightID = (type << 24) | (thread_ID.z & 0xFFFFFF);
            //Light type is encoded in the last 8bit of the
            //node.lightID and lightID in the first 24bits.
    linked_node.link = prev_offset;

    LinkedLightList[index_count] = linked_node;
  }
}
```

Listing 1.4. The complete compute shader for the fill pass.

The last part is the actual light data storage that can be set up in multiple ways as long as it can be indexed using a uint32. In this implementation, the light data is stored in structured buffers. The complete compute shader is outlined in Listing 1.4.

When the fill pass is complete, the linked light list contains all information necessary to shade any geometry in the scene. An example of a completely assigned cluster structure is illustrated in Figure 1.9.

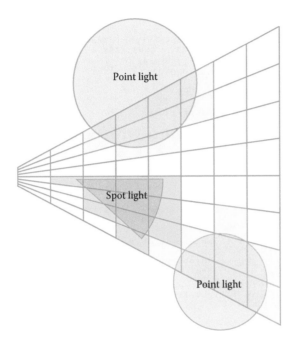

Figure 1.9. Two-dimensional top-down view of a fill pass.

1.4   Shading

The shading is done in the pixel shader by calculating in which cluster the pixel lies and getting the lights from that cluster. As the light types are stored sequentially in the light linked list, it is easy to loop through all lights without having to perform expensive branching. The pixel shader code is listed in Listing 1.5.

Finding out from which cluster the pixel should pull the lights is done by translating the screen-space x- and y-positions of the pixel into the cluster's x- and y-spaces. If the tile pixel size is a power of two, this can be done by a bit shift operation rather than using division. Finding the z-position of the cluster requires a depth value for the pixel, which could be sampled from a depth buffer in the case of deferred shading or could be the z-position of the interpolated geometry in the case of forward shading. The sampled depth is then translated into the Z-cluster space by applying the same depth distribution function used in the shell pass. Figure 1.10 shows what clusters are used for shading in an example scene using the assigned lights from Figure 1.9.

Each light type has its own `while` loop, and the `while` loops are in the reversed order from how the light types were assigned due to the the light linked list having its head pointing at the end of the linked sequence. For example, if point lights are assigned before spot lights, the spot lights will be before the point lights in

```
uint light_index = start_offset_buffer[clusterPos.x + CLUSTERSX *↵
    clusterPos.y + CLUSTERSX * CLUSTERSY * zcluster];

float3 outColor = float3(0,0,0);

LinkedLightID linked_light;

if(light_index != 0xFFFFFFFF)
{
    linked_light = light_linked_list[light_index];

    //Spot light
    while((linked_light.lightID >> 24) == 1)
    {
        uint lightID = (linked_light.lightID & 0xFFFFFF);

        outColor += SpotLightCalc(pos, norm, diff, spotLights[↵
            lightID]);

        light_index = linked_light.link;

        if(light_index == 0xFFFFFFFF)
            break;

        linked_light = light_linked_list[light_index];
    }
    //Point light
    while((linked_light.lightID >> 24) == 0)
    {
        uint lightID = (linked_light.lightID & 0xFFFFFF);

        outColor += PointLightCalc(pos, norm, diff, pointLights[↵
            lightID]);

        light_index = linked_light.link;

        if(light_index == 0xFFFFFFFF)
            break;

        linked_light = light_linked_list[light_index];
    }
}

return float4(outColor, 1.0f);
```

Listing 1.5. Pixel shader code for going through the light linked list for shading a pixel.

the linked sequence. See Figure 1.8, where the node pointer arrows show how the linked list will be traversed.

1.5 Results and Analysis

This section will show results from the performed experiments and presents an analysis of performance, memory, number of assigned clusters, and depth distri-

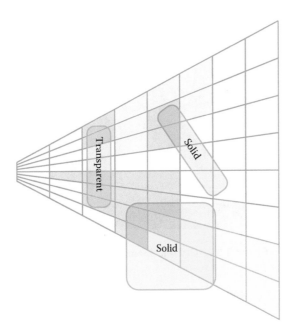

Figure 1.10. Two-dimensional top-down view of sampled clusters in a scene with objects. Note that transparent objects are shaded the same way as opaque objects. Colored clusters contain lights, and the blue clusters are used for shading the geometry.

bution in separate sections. The charts compare many different cluster structure setups, and in some of them the key legend describes the cluster structure dimensions and the depth distribution function used. The suffixes "-L" and "-E" mean linear and exponential, respectively. Performance is measured in milliseconds, and all measurements are done on the GPU.

The test scene is the CryTek Sponza Atrium with up to 4096 lights, and the test scenario is set up exactly as AMD's Forward+ demo [Harada et al. 13], which is also used as a comparison in the light assignment results. A screenshot of the test scene can be seen in Figure 1.11. All tests are performed on an NVIDIA GTX970 graphics card running DirectX 12 on Windows 10 build 10130. The resolution is 1536×768.

1.5.1 Performance

Apart from the performance inconsistencies between depth distribution functions, which are analysed in detail in Section 1.5.4, the performance results are consistent. A few observations can be made by examining Figures 1.12, 1.13 and 1.14: The shell pass remains constant in time when the x- and y-dimensions change, the fill pass increases in time when any of the three dimensions of the cluster

Figure 1.11. CryTek Sponza Atrium test scene.

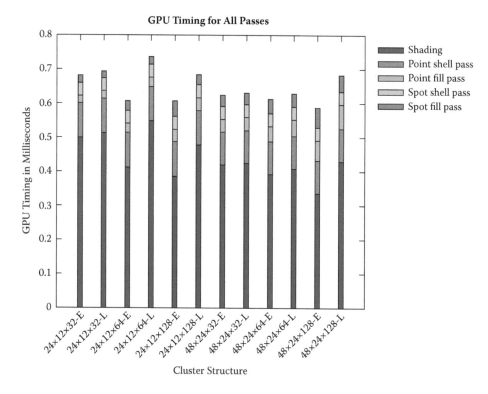

Figure 1.12. Total GPU timings in milliseconds split up into the different passes of the algorithm at 1024 lights. Lower is better.

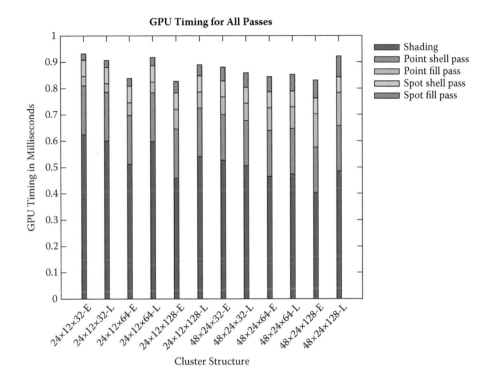

Figure 1.13. Total GPU timings in milliseconds split up into the different passes of the algorithm at 2048 lights. Lower is better.

structure increases, and the total time increases close to linearly with regards to the number of lights.

The times for the two shell passes remain constant when going from 24×12 to 48×24 tiles, but there is a significant difference between them in time. The light shape mesh vertex count used for the respective shell passes are 42 and 10, which indicates that the pixel shader is not the bottleneck. This observation is further strengthened by the fact that going from 24×12 tiles to 48×24 will yield up to four times the number of pixel shader invocations for any number of triangles, which in turn means that the constant time for the shell passes is caused by the triangle processing and data transfer being the bottleneck. Packing data for transfer between shader stages has given the best performance increases when optimizing the shaders.

The fill pass suffers from bad scaling with being up to 6.5 times slower between $24 \times 12 \times 32$ and $48 \times 24 \times 128$ at 4096 lights; see Figure 1.14. As opposed to the pixel shader in the shell pass, which uses mostly ALU instructions, the fill pass writes a lot of data to the light linked list and becomes bandwidth intensive at a

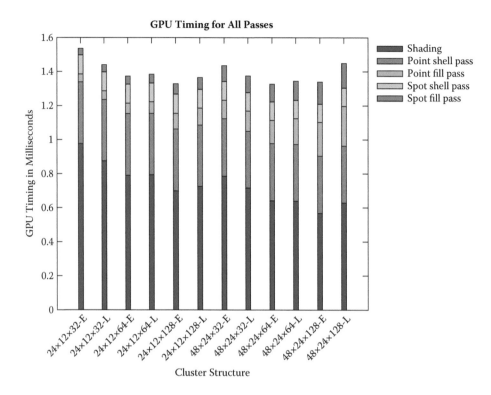

Figure 1.14. Total GPU timings in milliseconds split up into the different passes of the algorithm at 4096 lights. Lower is better.

large number of lights and clusters. The compute shader in the fill pass has low thread coherency and occupancy due to the shape of the cluster structure: lights close to the camera fill up most of their render targets while lights far away from the camera only fill a minimal part the their render targets. The compute shader will invoke threads for all texels, where empty texels cause an early exit for a thread. When using exponential depth, the lights close to the camera will be assigned to a large majority of the clusters. The shape and size of the lights also directly affects the thread coherency of the compute shader as lights that cover many clusters in the z-dimension will write more data as each thread writes data from the near to far clusters in each tile. This is also why the largest relative increases in time occur when adding more slices to the cluster structure. On top of those general observations, all the data writing is done by using atomic functions, which limits the level of parallel efficiency of the compute shader. The spot light fill pass goes from being one of the cheapest passes at a low cluster count to one of the most expensive passes at a high cluster count. The reason for having the fill

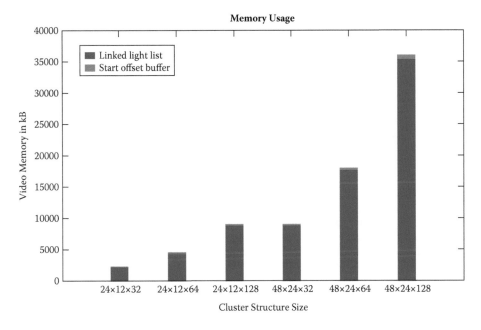

Figure 1.15. Video memory used by the cluster structure and light linked list at 4096 lights. Lower is better.

pass is because of the choice of data structure, the light linked list. The fill pass is decoupled from the shell pass and can be replaced by something else if another data structure is desired, this adds to the flexibility of the algorithm and could be a possible optimization. Another performance optimization possibility is to use fixed-size arrays for each cluster, but this will severely limit the number of lights as it would significantly increase the needed memory to store light pointers.

1.5.2 Memory

The memory model of this implementation is simple; it consists of the light linked list and the render targets for the lights. Figure 1.15 shows the memory used by the linked light list for the tested cluster structure sizes with 64-bit list nodes. The start offset buffer is always `numberOfClusters * 4` bytes large, and the light linked list is initialized to a safe size because it works like a pool of light pointers. In this case, the light linked list is `numberOfClusters * 8 * 30` bytes large; 30 is an arbitrarily chosen multiplier that provides a safe list size for this particular scenario. If the list size is not large enough, there will be lights missing at shading time. The missing lights will be noticeable: a light pointer could be missing from one cluster and correctly assigned to a neighbouring cluster, creating a hard edge at the tile border. Visually, missing light assignments will show up as darker

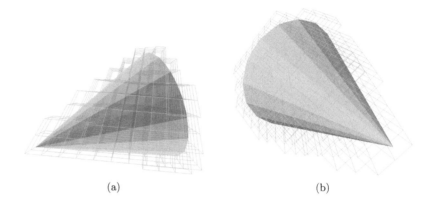

(a)   (b)

Figure 1.16. Clusters that were assigned to a spot light are visualized and viewed from two different angles. Perfect clustering with exponential depth distribution was captured from a medium distance at a clustered structure size of $24 \times 12 \times 64$.

blocks in the final shaded image. As can be seen in Figure 1.15, the actual linked list is a large majority of the memory usage at 4096 lights. Using a 32-bit node would only use half the memory of the linked list, but as previously shown in Table 1.1, only 1048576 linked nodes would fit at a 20-bit link size, which would limit the maximum cluster structure size depending on the concentration of lights in a scene.

The render target memory usage is not dependent on the cluster structure slice depth; it is dependent on the number of lights and the number of tiles. Each light needs `numberOfTiles * 2` bytes, and at 4096 lights with 24×12 tiles, this adds up to 2,359,296 bytes.

If memory is an issue, there is the alternative to use a 32-bit node in the light linked list and choosing an appropriate cluster structure size. Comparing the $24 \times 12 \times 128$ structure with 32-bit nodes to the $48 \times 24 \times 32$ structure with 64-bit nodes results in 6.87 MB and 18.2 MB, respectively. In this implementation, the $24 \times 12 \times 128$ structure even achieves better shading and light assignment times. This goes to show that knowing the use case of the application and choosing the right setup for this technique is important.

1.5.3   Light Assignment

Figure 1.16 shows a perfectly clustered spot light and how it fits in the cluster structure. Perfect clustering refers to the fact that a light shape is never assigned to clusters it does not intersect. Even with perfect clustering the shading pass will perform some unnecessary shading calculations due to parts of the clusters not being covered by the shape, as can be seen in the Figure 1.16. Smaller clusters will give less empty space for an assigned shape and give better shading times.

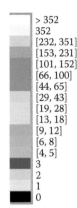

> 352
352
[232, 351]
[153, 231]
[101, 152]
[66, 100]
[44, 65]
[29, 43]
[19, 28]
[13, 18]
[9, 12]
[6, 8]
[4, 5]
3
2
1
0

Figure 1.17. Weather radar colors corresponding to the number of lighting calculations.

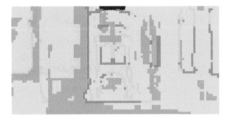

(a) Clustered shading using 24 × 12 × 128-E cluster structure.

(b) Tiled shading using 96 × 48 tiled structure.

Figure 1.18. Comparison between AMD's Forward+ tiled light culling demo using 2048 point lights and 2048 spot lights. Legend can be viewed in Figure 1.17.

The results from comparing AMD's Forward+ tiled light culling with the 24 × 12 × 128-E cluster structure (following the legend in Figure 1.17) are demonstrated in Figures 1.18, 1.19, and 1.20. The colors correspond to the number of lighting calculations, where lower is better. AMD's tiled light culling implementations uses 96 × 48 tiles, using 6488064 bytes video memory and performing the light assignment in 0.6 ms on average. The 24 × 12 × 128-E cluster structure uses a total of 8349696 bytes video memory including the 4096 render targets, as this comparison uses 2048 point lights and 2048 spot lights with the same light setup as AMD's demo. The clustered light assignment case takes 0.63 ms on average.

Figure 1.18 clearly shows that tiled light culling suffers from depth discontinuities and that at comparable performance the clustered light assignment performs better light assignment over all as well as having no depth discontinuities. The same is true when looking at the light types individually in Figures 1.19 and 1.20, but the spot light comparison also shows a significant reduction in lighting

(a) Clustered shading using 24 × 12 × 128-E cluster structure.

(b) Tiled shading using 96 × 48 tiled structure.

Figure 1.19. Comparison between AMD's Forward+ tiled light culling demo using 2048 point lights and no spot lights. Legend can be viewed in Figure 1.17.

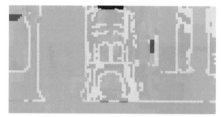

(a) Clustered shading using 24 × 12 × 128-E cluster structure.

(b) Tiled shading using 96 × 48 tiled structure.

Figure 1.20. Comparison between AMD's Forward+ tiled light culling demo using no point lights and 2048 spot lights. Legend can be viewed in Figure 1.17.

calculations when using clustered light assignment. This proves both that approximating light types as spheres is detrimental to shading performance when using non-spherical light types and that using conservative rasterization with light meshes is efficient.

1.5.4 Depth Distribution

Figure 1.21 displays the negative side of having a perspective cluster structure with exponential depth distribution. Clusters far away will always be larger than the ones up close, and they will accumulate more lights, causing a large worst-case shading time for pixels in the red zone. Using a cluster structure with a large amount of clusters will mitigate the worst case, but the same ratio between worst and best case is still present. Using a linear depth distribution will reduce the worst case but at the same time increase the best case times. Figure 1.22 shows how linear depth distribution covers more empty space where the exponential depth distribution is very fine grained and follows the structure of the pillar. The small clusters are what create a very good best case, but as can

 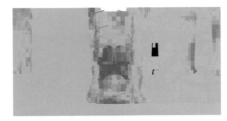

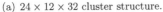

(a) $24 \times 12 \times 32$ cluster structure.   (b) $48 \times 24 \times 128$ cluster structure.

Figure 1.21. Two screen captures that show the number of lights used for shading each pixel. In this scene, 4096 lights are used: Green is 1 light, blue is 19 lights, and red is 38 or more lights. Values in between are interpolated colors.

 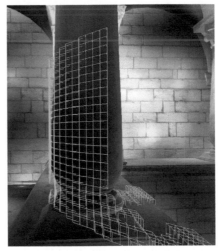

(a) Linear depth distribution.   (b) Exponential depth distribution.

Figure 1.22. Two screen captures that show clusters close to the camera. Side view. Cluster structure size is $48 \times 24 \times 128$.

be seen in Figure 1.23, the exponential depth distribution causes large clusters far from the camera as opposed to the linear distribution. Note that the depth distribution only affects the slice depth of the clusters, and even when increasing the number of cluster slices, making them thinner, the x- and y-size will remain the same. Increasing the number of slices will give better light assignment but will experience diminishing returns at a certain point due to the clusters still being large in the x- and y-dimensions and capturing many lights.

(a) Linear depth distribution.   (b) Exponential depth distribution.

Figure 1.23. Two screen captures that show clusters far from the camera. Top-down view. Cluster structure size is $48 \times 24 \times 128$.

Figure 1.12 shows that the exponential depth distribution, compared to linear depth distribution, results in better shading times in all cases. This is, however, not the case when looking at Figure 1.14, where both the $24 \times 12 \times 32$ and $24 \times 12 \times 64$ cluster structures have better shading times when using a linear depth distribution. This is caused by the fact that those cluster structures contain large clusters far away from the camera. This does not become an issue in a scene with few lights as the worst case large clusters only make up a minority of the shading cost. When a large amount of lights are used in the scene, the worst-case large clusters will be a majority of the shading cost. As can be seen in the cases where the clusters are smaller, the exponential depth distribution gives a better shading time.

There is a correlation between cluster shape and light assignment results where a cube-like cluster shape provides a good base shape. Looking at clusters structures $24 \times 12 \times 128$-E and $48 \times 24 \times 32$-E in Figure 1.14, where both contain the same amount of clusters, it is evident that the more cube-like clusters in $24 \times 12 \times 128$-E results in better performance. The performance increase gained when going from $24 \times 12 \times 128$-L to $24 \times 12 \times 128$-E is attributed to the exponential distribution creating cube-like clusters as opposed to the linear distribution, but 48x24x32-L does not benefit from going to $48 \times 24 \times 32$-E as the clusters will still have a dominant slice depth compared to the x- and y-dimensions.

1.6   Conclusion

This chapter has presented a novel technique for assigning arbitrarily shaped convex light types to clusters using conservative rasterization with good results and performance. The technique is not limited to clusters as many steps can be shared with a tiled shading implementation, nor is the technique limited to deferred shading. Using the technique to shade transparent object works without having to modify anything, and there is no requirement for a depth prepass.

Looking at the results in Section 1.5, it can be concluded that doing a finer clustering will be worthwhile as the shading pass becomes faster. Using costly shading models with many lights will increase the shading time significantly, while the light assignment will stay constant and be a minor part of the entire cost. With that said, there is a drawback of doing fine clustering: the memory usage. The total memory usage for the $48 \times 24 \times 128$ cluster structure at 4096 lights adds up to 45.4 MB, while the $24 \times 12 \times 64$ cluster structure uses 6.9 MB. The larger cluster structure achieves 28.3% better shading performance at a cost of using 6.6 times more memory.

As for finding the right cluster setup, the results have proven that cluster shape and size matters and that large and unevenly shaped clusters will be detrimental to the shading performance compared to cube-like clusters. Using an exponential depth distribution can help create cube-like clusters and gain some performance compared to linear depth distribution. However, if there are too few slices, the exponential structure will suffer from very large, far away clusters and provide worse light assignment.

Bibliography

[Andersson 09] Johan Andersson. "Parallel Graphics in Frostbite—Current and Future." Beyond Programmable Shading, SIGGRAPH Course, New Orleans, LA, August 3–7, 2009.

[Balestra and Engstad 08] Christophe Balestra and Pål-Kristian Engstad. "The Technology of Uncharted: Drake's Fortune." Game Developers Conference, San Francisco, CA, February 18–22, 2008.

[Fauconneau 14] Mark Fauconneau. "Forward Clustered Shading." https://software.intel.com/sites/default/files/managed/27/5e/Fast%20Foward%20Clustered%20Shading%20(siggraph%202014).pdf, 2014. Accessed May 20, 2015.

[Harada et al. 13] Takahiro Harada, Jay McKee, and Jason C. Yang. "Forward+: A Step Toward Film-Style Shading in Real Time." In *GPU Pro 4: Advanced Rendering Techniques*, edited by Wolfgang Engel, pp. 115–135. Boca Raton: A K Peters/CRC Press, 2013.

[Leadbetter 14] Richard Leadbetter. "The Making of Forza Horizon 2." http: //www.eurogamer.net/articles/digitalfoundry-2014-the-making-of-forza -horizon-2, 2014. Accessed May 18, 2015.

[Microsoft] Microsoft. "Floating-Point Rules." https://msdn.microsoft.com/ en-us/library/windows/desktop/jj218760(v=vs.85).aspx. Accessed May 18, 2015.

[Möller and Trumbore 05] Tomas Möller and Ben Trumbore. "Fast, Minimum Storage Ray/Triangle Intersection." In *ACM SIGGRAPH 2005 Courses,* article no. 7. New York: ACM, 2005.

[Olsson and Assarsson 11] Ola Olsson and Ulf Assarsson. "Tiled Shading." *Journal of Graphics, GPU, and Game Tools* 15:4 (2011), 235–251.

[Olsson et al. 12] Ola Olsson, Markus Billeter, and Ulf Assarsson. "Clustered Deferred and Forward Shading." In *Proceedings of the Fourth ACM SIGGRAPH/Eurographics Conference on High-Performance Graphics,* pp. 87– 96. Aire-la-Ville, Switzerland: Eurographics Association, 2012.

[Persson and Olsson 13] Emil Persson and Ola Olsson. "Practical Clustered Deferred and Forward Shading." Advances in Real-Time Rendering in Games, SIGGRAPH Course, Anaheim, CA, July 23, 2013. Available online (http://s2013.siggraph.org/attendees/courses/ session/advances-real-time-rendering-games-part-i).

[Swoboda 09] Matt Swoboda. "Deferred Lighting and Post Processing on Playstation 3." Game Developers Conference, San Francisco, CA, March 23–27, 2009.

[Thomas 15] Gareth Thomas. "Advanced Visual Effects with DirectX 11 and 12: Advancements in Tile-Based Compute Rendering." Game Developers Conference, San Francisco, CA, March 2–6, 2015. Available online (http:// www.gdcvault.com/play/1021764/Advanced-Visual-Effects-With-DirectX).

[Yang et al. 10] Jason C. Yang, Justin Hensley, Holger Grün, and Nicolas Thibieroz. "Real-Time Concurrent Linked List Construction on the GPU." *Computer Graphics Forum* 29:4 (2010), 1297–1304.

Fine Pruned Tiled Light Lists
Morten S. Mikkelsen

2.1 Overview

In this chapter we present a new tiled lighting variant with a primary focus on optimization for the AMD Graphics Core Next (GCN) architecture. Our approach was used for the game *Rise of the Tomb Raider*. In particular, we leverage asynchronous compute by interleaving light list generation with rendering of shadow maps. Light list generation is done per tile in two steps within the same compute kernel. An initial coarse pass that generates a light list in local storage using simple screen-space AABB bounding volume intersection testing regardless of light type. The second step is fine pruning, which performs further testing on the coarse list by testing each pixel in the tile if the point in 3D space is inside the true shape of the light source.

Furthermore, we present an efficient hybrid solution between tiled deferred and tiled forward.

2.2 Introduction

Traditionally, real-time deferred lighting is done using alpha blending to accumulate lighting contributions one light at a time. The main big advantage is the ability to assign and apply lights specifically to pixels representing points in 3D space inside the light volume. With a basic forward-lit shading model, on the other hand, light lists are built on the CPU per mesh instance based on bounding volume intersection tests between the mesh instance and the light volumes. This approach often results in a significant overhead in light count to process per pixel, particularly for large meshes because the light list is shared for all pixels occupied on screen by the mesh instance.

Recently, since the introduction of DirectX 11, compute-based tiled lighting has become a popular alternative to deferred lighting. Tiled lighting works by representing the frame buffer as an $n \times m$ grid of tiles where the tiles are of a fixed resolution. The GPU is used to generate a list of indices per tile containing

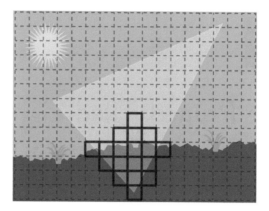

Figure 2.1. The screen separated into tiles. A spot light is shown intersecting with the foreground. This light is added to the light list of every tile containing a valid intersection, which is indicated here with a solid tile boundary.

references to the lights overlapping screen boundaries of a tile. A lighting pass pulls the light list from the tile containing the currently processed pixel (see Figure 2.1).

This is a high-level overview of how a basic tiled lighting scheme works in compute:

1. Per tile

   (a) For each tile find a minimum and a maximum depth in the depth buffer.

   (b) Each thread checks a disjoint subset of lights by bounding sphere against tile bounds.

   (c) Indices to lights intersecting the tile are stored in local data storage (LDS).

   (d) Final list is available to all threads for further processing.

Recently several proposed methods for tiled lighting have emerged such as AMD's Forward+ Tiled Lighting [Harada et al. 12], which is primarily aimed at moving away from traditional deferred lighting in order to leverage EQAA. This method partitions tiles evenly by depth into cells, thus making it a 3D grid of light lists $n \times m \times l$. Culling is performed by testing the bounding sphere of the light against the side planes of the tile frustum and the near and far plane of the cells. Another known variant is Insomniacs' Light Linked List [Bezrati 14], which proposes a solution where the footprint of the light lists is reduced/managed using linked lists on the GPU. Another variant is Clustered Deferred and Forward

Shading [Olsson et al. 12], which reduces tile occupancy further by clustering. This achieves a more ideal partitioning of tiles into cells.

Among main advantages of tiled lighting are the following:

1. Tiled deferred lighting is single pass since each pixel is lit simply by looping over the lights referenced by the list stored in the corresponding tile. This makes the approach more resilient to overlapping lights than traditional deferred lighting because the data in the G-buffer is only pulled once and because the resulting color is only written to the frame buffer once.

2. Unlike traditional deferred lighting, there exists a forward variant when using tiled lighting. The reason is that as we draw the polygonal meshes, we can pull the same light list in-process from the tile containing the pixel being shaded.

3. A less commonly known advantage to using tiled lighting is that the light list generation is an ideal candidate for asynchronous compute, which allows us to interleave this processing with unrelated graphics work earlier in the frame update.

Previous methods such as [Harada et al. 12] and [Olsson et al. 12] have excess lights in the per tile light lists because these are built based on a simple bounding spheres intersection test. Additional redundancy exists with all previous techniques because the cells contain significant amounts of unoccupied space. In AAA games many of our lights are not spheres, and in fact, we must support several light shapes such as cones, capsules, and boxes with different features. Building lists based on bounding volumes and partitioned tile bounds alone leaves much redundancy in the light lists compared to the final list we end up with when fine pruning.

We found that by writing a lean dedicated compute shader to perform fine pruning, we were able to achieve significant gains due to the more complex shader used for lighting not having to deal with the redundant lights in the list. Furthermore, the separation between light list building and actual lighting allowed us to run the list building in asynchronous compute during rendering of shadow maps, which in practice gives us fine pruned lists for free.

Furthermore, our approach is a hybrid between tiled deferred and tiled forward lighting. This allows us to light the majority of pixels by a deferred approach using a narrow G-buffer, which is more hardware efficient, and then deviate from this for cases where we need a material-specific lighting model by using tiled forward.

2.3 Our Method

Previous papers on tiled lighting such as [Harada et al. 12] and [Olsson et al. 12] are particularly aimed at processing high quantities of sphere lights. The numbers quoted are in the 1–2 thousand range. Furthermore, these papers describe algorithms that are designed to handle scenarios where the lights have a relatively optimal distribution in space. While our method is also capable of handling high numbers of lights, we found we generally have no more than 40–120 lights inside the camera frustum in our real world levels. In our case we found that we often have fewer very large lights that occupy the same space. Many of our lights are large spot lights that are narrow to achieve a good distribution of pixels in the shadow map. The bounding sphere is a bad representation in this case. Ultimately, without additional culling, our light lists would contain high numbers of lights, several of which do not affect any of the actual tile pixels.

In every frame we receive a set of lights that have been classified visible (inside the camera frustum) by the cell and portal system. For each tile on the screen, we generate a *fine pruned light list*. Each light is included only if at least one pixel in the tile represents a point in 3D space that is inside the light volume. Testing all pixels in a tile against all visible lights is prohibitively expensive. To solve this, we first build a *coarse light list* containing lights whose screen-space axis aligned bounding box (AABB) intersects the tile boundary. The tile boundary is trivially defined by its xy-region on the screen and minimum and maximum depths in the depth buffer within tile region. We determine, on the GPU, the screen-space AABB around each visible light.

The process is described below in pseudo-code.

1. Per camera

    (a) On the CPU find lights that intersect the camera frustum.

    (b) Sort this set of lights by shape.

    (c) On the GPU find the tight screen-space AABB per light source regardless of shape. This is done by finding the intersection volume between the camera and a convex hull for the light. We further constrain the AABB using a bounding sphere of the light.

2. Per 16×16 pixel tile

    (a) For each tile find a minimum and a maximum depth in the depth buffer.

    (b) Each compute thread tests the intersection of a disjoint subset of lights by an AABB against tile bounds.

    (c) Indices to lights intersecting the tile are stored in LDS. We refer to this as the *coarse list*.

    (d) In the same kernel loop over the coarse list of lights.

        i. Each thread tests four pixels of the tile depth buffer to see if these are inside the true shape of the light.

ii. The status of the test is stored in a bit field maintained by each thread where each bit represents the corresponding coarse light.

(e) Perform a bitwise OR of all bit fields into a single bit field and use it to generate a *fine pruned light list*.

The distinction between fine pruning and performing an early out during lighting is, in concept, subtle. However, the difference is significant for two reasons. First, the shader associated with lighting consumes more resources relative to a lean shader dedicated to culling, which, as we describe in the next section, has implications on performance. Second, by using asynchronous compute, we can absorb most of the cost of fine pruning, which includes the cost of looping through redundant lights.

2.4 Implementation Details

In the following we are targeting the AMD GCN architecture specifically, though the practices are generally good for any modern-day GPU. A modern GPU core hides latency by shuffling through jobs. We will refer to these cores as a CU (compute unit). All work is packaged into wavefronts. Whether it is compute, vertex shading, pixel shading, etc., each CU can harbor up to 40 wavefronts, and each wavefront represents 64 threads. These threads run in lock-step similar to how SSE4 is 4 wide running in lock-step. The pool of resources such as registers and local store LDS are shared on each CU, which implies that the more you consume these, the fewer jobs get to occupy each CU, which means the GPU's ability to hide latencies deteriorates dramatically.

As it turns out, the rendering of shadow maps and generation of fine pruned light lists are a great match. According to our timings, shadow map rendering generally takes 2–4 ms in our game. Furthermore, it is a process that generates very few wavefronts of work and relies primarily on the primitive scan converter and trafficking of data. The reason for this is that shadow map rendering is a depth-only pass, which means no actual pixel shading CU work is generated for opaque meshes. Generating fine pruned light lists, on the other hand, is primarily propagating ALU-heavy wavefronts. This allows us to absorb most of the time spent on generating the lists using asynchronous compute.

Let us describe the algorithm steps in detail. First, Step 1(a) is to gather all visible lights in the frame. We do this using a typical cell and portal system on the CPU.

In Step 1(b) we sort, on the CPU, the visible lights by their type of shape. This allows us to process the lights using a fixed sequence of loops where each loop is dedicated to a specific light type. This is particularly important in the context of tiled forward lighting since in this case the 64 pixels being processed in a wavefront do often not exist in the same tile. Because the 64 threads run in lock-step, a divergence in execution path is inefficient. Having sorted the lights by type maximizes the likelihood that all threads are in alignment execution path-wise. In our case sphere/capsule is one type/execution path, cone/wedge is a type, and box is the final type.

Next, in Step 1(c) we find the screen-space AABB for each light in the visible set. As input each light source is represented by an oriented bounding box (OBB) with a nonuniform scale at the top four vertices, which allows us to represent narrow spot lights and wedges better. To determine the AABB for the light, we find the point set to the intersection volume between the camera frustum and the convex bounding volume. This is done by frustum clipping the quads of the scaled OBB and using the final point set of each resulting fan to update the AABB. Any of the eight points of the camera frustum that are inside the convex bounding volume must also be applied to the fitting of the AABB. Last, we determine the AABB around the bounding sphere of the light and then store the intersection between this and the already established AABB as the final result. It should be noted that though this is a lot of processing, it is done once per camera and *not per tile*. This work can be done on the CPU but we do it on the GPU as an asynchronous compute shader.

In Step 2 the work of generating the final per-tile light list is performed, and we describe the various components to it in the following. All the parts within Step 2 are performed on a per-tile level within one compute kernel. Since the tile size is 16×16 pixels, the dispatch of the kernel is executed using the following threadgroup counts: $(\text{width} + 15)/16$, $(\text{height} + 15)/16$, and 1. The kernel is declared as a single wavefront threadgroup: $64 \times 1 \times 1$.

First, in Step 2(a) we must establish the screen-space AABB associated with the tile being operated on by the threadgroup. Each of the 64 threads reads four individual depths of the tile and establish the minimum and maximum of the four samples. Next, the collective minimum and maximum of the tile is established using `InterlockedMin()` and `InterlockedMax()`, which are HLSL intrinsic functions.

In Steps 2(b)–(c) we perform the initial coarse pruning test. Each of the visible lights will have its screen-space AABB tested for intersection against the AABB of the tile regardless of the true light shape. Each thread handles a disjoint subset of lights and thus performs `numVisibleLights`/64 iterations. Furthermore, using a single wavefront threadgroup allows us to preserve the order of the lights passing the coarse test because the 64 threads run in lock-step. The resulting coarse list of indices to lights is stored in LDS.

It is worth noting that the screen-space AABB corresponds to a sheared sub-frustum in the camera space, as shown in Figure 2.2. In [Harada et al. 12] and [Olsson et al. 12] tiled lighting is implemented such that the bounding sphere around each light is tested against the frustum planes associated with each tile. However, we can do the same test faster when we already know the screen-space AABB for each light. This also allows for a tighter fit than a bounding sphere around certain light types, such as a spot light, which allows us to spend less

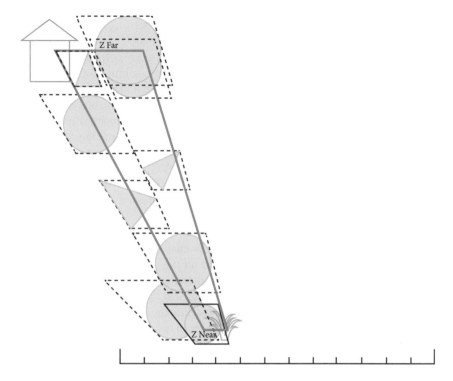

Figure 2.2. The sheared frustum associated with a tile from the frontmost pixel to the one farthest away. In this case there are six sphere lights and three spot lights. All nine lights pass the coarse intersection test but only one passes the fine pruned intersection test.

time on fine pruning. Potentially using AABB for the test also leads to a lower register count since we no longer need to keep six frustum planes for the tile in registers during iteration through the lights.

Finally, in Steps 2(d)–(e) we perform fine pruning. The fine pruned light list is a subset of the coarse light list. Each pixel in the tile is tested to see if the corresponding point in 3D space is inside the true shape of the light volume. Lights that contain one or more such points are put in the fine pruned light list. Each thread is responsible for testing 2×2 pixels of the 16×16 tile (1×1 for half-resolution lighting), and each thread maintains a record in the form of a 64-bit mask where each bit is enabled if the volume of the corresponding light contains at least one of the four points managed by the thread. Once we have processed all coarse lights in this manner, we finally determine the collective 64-bit mask by using the HLSL intrinsic `InterlockedOr()`. The resulting bit mask is used to remove redundancies from the coarse light list and write the final fine pruned list to memory. The effect of fine pruning is shown in Figure 2.2.

A CU has both vector and scalar registers. For a vector register VGPR, every thread has an individual dword, which gives a total footprint of 256 bytes per register. A scalar register SGPR is a dword that is shared for all threads with a total of 4 bytes per register. As mentioned at the beginning of this section, a high consumption of resources by a shader has a negative impact on performance. A shader used for lighting often consumes a relatively high amount of vector registers due to the overall complexity in code. If we can ensure during lighting that every thread of a wavefront represents a pixel in the same tile and thus pulls the same light list, then the attributes of the light such as color, position, fall-off, etc. can be pulled into SGPRs instead of VGPRs. It is easy to organize the treads accordingly in a compute shader; however, as will be discussed in the next section, we are using a full-screen stencil tested pixel shader for the final deferred lighting pass. This means that we are no longer in direct control of how the wavefronts are packaged. For a full-screen primitive we can ensure that the pixel shader wavefronts are fully packaged as 8×8 pixels by calling `SetScanConverterModeControl(false, false)` on the pixel shader used for deferred tiled lighting at initialization time. In addition to this, we must also run the pass after high stencil testing but before the low stencil test to maintain the execution in blocks of 8×8. Finally, we must inform the shader compiler to pull the attributes as scalar as opposed to vector. This is done by using the HLSL intrinsic `__XB_MakeUniform()` wherever we pull data from the tile.

For us this resulted in a drop from 76 to 52 in VGPRs and up to about a 1.3-ms reduction in execution time. In comparison, our kernel for generating fine pruned light lists consumes only 28 VGPRs, which as expected is much less.

The API calls mentioned above are for Xbox One only, though we suspect the equivalent API calls exist for Playstation 4 as well. No equivalent exists in the generic DirectX 11 API, though, so in this case there are two options: Either settle for vector registers on this platform, which preserves the stencil optimize, or alternatively implement the deferred lighting as a compute shader. In the latter case we would read the stencil as a texture look-up in the compute shader and perform the stencil test manually to avoid lighting the pixel twice.

2.5   Engine Integration

In order to achieve greater flexibility in shaders, it has become common to use a wide G-buffer to allow storage of more parameters. However, this consumes larger amounts of memory and puts a significant strain on the bus. It was an early decision that our game must run at 1920×1080; to achieve this, we decided to use a prepass deferred implementation, which is described in [Engel 09], with a narrow G-buffer. Our G-buffer contains a depth buffer and normal and specular power in signed R8G8B8A8 format. The sign bit of the specular power is used to indicate whether Fresnel is to be enabled or disabled on the specular reflection. The lean footprint allows us to leverage fast ESRAM on Xbox One.

77

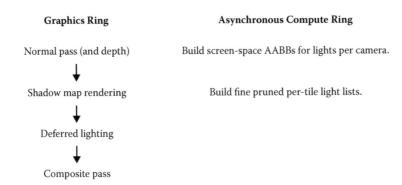

Figure 2.3. Our primary stages running on the main command buffer (left) and our asynchronous compute work (right). Generation of AABBs is interleaved with the normal-depth pass, and generation of fine pruned per-tile light lists is interleaved with rendering of the shadow maps.

The stages of our prepass rendering pipeline are shown on the left side of Figure 2.3. The geometry is rendered to the screen twice. The first time is the normal-depth pass that creates the G-buffer as depth, with world-space normal and specular power. The second time the geometry is rendered to the screen is the composite pass, which is the last stage. This stage does the shading and folds in the lighting. Rendering of shadow maps comes after the normal-depth pass, while generation of per-tile light lists is scheduled to run at the same time as an asynchronous compute job. The next stage is deferred lighting, which runs as a full-screen pass. Each pixel is lit by accumulating contributions from lights stored in the list associated with the tile to which the pixel belongs. We write the final diffuse and specular results to separate render targets, which allows us to modulate these by different textures during the final composite pass.

To achieve custom lighting on certain materials such as eyes, skin, and cloth, we use tiled forward lighting. In this case the lighting is done in-process during the composite pass by pulling and processing the light list for the tile similar to how we do this during deferred lighting. This presents a problem since we will pay the cost of lighting the pixel both deferred and forward. To solve this problem, we mark every pixel in the stencil buffer that is lit as tiled forward. During deferred lighting, we skip such pixels by using stencil testing.

In regards to the format of the per-tile light list, it can be stored in a number of ways. The obvious option is one buffer for the whole screen where each tile consumes some fixed number of 8-bit or 16-bit entries for the light indices. Using 8 bits will only allow for 256 lights on screen, and 16 bits give more range than we need. To achieve a more compact footprint, we chose to store the list as blocks of `R10G10B10A2_UINT`, where the 10-bit components each store an index to a light and the 2-bit component tells us how many of the three indices are active. We store eight such blocks per tile, which results in a final limit of 24 lights per tile after fine pruning. As previously mentioned, we allow up to 64 lights in the coarse list while in LDS. The total footprint for eight such blocks is 32 bytes per tile and thus 1 bit per pixel on screen. Note that 10-bit indices indicate a limit of 1024 lights intersecting the camera frustum per frame.

In our implementation we use separate light lists for direct lights and probe lights, each with a limit of 24 per tile. It is important to note that the light list generation is executed *once only*. This is possible since up to 64 fine pruned lights may exist temporarily on the compute side during the execution of Step 2(e). Subsequently, in this step we separate these in LDS according to their designated light list.

As mentioned in the introduction, it is common for a tiled lighting implementation to partition the tile farther along depth into cells, as is done in [Olsson et al. 12]. This grows the footprint further because each cell stores a separate list of lights. A different problem with this strategy during deferred lighting is that each thread may pull the list of lights from a different cell than other threads in the wavefront. This forces us to pull the attributes of the lights into vector registers instead of scalar registers, which as mentioned in the previous section reduces our ability to populate more wavefronts per CU, which reduces our ability to hide latency on the GPU. Ultimately, we found that the act of fine pruning our lists of lights removes most redundancies in practice, which negates the need for partitioning into cells. This is also indicated in Figure 2.2 and evident from the heat map in the next section.

One limitation when using our method is that the generated lists only work for opaque surfaces that write to a depth buffer. In our case the majority of transparencies are particle effects with many stacked layers occupying the same local space. We concluded that we could not afford to light these per pixel as it would be too costly, and we decided to light these using vertex lighting.

For regular mesh-based transparencies, we decided to use traditional forward lighting where light lists are built on the CPU for each mesh based on a bounding volume intersection. Since our transparent surfaces are sorted on a per-material basis, these are not large meshes and thus do not benefit as much from tiled light lists. Additionally, we support *light groups*, which allow artists to manually remove specific lights from the light lists of traditionally forward-lit objects. This feature allows them to prune the list to the most essential set of lights that intersect the transparent surface.

2.6   Results

In this section we show an interior scene running at 1920×1080 with and without fine pruning. Figure 2.4 shows the results of coarse culling. The coarse list generation takes 0.5 ms and runs asynchronously. Figure 2.5 shows the results

Figure 2.4. Number of lights per tile after coarse culling.

after fine pruning, which costs 1.7 ms in list generation. The cost is however well hidden because of asynchronous compute. The heat map in Figure 2.6 indicates the occupancy of lights per tile in Figures 2.4 and 2.5. We can see that the light counts without fine pruning are significantly higher in almost every tile. As expected, we see a significant drop in execution time of deferred lighting, dropping from 5.4 ms to 1.4 ms with fine pruning enabled.

2.7 Conclusion

We have demonstrated a new tiled lighting variant that performs light list generation per tile in two steps within the same compute kernel. The initial coarse pass generates a light list in local storage based on simple screen-space AABB bounding volume intersection testing regardless of light type. The second step is fine pruning, which performs further testing on the coarse list by testing each pixel in the tile if the corresponding point in 3D space is inside the true shape of the light source. Lights that contain one or more such points are put in the fine pruned list, which is written to memory. We have found that in practice this process reduces the light count per tile significantly.

On the AMD GCN architecture a depth-only pass of opaque meshes generates very little work for the GPU cores. We take advantage of this fact by using asynchronous compute to hide most of the combined cost of the coarse and the fine pruning steps by interleaving this work with the rendering of shadow maps, which gives no redundancy light lists for free.

Figure 2.5. Number of lights per tile after fine pruning.

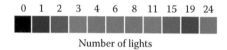

Number of lights

Figure 2.6. Color heatmap with number of lights per tile.

While supporting multiple light types, the final footprint for the light list is 1 bit per pixel with a maximum number of 24 fine pruned lights per tile.

Finally, an efficient hybrid between tiled deferred and tiled forward is presented where tiled deferred lighting is done as a stencil tested full-screen pass to avoid lighting twice for pixels that are lit by tiled forward materials. To further accelerate tiled forward, we keep the light list sorted by type in a fixed order. This allows us to maximize the chance that all pixels in a wavefront are processing lights in the same light loop.

2.8 Acknowledgments

Thank you to editor Michal Valient for his support in the development of this chapter and for his reviews. Additionally, thank you to Manchor Ko and Kasper H. Nielsen for proofreading the chapter. I would also like to thank Paul Houx at Nixxes for his excellent work and collaboration on integrating this method into the foundation engine at Crystal Dynamics. And finally, thanks go to Scott Krotz for his support and help getting asynchronous compute to work properly.

Bibliography

[Bezrati 14] Abdul Bezrati. "Real-Time Lighting via Light Linked List." Paper presented at SIGGRAPH, Vancouver, Canada, August 12–14, 2014.

[Engel 09] Wolfgang Engel. "The Light Pre-Pass Renderer: Renderer Design for Efficient Support of Multiple Lights." SIGGRAPH Course: Advances in Real-Time Rendering in 3D Graphics and Games, New Orleans, LA, August 3, 2009.

[Harada et al. 12] Takahiro Harada, Jay McKee, and Jason C. Yang. "Forward+: Bringing Deferred Lighting to the Next Level." Eurographics Short Paper, Cagliari, Italy, May 13–18, 2012.

[Olsson et al. 12] Ola Olsson, Markus Billeter, and Ulf Assarsson. "Clustered Deferred and Forward Shading." Paper presented at High Performance Graphics, Paris, France, June 25–27, 2012.

Deferred Attribute Interpolation Shading
Christoph Schied and Carsten Dachsbacher

3.1 Introduction

Deferred shading is a popular technique in real-time rendering. In contrast to a traditional rendering pipeline, deferred shading is split into two phases. First, the geometry is sampled and stored in the geometry buffer, which serves as input for the second phase where the shading is computed. Thereby, the complexity for shading is decoupled from the geometric complexity, and furthermore advanced geometry-aware screen-space techniques may be employed. However, deferred shading does not play well with multi-sample antialiasing. Multi-sample antialiasing samples the visibility of a primitive at several subpixel positions, however the shading is only evaluated once inside a pixel per primitive. Deferred shading samples the geometric attributes, and the shading is deferred into a second phase where the correspondence between primitives and visibility samples is lost, which makes it hard to avoid redundant shading. Furthermore, the geometry buffer can become prohibitively large in case of high screen resolutions and high visibility sampling because each sample needs to store all attributes.

In this chapter based on our publication [Schied and Dachsbacher 15], we present a technique to dramatically reduce the memory consumption of deferred shading in the aforementioned setting. Unlike deferred shading, our method samples solely visibility in the geometry phase and defers the attribute interpolation and material evaluation to the shading phase. This allows us to store the data needed for shading at per-triangle instead of per-sample frequency. Compared to a G-buffer sample, storing a triangle uses more memory, but since in practice most triangles will cover several pixels, the cost is amortized across several visibility samples, which leads to a significant reduction in the overall memory cost. Visible triangles are identified in the geometry phase and stored in the triangle buffer. The geometry buffer is replaced by a visibility buffer [Burns and Hunt 13],

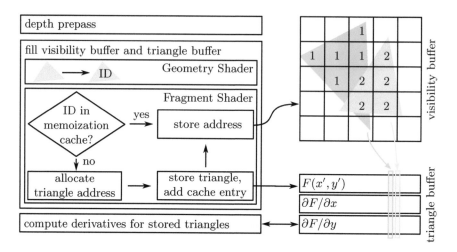

Figure 3.1. The first phase of our algorithm that samples the visibility of triangles. A depth prepass is performed to ensure that in the second geometry pass only visible triangles will generate fragment shader invocations. In the second pass, each triangle is first assigned an ID that is used in the fragment shader as a lookup into the memoization cache that stores mappings between triangle IDs and physical addresses. In case the cache does not contain the mapping yet, a new entry is allocated in the triangle buffer, the triangle is stored, and the new address is added to the cache. Finally, for each triangle the screen-space partial derivatives, needed for attribute interpolation, are computed in a separate pass.

which stores references in the triangle buffer. To enable efficient attribute interpolation during shading, triangles are represented using partial derivatives of the attributes.

3.2 Algorithm

Similar to deferred shading, the drawing of a frame is split into two phases. In the first phase all visible triangles are determined and stored in the triangle buffer. (See Figure 3.1.) Furthermore the visibility buffer is populated with references to these triangles. In the second phase the triangle attributes are interpolated and the shading is computed. Our method stores visible triangles after vertex transformations have been applied. Therefore, vertex transformations do not need to be carried out during the shading phase, and furthermore this makes our method compatible with the use of tessellation shaders. Compared to deferred shading, we introduce the cut in the pipeline at an earlier stage, i.e., before attribute interpolation and material evaluation. The following sections describe the attribute interpolation as well as the two rendering phases in more detail.

3.2.1 Attribute Interpolation Using Partial Derivatives

Interpolation of vertex attributes a_i with respect to a triangle is commonly done by barycentric weighting of all attributes. The barycentric coordinates λ_i of a point (x, y) with respect to a triangle with points $p_i = (u_i, v_i)$ can be computed as a ratio of areas by

$$
\begin{aligned}
\lambda_1(x, y) &= \frac{(v_2 - v_3)(x - u_3) + (u_3 - u_2)(y - v_3)}{D}, \\
\lambda_2(x, y) &= \frac{(v_3 - v_1)(x - u_3) + (u_1 - u_3)(y - v_3)}{D}, \\
\lambda_3(x, y) &= 1 - \lambda_1(x, y) - \lambda_2(x, y),
\end{aligned}
\tag{3.1}
$$

where $D = \det(p_3 - p_2, p_1 - p_2)$. The interpolated attribute is then determined as

$$
\tilde{a}(x, y) = \sum_{i=1}^{3} \lambda_i(x, y) \cdot a_i .
\tag{3.2}
$$

Because $\lambda_i(x, y)$ is linear in the x- and y-directions, the partial derivatives with respect to x, y are constant, and Equation (3.2) can be reformulated as

$$
\begin{aligned}
\tilde{a}(x, y) &= a_{x'y'} + (x - x') \sum_i \frac{\partial \lambda_i}{\partial x} \cdot a_i + (y - y') \sum_i \frac{\partial \lambda_i}{\partial y} \cdot a_i \\
&= a_{x'y'} + (x - x') \frac{\partial a}{\partial x} + (y - y') \frac{\partial a}{\partial y},
\end{aligned}
\tag{3.3}
$$

assuming that the attribute $a_{x'y'}$ is known for an arbitrary sample point (x', y'). (See Figure 3.2.)

For projected triangles defined in four-dimensional homogeneous coordinates with the vertices (x_i, y_i, z_i, w_i), a perspective correction needs to be applied when interpolating attributes. This correction is done by interpolating a_i/w_i and $1/w_i$ linearly in the screen space and dividing the interpolants afterward. This leads to an interpolation scheme defined as $a(x, y) = (\sum \lambda_i a_i / w_i) / (\sum \lambda_i / w_i)$. Reformulating this expression similar to Equation (3.3) leads to

$$
a(x, y) = \frac{\frac{a_{x'y'}}{w_{x'y'}} + (x - x') \frac{\partial a/w}{\partial x} + (y - y') \frac{\partial a/w}{\partial y}}{\frac{1}{w_{x'y'}} + (x - x') \frac{\partial 1/w}{\partial x} + (y - y') \frac{\partial 1/w}{\partial y}} .
\tag{3.4}
$$

Assuming that the triangle has been clipped and projected to the screen, the partial derivatives of the attributes can be computed as

$$
\frac{\partial a/w}{\partial x} = \sum_i \frac{\partial \lambda_i}{\partial x} \cdot \frac{a_i}{w_i}, \quad \frac{\partial a/w}{\partial y} = \sum_i \frac{\partial \lambda_i}{\partial y} \cdot \frac{a_i}{w_i},
\tag{3.5}
$$

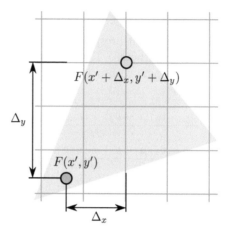

$$F(x' + \Delta_x, y' + \Delta_y) = F(x', y') + \Delta_x \frac{\partial F}{\partial x} + \Delta_y \frac{\partial F}{\partial y}$$

Figure 3.2. A sample of the attribute is stored at a sample point (green). The attribute can be interpolated at an arbitrary position (yellow) by weighting the partial derivatives in the x- and y-directions by their respective screen-space distances Δ_x and Δ_y.

whereas the partial derivatives of the barycentric coordinates are derived from Equation (3.1) as

$$
\begin{aligned}
\frac{\partial \lambda_1}{\partial x} &= \frac{y_2 - y_3}{D}, & \frac{\partial \lambda_2}{\partial x} &= \frac{y_3 - y_1}{D}, & \frac{\partial \lambda_3}{\partial x} &= \frac{y_1 - y_2}{D}, \\
\frac{\partial \lambda_1}{\partial y} &= \frac{x_3 - x_2}{D}, & \frac{\partial \lambda_2}{\partial y} &= \frac{x_1 - x_3}{D}, & \frac{\partial \lambda_3}{\partial y} &= \frac{x_2 - x_1}{D}.
\end{aligned}
\tag{3.6}
$$

3.2.2 Visibility Sampling Phase

The first phase employs two geometry passes to identify and store visible triangles. A depth prepass is performed that constrains the fragment shader execution in the second pass to visible surfaces. Therefore, we can use the fragment shader in the second geometry pass to store visible triangles. Since it is our goal to share the triangle data across several visibility samples, we need to ensure that triangles are uniquely stored. Additionally, the address of the stored triangle needs to be communicated to all fragment shader invocations, which store the address in the visibility buffer. We assign each triangle a unique ID and use a memoization cache that stores mappings between triangle IDs and physical addresses. This allows each fragment shader invocation to query the cache if the triangle is already stored, and thereby get the physical address of the triangle. If a requested triangle ID is not found in the cache, one invocation is selected to allocate space in the triangle buffer and to store the ID-to-address mapping in the cache. Finally, the triangle is stored by the same invocation in the triangle buffer. All invocations store the physical address in the visibility buffer.

3.2.3   Shading Phase

Because the geometry pass only samples visibility and does not capture the geometric attributes per visibility sample, these attributes need to be interpolated in the shading phase. A compute pass is used to determine the partial derivatives needed to interpolate attributes, as described in Section 3.2.1 for each visible triangle.

During shading the visible triangles can be determined per pixel using a lookup into the visibility buffer. The precomputed data needed for interpolation is loaded, the attributes are interpolated according to Equation (3.4), and finally the materials are evaluated.

3.2.4   Multi-rate Shading

Shading contributes a large part to the computational costs for rendering a frame and becomes increasingly expensive with growing screen resolutions. Since not all components of the shading signal are high frequency (such as, for example, indirect illumination, which is particularly costly to evaluate), such components can be sampled at reduced frequency. Our pipeline allows us to create shading samples that reference a primitive and store a screen-space position. These shading samples are referenced by an additional render target in the visibility buffer and are evaluated in a compute pass prior to shading. In the shading phase the results of the evaluated shading samples are combined with the full shading-rate signal. While it would be possible to achieve arbitrary shading-rates using a similar approach as proposed by Liktor et al. [Liktor and Dachsbacher 12], we use a simplified approach that relies on inter-thread communication inside of a shading quad.

3.3   Implementation

The following section explains our implementation that makes use of the OpenGL 4.5 API.

3.3.1   Visibility Sampling Phase

At first the depth buffer is populated with front-most surfaces by performing a depth prepass. Setting the depth test in the second geometry pass to GL_EQUAL allows us to perform alpha-clipping in the depth prepass and thus to ignore alpha in the second geometry pass. In the second pass the geometry shader is used to pass all vertices of the triangle through to the fragment shader. When using tessellation shaders, each triangle needs to be assigned a unique ID; otherwise, the language built-in variable `gl_PrimitiveID` may be used. To assign a unique ID, an atomic counter is incremented and passed through to the fragment shader. We use frustum culling in the geometry shader, which can be implemented efficiently using bit operations to reduce the number of atomic counter operations.

Early depth testing has to be enabled in the fragment shader to ensure that the fragment shader is executed for visible fragments only:

```
layout(early_fragment_tests) in;
```

In the fragment shader a lookup into the memoization cache is performed to get the physical address of the stored triangle. The return value of the lookup function tells if the triangle needs to be stored by the current invocation. Our implementation of the memoization cache closely follows the implementation by Liktor et al. [Liktor and Dachsbacher 12]. It is explained in depth in Section 3.3.2.

The fragment shader stores all vertices of the triangle in the triangle buffer, whereas in a later pass the vertices are overwritten by their partial derivatives, since the original vertex data is not needed anymore during shading. To reduce storage costs when storing the vertices, normal vectors are encoded to 32 Bit using a octahedral encoding [Cigolle et al. 14]. In the beginning of the triangle struct we store a material ID what enables the use of multiple storage formats.

3.3.2 Memoization cache

Our implementation of the memoization cache (refer to Listing 3.1) closely follows the implementation by Liktor et al. [Liktor and Dachsbacher 12]. The image buffer `locks` stores a lock for each cache bucket, where each entry can be either `LOCKED` or `UNLOCKED`. Furthermore, the `cache` image buffer stores two cache entries, each represented by a triangle ID and the corresponding address. Invalid addresses are represented by negative values. When an ID is found in a cache bucket, the found address is stored in the address variable. The return value of the function denotes if a new slot was allocated and therefore the data has to be stored by the current invocation. In the case that the cache does not contain the desired entry, a `imageAtomicExchange` operation is issued to gain exclusive access to the cache bucket. When exclusive access is granted, a new address is allocated and stored alongside the ID in the cache bucket. Older entries are removed in a FIFO manner. This strategy is reasonable because it is to be expected that fragment shader invocations are scheduled according to the rasterization order. For the same reason, a simple modulus hash-function works well with monotonically increasing triangle IDs. When the fragment shader invocation fails to gain access to the cache bucket, it waits a limited amount of time for the bucket to be unlocked and reloads the entry.

Graphics cards execute several threads in lock-step whereby diverging branches are always taken by all threads and the results are masked out accordingly af-

```
 1  layout(rgba32ui) coherent volatile restrict uimageBuffer cache;
 2  layout(r32ui)    coherent volatile restrict uimageBuffer locks;
 3
 4  bool lookup_memoization_cache(
 5    int id, int hash_mod, int triangle_size, out int address)
 6  {
 7    bool store_sample = false;
 8    int hash = id & hash_mod;
 9    uvec4 b = imageLoad(cache, hash);
10    address = get_address_from_bucket(id, b);
11    for(int k = 0; address < 0 && k < 1024; k++) {
12      // ID not found in cache, make several attempts.
13      uint lock = imageAtomicExchange(locks, hash, LOCKED);
14      if(lock == UNLOCKED) {
15        // Gain exclusive access to the bucket.
16        b = imageLoad(cache, hash);
17        address = get_address_from_bucket(id, b);
18        if(address < 0) {
19          // Allocate new storage.
20          address = int(atomicAdd(ctr_ssid[1], triangle_size));
21          b.zw = b.xy; // Update bucket FIFO.
22          b.xy = uvec2(id, address);
23          imageStore(cache, hash, b);
24          store_sample = true;
25        }
26        imageStore(locks, hash, uvec4(UNLOCKED));
27      }
28      // Use if(expr){} if(!expr){} construct to explicitly
29      // sequence the branches.
30      if(lock == LOCKED) {
31        for(int i = 0; i < 128 && lock == LOCKED; i++)
32          lock = imageLoad(locks, hash).r;
33        b = imageLoad(cache, hash);
34        address = get_address_from_bucket(id, b);
35      }
36    }
37    if(address < 0) { // Cache lookup failed, store redundantly.
38      address = int(atomicAdd(ctr_ssid[1], triangle_size));
39      store_sample = true;
40    }
41    return store_sample;
42  }
```

Listing 3.1. The memoization cache uses several `imageBuffers` to store locks as well as cache entries. An access to the cache bucket determines if the cache contains the requested ID. If it is not found, all invocations concurrently try to acquire exclusive access to the cache where the winner is allowed to allocate memory. All other invocations repeatedly poll the cache to retrieve the updated cache entry.

terward. Since an `if-else` statement does not carry any notions about the first executed branch in case of divergence, this statement must be explicitly sequenced by dividing it into two disjunct statements when it contains side effects that require explicit ordering. This is important when implementing the memoization cache because invocations should be waiting for the updated cache buckets strictly following the update step; otherwise, deadlocks might occur.

```
 1  void compute_attribute_derivatives(
 2    in Triangle triangle, out TriangleDerivatives d)
 3  {
 4    mat3x4 pos; mat3x2 tex_coord; mat3 normal;
 5    for(int i = 0; i < 3; i++) {
 6      pos[i]       = P * vec4(triangle.positions[i], 1.0);
 7      normal[i]    = triangle.normals[i];
 8      tex_coord[i] = triangle.tex_coords[i];
 9    }
10    // Clip triangle against all frustum planes.
11    for(int i = 0; i < 3; i++) {
12      shrink_triangle(pos, tex_coord, normal, i, true);
13      shrink_triangle(pos, tex_coord, normal, i, false);
14    }
15    vec3 one_over_w = 1.0 / vec3(pos[0].w, pos[1].w, pos[2].w);
16    vec2 pos_scr[3]; // projected vertices
17    for(int i = 0; i < 3; i++) {
18      pos_scr[i]    = pos[i].xy * one_over_w[i];
19      tex_coord[i] *= one_over_w[i];
20      normal[i]    *= one_over_w[i];
21    }
22    vec3 db_dx, db_dy; // Gradient barycentric coordinates x/y
23    compute_barycentric_derivatives(pos_scr, db_dx, db_dy);
24    // Compute derivatives in x/y for all attributes.
25    d.d_normal_dx = normal * db_dx;
26    d.d_normal_dy = normal * db_dy;
27    d.d_tex_dx    = tex_coord * db_dx;
28    d.d_tex_dy    = tex_coord * db_dy;
29    d.d_w_dx      = dot(one_over_w, db_dx);
30    d.d_w_dy      = dot(one_over_w, db_dy);
31    // Compute attributes shifted to (0,0).
32    vec2 o = -pos_scr[0];
33    d.one_by_w_fixed = one_over_w[0]
34                     + o.x * d.d_w_dx + o.y * d.d_w_dy;
35    d.tex_coord_fixed = tex_coord[0]
36                      + o.x * d.d_tex_dx + o.y * d.d_tex_dy;
37    d.normal_fixed = normal[0];
38                      + o.x * d.d_normal_dx + o.y * d.d_normal_dy;
39  }
```

Listing 3.2. Derivatives are computed according to Equation (3.5). First, the stored triangles are transformed into clip space and consecutively clipped against all view planes, which allows us to project them to the screen. The derivatives of the barycentric coordinates are computed according to Equation (3.1) to compute the partial derivatives for all attributes. Finally, the sample point of the attribute is extrapolated to the center of the screen to make the storage of the sample point's coordinate redundant.

3.3.3 Computing Partial Derivatives of Triangle Attributes

For the attribute interpolation, the partial derivatives need to be computed for each triangle. (Refer to Listing 3.2.) In theory it would be possible to compute the derivatives using the fragment shader built-in dFdx,dFdy functions. However, the numerical precision is not sufficient, and therefore the derivatives need to be

```
 1  void shrink_triangle(inout mat3x4 pos, // Positions in clip space
 2               inout mat3x2 tex,             // Texture coordinates
 3               inout mat3   normal,          // Normals
 4               const int axis, const bool is_min) // Clip plane
 5  {
 6    const int V0 = 1, V1 = 2, V2 = 4;
 7    uint clipmask = 0;
 8    if(is_min) {
 9      clipmask |= pos[0][axis] < -pos[0].w ? V0 : 0;
10      clipmask |= pos[1][axis] < -pos[1].w ? V1 : 0;
11      clipmask |= pos[2][axis] < -pos[2].w ? V2 : 0;
12    } else {
13      clipmask |= pos[0][axis] >  pos[0].w ? V0 : 0;
14      clipmask |= pos[1][axis] >  pos[1].w ? V1 : 0;
15      clipmask |= pos[2][axis] >  pos[2].w ? V2 : 0;
16    }
17    float a, b1, b2;
18  // Push the vertex on the edge from->to.
19  #define PUSH_VERTEX(from, to)                                          \
20      b1 = is_min ? pos[to  ][axis] : -pos[to  ][axis]; \
21      b2 = is_min ? pos[from][axis] : -pos[from][axis]; \
22      a = (pos[to].w + b1)                               \
23        / (pos[to].w - pos[from].w + b1 - b2);           \
24      pos[from]    = mix(pos[to],    pos[from],    a); \
25      tex[from]    = mix(tex[to],    tex[from],    a); \
26      normal[from] = mix(normal[to], normal[from], a);
27
28    // Only two vertices may be outside; otherwise,
29    // the triangle would not be visible.
30    switch(clipmask) {
31    case V2|V0: PUSH_VERTEX(2, 1);
32    case V0:    PUSH_VERTEX(0, 1); break;
33    case V0|V1: PUSH_VERTEX(0, 2);
34    case V1:    PUSH_VERTEX(1, 2); break;
35    case V1|V2: PUSH_VERTEX(1, 0);
36    case V2:    PUSH_VERTEX(2, 0); break;
37    }
38  }
```

Listing 3.3. Shrinking a triangle to make it fit into the frustum. First, a bitmask is computed that indicates for each vertex if it is outside with respect to the current clip plane. This bitmask is used to determine which of the edges alongside the respective vertices are pushed.

computed manually in a separate pass after visibility of the triangles has been established.

For computing the partial derivatives of the attributes as described in Section 3.2.1, the triangles need to be projected to the screen, which necessitates clipping against the view frustum. Our implementation uses homogeneous clipping, however we do not create additional triangles since the derivatives are identical for all resulting clipped triangles.

A bitmask is computed (refer to Listing 3.3) that stores per vertex if it is outside with respect to the current clip plane. Since this computation considers only visible triangles, at most two vertices may be outside with respect to a single clip plane. The bitmask is used to determine which vertices need to be pushed, and furthermore the corresponding triangle edge to the vertex lying inside the frustum is found. The intersection of the edge with the clip plane is computed, and the vertex is moved to the intersection point.

3.3.4 Shading

Attributes are interpolated according to Equation (3.3). By storing a material ID in the first field of the triangle struct, different materials and triangle storage formats can be identified. Akin to deferred shading, the world-space position could be reconstructed from the depth buffer; however, we reconstruct the world-space position from the $1/w$ attribute, allowing us to reconstruct the attribute precisely for arbitrary screen positions. First, the position $p_{\mathrm{NDC}} = (x, y, z, 1)^T_{\mathrm{NDC}}$ is computed from the screen-space coordinate; z_{NDC} is computed from the w-component as $z_{\mathrm{NDC}} = P_{34}/w - P_{33}$, where P is the projection matrix. The world-space position p thus can be computed as $p = w \cdot (PV)^{-1} p_{\mathrm{NDC}}$ with V as the view matrix.

For the shading the materials need to be evaluated. We use OpenGLs bindless texture mechanism for random access to the resources needed by the materials. A gradient is needed for the texture access to ensure proper texture filtering, which can be computed by interpolating the attribute offset to the neighboring pixel and by computing the difference to the attribute at the shaded pixel. We do not store the tangent space as an additional attribute but rather compute the tangent using screen-space derivatives [Schueler 07].

3.3.5 Linked List of Visibility Samples

Since, for most pixels, only a small number of different triangles is referenced, it is more memory efficient to dynamically allocate memory for a linked list and to reference that linked list using a per-pixel head pointer. Each linked list element stores a pointer to the next list element as well as a reference to the triangle. The coverage mask reported in the fragment shader is used to determine if a pixel is fully covered by the current triangle. The depth prepass ensures that correct coverage information is determined; however, the coverage information needs to take the depth test into account. The following code fragment shows how to determine the correct number of covered samples:

```
#extension GL_ARB_post_depth_coverage : require
layout(post_depth_coverage) in;
uint num_samples_covered = bitCount(gl_SampleMaskIn[0]);
```

In the case of full coverage, the head pointer is used to directly encode the triangle reference, which is indicated using a special bit in the head pointer. Otherwise,

```
 1  #extension GL_NV_shader_thread_group: enable
 2  uint sid = 0; // Shading sample address
 3  if (( gl_ThreadInWarpNV & 3) == 0) // One thread allocates memory.
 4      sid = atomicCounterIncrement(ctr_shading_samples);
 5  // Communicate to all invocations.
 6  uint sid_sw = floatBitsToUint(
 7      quadSwizzle0NV(uintBitsToFloat(sid)));
 8  if (sid_sw == 0) { // Fails when there are helper-invocations.
 9    if (sid == 0) // Allocate shading samples for all invocations.
10      sid = atomicCounterIncrement(ctr_shading_samples);
11    store_shading_sample(sid);
12  } else if ((gl_ThreadInWarpNV & 0x03) == 0) {
13    sid = sid_sw;
14    store_shading_sample(sid);
15  } else { // Communication worked, do not need to store.
16    sid = sid_sw;
17  }
```

Listing 3.4. Multi-rate shading samples are created in the fragment shader by a specific invocation that then tries to broadcast this address to all invocations in the shading quad. If the broadcast fails, each invocation creates a shading sample, which might happen if there are helper-invocations.

the linked list is build similar to *order independent transparency* techniques by allocating samples using an atomic counter and performing an atomic exchange operation on the list head pointer. Alongside the triangle address, the number of covered samples is stored to allow for correct weighting of the samples in the shading phase.

3.3.6 Multi-rate Shading

Our multi-rate shading approach requires shading samples to be spawned that are referenced by the visibility buffer. Each of the shading samples stores a reference to the triangle to be shaded, as well as the screen-space coordinate to enable attribute interpolation. Our approach uses inter-shading-quad communication to determine which fragment shader invocation creates the shading sample and to communicate the address of the sample to all four invocations. Listing 3.4 shows our approach to communicate the shading sample address. First, one invocation allocates memory and tries to communicate the address to all other invocations in the quad. Next, all invocations check if the communication succeeded, as it might fail in case there are helper-invocations inside the shading quad. If the communication of the sample failed, each invocation creates a separate shading sample.

We issue a compute pass for all samples and compress the computed shading into the LogLuv [Larson 98] representation. The compressed result replaces the input needed for shading in-place. In the final shading phase, these samples are read by looking up the visibility buffer and are combined with the full shading.

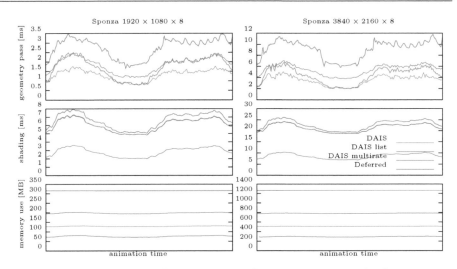

Figure 3.3. Timings and total memory usage for an animation in the Sponza scene. The geometry pass corresponds to the visibility sampling phase and includes the depth prepass. The memory consumption includes all buffers needed for shading. Note the varying y-axis scaling.

3.4 Results

We compare the performance characteristics and memory consumption of three versions of our algorithm to a standard deferred shading implementation. *DAIS* uses a standard multi-sample render target, whereas *DAIS list* employs a per-pixel linked list of visibility samples. Furthermore, we test our multi-rate shading implementation that reduces the shading rate for indirect illumination evaluated using reflective shadow maps [Dachsbacher and Stamminger 05] to 50%. Our deferred shading implementation uses a G-buffer format of 20 bytes per visibility sample.

Figure 3.3 shows our measurements for a camera animation in the Sponza scene, which has 262,267 triangles. Furthermore, we performed the measurements (refer to Figure 3.4) using the San Miguel scene, which has 8,145,860 triangles. On the Sponza scene our method is consistently able to outperform deferred shading while at the same time significantly reducing the storage consumption. Due to the large number of triangles, the San Miguel scene stresses our method, which is not able to meet the performance of deferred shading at a resolution of $1920 \times 1080 \times 8$; however, our method is able to outperform deferred shading at the higher screen resolution.

We furthermore evaluated our method using tessellation shaders (refer to Figure 3.5) to spawn equally-sized triangles in screen space on the Sponza scene. The performance characteristics are similar to the San Miguel scene as shown in Figure 3.4.

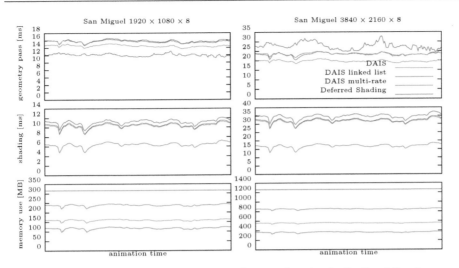

Figure 3.4. Timings and total memory usage for an animation in the San Miguel scene. The geometry pass corresponds to the visibility sampling phase and includes the depth prepass. The memory consumption includes all buffers needed for shading. Note the varying y-axis scaling.

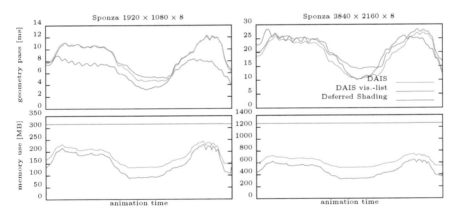

Figure 3.5. Timings and total memory usage for an animation in the Sponza scene. A tessellation shader was used to create triangles with approximately equal screen-space size, generating up to 13 and 26 million triangles for the resolutions of $1920 \times 1080 \times 8$ and $3840 \times 2160 \times 8$, respectively.

3.5 Conclusion

In this chapter we presented a memory-efficient deferred shading algorithm that makes the usage of multi-sample antialiasing in conjunction with high screen resolutions viable. Storing data per triangle instead of per visibility sample significantly reduces the memory usage and allows us to employ caches efficiently, which makes the method faster and more memory efficient compared to deferred shading. The visibility buffer is of low entropy since many visibility samples store the same reference, which allows the GPU to effectively apply transparent memory compression to further reduce the memory bandwidth usage.

Bibliography

[Burns and Hunt 13] Christopher A. Burns and Warren A. Hunt. "The Visibility Buffer: A Cache-Friendly Approach to Deferred Shading." *Journal of Computer Graphics Techniques (JCGT)* 2:2 (2013), 55–69. Available online (http://jcgt.org/published/0002/02/04/).

[Cigolle et al. 14] Zina H. Cigolle, Sam Donow, Daniel Evangelakos, Michael Mara, Morgan McGuire, and Quirin Meyer. "A Survey of Efficient Representations for Independent Unit Vectors." *Journal of Computer Graphics Techniques (JCGT)* 3:2 (2014), 1–30. Available online (http://jcgt.org/published/0003/02/01/).

[Dachsbacher and Stamminger 05] Carsten Dachsbacher and Marc Stamminger. "Reflective Shadow Maps." In *Proceedings of the 2005 Symposium on Interactive 3D Graphics and Games, I3D '05*, pp. 203–231. New York: ACM, 2005.

[Larson 98] Gregory Ward Larson. "LogLuv Encoding for Full-Gamut, High-Dynamic Range Images." *Journal of Graphics Tools* 3:1 (1998), 15–31.

[Liktor and Dachsbacher 12] Gábor Liktor and Carsten Dachsbacher. "Decoupled Deferred Shading for Hardware Rasterization." In *Proceedings of the ACM SIGGRAPH Symposium on Interactive 3D Graphics and Games*, pp. 143–150. New York: ACM, 2012.

[Schied and Dachsbacher 15] Christoph Schied and Carsten Dachsbacher. "Deferred Attribute Interpolation for Memory-Efficient Deferred Shading." In *Proceedings of the 7th Conference on High-Performance Graphics*, pp. 1–5. New York: ACM, 2015.

[Schueler 07] Christian Schueler. "Normal Mapping without Pre-Computed Tangents." In *ShaderX5: Advanced Rendering Techniques*, edited by Wolfgang F Engel. Boston: Charles River Media, 2007.

Real-Time Volumetric Cloudscapes

Andrew Schneider

4.1 Overview

Real-time volumetric clouds in games usually pay for fast performance with a reduction in quality. The most successful approaches are limited to low-altitude fluffy and translucent stratus-type clouds. We propose a volumetric solution that can fill a sky with evolving and realistic results that depict high-altitude cirrus clouds and all of the major low-level cloud types, including thick, billowy cumu-

Figure 4.1. Several cloudscapes that were drawn in real time for the game *Horizon: Zero Dawn*.

lus clouds. Additionally, our approach approximates several volumetric lighting effects that have not yet been present in real-time cloud rendering solutions. And finally, this solution performs well enough in memory and on the GPU to be included in a AAA console game. (See Figure 4.1.)

4.2 Introduction

The standard solutions for rendering clouds in AAA console games involve assets of some kind, either 2D billboards, polar sky dome images, or volumetric libraries that are instanced at render time. For games that require a constantly changing sky and allow the player to cover vast distances, such as open world, the benefits of highly detailed assets are overshadowed by the cost of storing and accessing data for multiple camera angles, times of day, and lighting conditions. Additionally, the simulation of cloud system evolution is limited to tricks or fakes such as rotating the sky dome or distorting images using 2D noise.

Numerous techniques for procedural cloud systems do not rely on assets. Several good examples are freely available on ShaderToy.com, such as "Clouds" [Quilez 13]. Evolution studios used middleware called TrueSky to deliver impressive atmospheric weather effects for the game *Drive Club* [Simul 13].

Yet, there are several limitations with these approaches:

- They all only describe low-altitude stratus clouds and not the puffy and billowy stratocumulus or cumulus clouds.

- Current volumetric methods do not implement realistic lighting effects that are specific to clouds.

- Real-time volumetric clouds are often quite expensive in terms of performance and memory and are not really worth the quality of the results produced.

For the game *Horizon: Zero Dawn*, we have developed a new solution that addresses these problems. We submit new algorithms for modeling, lighting, and rendering, which deliver realistic and evolving results while staying within a memory budget of 20 MB and a performance target of 2 ms.

4.3 Cloud Modeling

Figure 4.2 shows the various cloud types and their height ranges. There are two layers that we render volumetrically: the low stratus clouds, which exist between 1.5 km and 4 km, and the cumulonimbus clouds, which span the entire lower atmosphere from 1 km to 8 km. The alto and cirro class clouds are usually very thin in height and can be rendered for less expense with a 2D texture lookup.

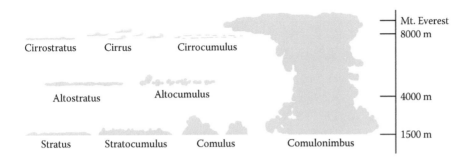

Figure 4.2. A map of the major cloud types.

As the day progresses and the sun heats the earth, water vapor rises from the surface and travels through these layers of atmosphere. Each layer has its own wind direction and temperature. As the vapor travels higher in the atmosphere, the temperature decreases. As temperature decreases the vapor condenses into water or ice around particles of dust it encounters. (Sometimes this comes back down as rain or snow.) The great deal of instability in the flow of this vapor introduces turbulence. As clouds rise, they tend to make billowing shapes. As they diffuse, they stretch and dissipate like fog [Clausse and Facy 61].

Clouds are really amazing examples of fluid dynamics in action, and modeling this behavior requires that the designer approach clouds in a way that approximates the underlying physics involved. With these concepts in mind, we define several techniques that will be used in our ray march to model clouds.

Sections 4.3.1 through 4.3.3 detail some concepts that are used to model clouds and Section 4.3.4 explains how they are all used together.

4.3.1 Modified Fractal Brownian Motion

The standard approach for modeling volumetric cloud systems in real time involves using a ray march with a technique called *fractal Brownian motion*, or FBM for short [Mandelbrot and van Ness 68]. (See Figure 4.3.) FBM is the sum of a series of octaves of noise, each with higher frequency and lower amplitude.

Perlin noise [Perlin 85] is commonly used for this purpose. While this is a reliable model for producing the fog-like shapes of stratus clouds, it fails to describe the round, billowy shapes in cumulus clouds or give them an implied sense of motion as seen in Figure 4.4.

Perlin noise can be flipped over in the middle of its range to create some puffy shapes, but because it is just one flavor of noise, it still lacks the packed cauliflower pattern seen in clouds. Figure 4.5 shows Perlin noise, the result of `abs(Perlin * 2 + 1)`, and photographic reference of the fractal billowing pattern found in clouds.

Figure 4.3. Procedural clouds generated with a ray march and an FBM noise.

Figure 4.4. Photographic reference showing round billowing shapes, similar to puffs of smoke from a factory vent.

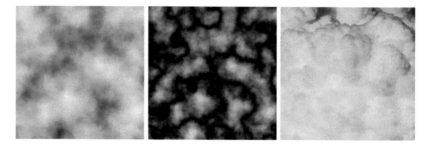

Figure 4.5. Seven-octave Perlin noise (left), Perlin noise made to look "puffy" (center), and photographic reference of the packed cauliflower shapes in clouds (right).

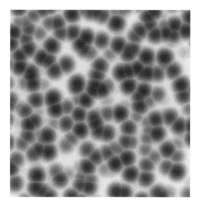

Figure 4.6. Worley noise.

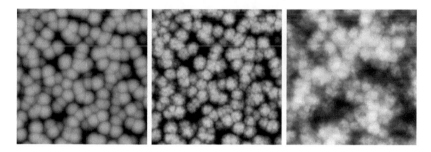

Figure 4.7. Inverted Worley noise (left), FBM composed of Worley noise (center), and Perlin-Worley noise (right).

Another flavor of noise, Worley noise, was introduced in 1996 by Steven Worley [Worley 96] and is often used in rendering caustics and water effects, as seen in Figure 4.6.

If inverted and used in a FBM, Worley noise approximates a nice fractal billowing pattern. It can also be used to add detail to the low-density regions of the low-frequency Perlin noise. (See Figure 4.7, left and center.) We do this by remapping the Perlin noise using the Worley noise FBM as the minimum value from the original range.

```
OldMin = Worley_FBM
PerlinWorley = NewMin + (((Perlin - OldMin) / (OldMax - OldMin))
    * (NewMax - NewMin))
```

This method of combining the two noise types adds a bit of billowing to the connectedness produced in Perlin noise and produces a much more natural result.

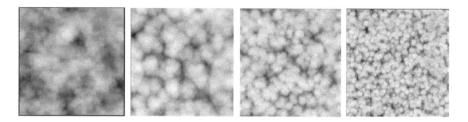

Figure 4.8. A slice of the low-frequency noise's RGBA channels. The first slice is Perin-Worley noise. The last three are Worley noises at increasing frequencies. (Resolution: 128^3.)

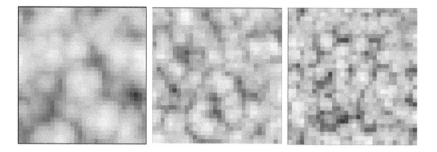

Figure 4.9. From left to right, a slice of the high-frequency noise's RGB channels and Worley noise at increasing frequencies. (Resolution: 32^3.)

We refer to this as our low frequency Perlin-Worley noise and it is the basis for our modeling approach. (See Figure 4.7, right.)

Instead of building the FBM using one texture read per octave, we precompile the FBM so we only have to read two textures. Figure 4.8 shows our first 3D texture, which is made of the Perlin-Worley noise FBM and three octaves of Worley noise FBM's. Figure 4.9 shows our second 3D texture, which consists of three more octaves of Worley noise.

The first 3D texture defines our base cloud shape. The second is of higher frequency and is used to erode the edges of the base cloud shape and add detail, as explained further in Section 4.3.4.

4.3.2 Density-Height Functions

Previous work in this area creates a specific cloud type by biasing or scaling the cloud density value, based on height [Quilez 13].

This function is used to bias or scale the noise signal and produce a cloud. This has limited the types of clouds seen in other work to one type because the maximum height of the clouds never changes.

Figure 4.10. The gradients produced by three density height functions to represent stratus (left), cumulus (center), and cumulonimbus (right) clouds.

Figure 4.11. Results of three functions used to represent stratus (left), cumulus (center), and cumulonimbus (right) clouds.

We extend this approach by using three such functions, one for each of the three major low-level cloud types: stratus, stratocumulus, and cumulus. Figure 4.10 shows the gradient functions we used. Figure 4.11 shows the results of using these functions to change cloud density over height.

At runtime we compute a weighted sum of the three functions. We vary the weighting using a weather texture to add more or less of each cloud type—details are in the next section.

4.3.3 Weather Texture

For our purposes we want to know three things at any point in the domain of our cloud system:

1. Cloud coverage: The percentage of cloud coverage in the sky.

2. Precipitation: The chance that the clouds overhead will produce rain.

3. Cloud type: A value of 0.0 indicates stratus, 0.5 indicates stratocumulus, and 1.0 indicates cumulus clouds.

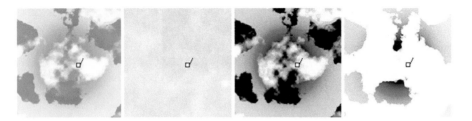

Figure 4.12. Weather texture (left), then (from left to right) coverage signal (red), precipitation signal (green), and cloud type signal (blue).

These attributes can all be expressed as a probability between zero and one, which makes them easy to work with and to preview in a 2D texture. This buffer can be sampled to get a value for each attribute at any point in world space.

Figure 4.12 breaks the weather map for this scene down into its components. The scale of this map is 60,000 × 60,000 meters, and the arrows indicate camera direction.

In reality, rain clouds are always present where it is raining. To model this behavior, we bias cloud type to cumulonimbus and cloud coverage to at least 70% where the chance of rain is 100%.

Additionally, we allow the artist to override the weather texture to produce art-directed skies for cutscenes or other directed experiences [Schneider 15, slide 47].

4.3.4 Cloud Sampler

Having established the components of the cloud density function, we will now move on to the cloud model.

Like all other volumetric cloud solutions to date, we use a ray march. A ray march takes steps through a domain and samples density values for use in lighting and density calculations. These data are used to build the final image of the volumetric subject. Our cloud density sample function does most of the work of interpreting the sample position and the weather data to give us the density value of a cloud at a given point.

Before we start working in the function, we calculate a normalized scalar value that represents the height of the current sample position in the cloud layer. This will be used in the last part of the modeling process.

```
// Fractional value for sample position in the cloud layer.
float GetHeightFractionForPoint(float3 inPosition,
                                float2 inCloudMinMax)
{
    // Get global fractional position in cloud zone.
    float height_fraction = (inPosition.z - inCloudMinMax.x ) /
```

```
                                    (inCloudMinMax.y - inCloudMinMax.x);

        return saturate(height_fraction);
}
```

We also define a remapping function to map values from one range to another, to be used when combining noises to make our clouds.

```
// Utility function that maps a value from one range to another.
float Remap(float original_value, float original_min,
            float original_max, float new_min, float new_max)
{
    return new_min + (((original_value - original_min) /
            (original_max - original_min)) * (new_max - new_min))
}
```

The first step of our sampling algorithm is to build a basic cloud shape out of the low-frequency Perlin-Worley noise in our first 3D texture. The process is as follows:

1. The first step is to retrieve the four low-frequency noise values required to build a basic cloud shape. We sample the first 3D texture, containing low-frequency octaves.

2. We will use the first channel, which contains the Perlin-Worley noise, to establish our base cloud shape.

3. Though the basic Perlin-Worley noise provides a reasonable cloud density function, it lacks the detail of a realistic cloud. We use a remapping function to add the three other low-frequency noises to the edges of the Perlin-Worley noise. This method of combining noises prevents the interior of the Perlin-Worley cloud shape from becoming non-homogenous and also ensures that we only add detail in the areas that we can see.

4. To determine the type of cloud we are drawing, we compute our density height function based on the cloud type attribute from our weather texture.

5. Next, we multiply the base cloud shape by the density height function to create the correct type of cloud according to the weather data.

Here is how it looks in code:

```
float SampleCloudDensity(float3 p, float3 weather_data)
{
    // Read the low-frequency Perlin-Worley and Worley noises.
    float4 low_frequency_noises = tex3Dlod(Cloud3DNoiseTextureA,
        Cloud3DNoiseSamplerA, float4 (p, mip_level) ).rgba;

    // Build an FBM out of  the low frequency Worley noises
```

Figure 4.13. The low-frequency "base" cloud shape.

```
// that can be used to add detail to the low-frequency
// Perlin-Worley noise.
float low_freq_FBM = ( low_frequency_noises.g * 0.625 )
                   + ( low_frequency_noises.b * 0.25 )
                   + ( low_frequency_noises.a * 0.125 );

// define the base cloud shape by dilating it with the
// low-frequency FBM made of Worley noise.
float base_cloud = Remap( low_frequency_noises.r, -
    ( 1.0 - low_freq_FBM), 1.0, 0.0, 1.0 );

// Get the density-height gradient using the density height
// function explained in Section 4.3.2.
float density_height_gradient =
    GetDensityHeightGradientForPoint( p, weather_data );

// Apply the height function to the base cloud shape.
base_cloud *= density_height_gradient;
```

At this point we have something that already resembles a cloud, albeit a low-detail one (Figure 4.13).

Next, we apply the cloud coverage attribute from the weather texture to ensure that we can control how much the clouds cover the sky. This step involves two operations:

1. To make the clouds realistically grow as we animate the coverage attribute, we expand the base cloud shape that was produced by the previous steps using the cloud coverage attribute in the remapping function.

2. To ensure that density increases with coverage in an aesthetically pleasing way, we multiply this result by the cloud coverage attribute.

Figure 4.14. The "base" cloud shape with coverage applied.

Here is how it looks in code:

```
// Cloud coverage is stored in weather_data's red channel.
float cloud_coverage = weather_data.r;

// Use remap to apply the cloud coverage attribute.
float base_cloud_with_coverage  = Remap(base_cloud,
    cloud_coverage, 1.0, 0.0, 1.0);
// Multiply the result by the cloud coverage attribute so
// that smaller clouds are lighter and more aesthetically
// pleasing.
base_cloud_with_coverage *= cloud_coverage;
```

The result of these steps is shown in Figure 4.14. The base cloud is still low detail but it is beginning to look more like a system than a field of noise.

Next, we finish off the cloud by adding realistic detail ranging from small billows created by instabilities in the rising water vapor to wispy distortions caused by atmospheric turbulence (see examples in Figure 4.15).

We model these effects using three steps:

1. We use animated curl noise to distort the sample coordinate at the bottom of the clouds, simulating the effect of turbulence when we sample the high-frequency 3D texture using the distorted sample coordinates.

2. We build an FBM out of the high-frequency Worley noises in order to add detail to the edges of the cloud.

3. We contract the base cloud shape using the high-frequency FBM. At the base of the cloud, we invert the Worley noise to produce wispy shapes in

Figure 4.15. Photographic reference of billowy shapes and wispy shapes created by atmospheric turbulence.

this region. Contracting with Worley noise at the top produces billowing detail.

Here is how it looks in code:

```
// Add some turbulence to bottoms of clouds.
p.xy += curl_noise.xy * (1.0 - height_fraction);

// Sample high-frequency noises.
float3 high_frequency_noises = tex3Dlod(Cloud3DNoiseTextureB,
    Cloud3DNoiseSamplerB,  float4 (p * 0.1, mip_level) ).rgb;

// Build-high frequency Worley noise FBM.
float high_freq_FBM = ( high_frequency_noises.r * 0.625 )
                    + ( high_frequency_noises.g * 0.25 )
                    + ( high_frequency_noises.b * 0.125 );

// Get the height_fraction for use with blending noise types
// over height.
float height_fraction  = GetHeightFractionForPoint (p,
                                        inCloudMinMax );

// Transition from wispy shapes to billowy shapes over height.
float high_freq_noise_modifier = mix(high_freq_FBM,
    1.0 - high_freq_FBM, saturate(height_fraction * 10.0));

// Erode the base cloud shape with the distorted
```

Figure 4.16. The final cloud shape.

```
// high-frequency Worley noises.
float final_cloud = Remap(base_cloud_with_coverage,
    high_freq_noise_modifier * 0.2 , 1.0, 0.0, 1.0);

return final_cloud;
}
```

The result of these steps is shown in Figure 4.16. This series of operations is the framework that our sampler uses to create cloudscapes in the ray march, but we take additional steps to add that implied sense of motion that traditional noise-based solutions for cloudscapes lack.

To simulate the shearing effect as a cloud rises from one atmosphere layer to another, we offset the sample position in the wind direction over altitude. Additionally, both 3D texture samples are offset in the wind direction and slightly upward over time, but at different speeds. Giving each noise its own speed produces a more realistic look to the motion of the clouds. In a time lapse, the clouds appear to grow upward.

```
// Wind settings.
float3 wind_direction = float3(1.0, 0.0, 0.0);
float cloud_speed = 10.0;

// cloud_top offset pushes the tops of the clouds along
// this wind direction by this many units.
float cloud_top_offset = 500.0;

// Skew in wind direction.
p += height_fraction * wind_direction * cloud_top_offset;
```

Figure 4.17. Sample cloudscapes, captured on the Playstation 4.

```
// Animate clouds in wind direction and add a small upward
// bias to the wind direction.
p+= (wind_direction + float3(0.0, 0.1, 0.0)  ) * time
    * cloud_speed;
```

This code must be located before any 3D texture samples in the `CloudDensity-Sample()` function.

4.3.5 Results

Some volumetric cloudscapes created using different weather settings are illustrated in Figure 4.17.

This modeling approach allows us to sculpt numerous unique cloudscapes. When a rain signal approaches the camera along the wind direction, it gives the effect of an approaching storm front [Schneider 15, slide 43–44].

4.4 Cloud Lighting

Volumetric cloud lighting is a very well researched area of computer graphics. Unfortunately for game developers, the best results come from taking high numbers of samples. This means that we have to find ways to approximate the complicated and expensive processes that take place when producing film-quality clouds.

Figure 4.18. Photographic reference of directional scattering (left), the silver lining effect (center), and the dark edges effect (right).

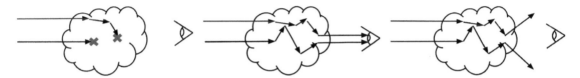

Figure 4.19. Examples of three light behaviors in a cloud: absorption (left), in-scattering (center), and out-scattering (right).

There are three effects in particular for which our approach solves with approximations: the multiple scattering and directional lighting in clouds, the silver lining effect when we look toward the sun, and the dark edges on clouds when we look away from the sun. Figure 4.18 shows photographic references of these three effects.

4.4.1 Volumetric Scattering

When light enters a cloud, the majority of the light rays spend their time refracting through water droplets and ice inside of the cloud before scattering toward our eyes [Van De Hulst 57]. There are three things that can happen to a photon entering a cloud (see also Figure 4.19):

1. It can be absorbed by water or non-participating particles in the cloud such as dust; this is *extinction* or *absorption*.

2. It can exit the cloud toward the eye; this is *in-scattering*.

3. It could exit the cloud traveling away from the eye; this is *out-scattering*.

Beer's law is a standard method for approximating the probability of each of these three outcomes.

4.4.2 Beer's Law

Originally conceived of as a tool for chemical analysis, Beer's law models the attenuation of light as it passes through a material [Beer 52]. (See Figure 4.20.)

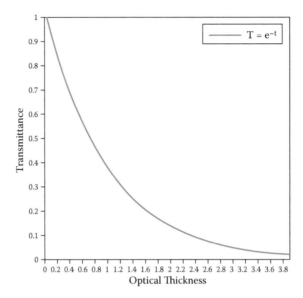

Figure 4.20. Beer's law: Transmittance as a function of optical depth.

In the case of volumetrics, it can be used to reliably calculate transmittance based on optical thickness [Wrenninge 13].

If our participating media are non-homogenous, like clouds, we must accumulate optical thickness along the light ray using a ray march. This model has been used extensively in film visual effects, and it forms the foundation of our lighting model.

Here is how it is implemented in code:

```
light_energy = exp( - density_samples_along_light_ray );
```

4.4.3 Henyey-Greenstein Phase Function

In clouds, there is a higher probability of light scattering forward [Pharr and Humphreys 10]. This is responsible for the silver lining in clouds. (See Figure 4.21.)

In 1941, the Henyey-Greenstein phase function was developed to mimic the angular dependence of light scattering by small particles, which was used to describe scattering of light by interstellar dust clouds [Henyey and Greenstein 41]. In volumetric rendering the function is used to model the probability of light scattering within participating media. We use a single Henyey-Greenstein phase function with an eccentricity (directional component) g of 0.2, to make sure that

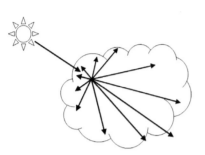 

Figure 4.21. Illustration of forward scattering of light in a cloud (left), and photographic reference of the silver lining effect (right).

more light in our clouds scatters forward:

$$p_{\mathrm{HG}}(\theta, g) = \frac{1}{4\pi} \frac{1 - g^2}{1 + g^2 - 2g\cos(\theta)^{3/2}}.$$

And here is how it looks implemented in code:

```
float HenyeyGreenstein(float3 inLightVector, float3 inViewVector,
                       float inG)
{
    float cos_angle = dot(normalize(inLightVector),
                          normalize(inViewVector));
    return ((1.0 - inG * inG) / pow((1.0 + inG * inG -
        2.0 * inG * cos_angle), 3.0 / 2.0)) / 4.0 * 3.1415;
}
```

The results are shown in Figure 4.22.

Figure 4.22. Clouds without the Henyey-Greenstein phase function (left), and clouds with the Henyey-Greenstein phase function (right).

Figure 4.23. A diagram showing the 180-degree view angle where the dark edge effect is apparent (left), and photographic reference of the dark edge effect (right).

4.4.4   In-Scattering Probability Function (Powdered Sugar Effect)

Beer's law is an extinction model, meaning that it is concerned with how light energy attenuates over depth. This fails to approximate an important lighting effect related to in-scattering on the sun-facing sides of clouds. This effect presents itself as dark edges on clouds when a view ray approaches the direction of the light ray. There is a similar effect in piles of powdered sugar, the source of our nickname for this effect. See Figure 4.23 for an illustration.

This effect is most apparent in round, dense regions of clouds, so much so that the creases between each bulge appear brighter than the bulge itself, which is closer to the sun. These results would appear to be the exact opposite of what Beer's law models.

Recall that in-scattering is an effect in which light rays inside a cloud bounce around until they become parallel and then exit the cloud and travel to our eyes. This phenomenon even occurs when we look at a sunlit side of a cloud (Figure 4.24).

Also recall that more light scatters forward, along the original light ray direction, due to forward scattering. However, a relatively large optical depth must exist for there to be a reasonable chance for a photon to turn 180 degrees. Paths around the edge of the cloud won't pass through a sufficiently large optical depth to turn a noticeable fraction of the photons completely around. Paths that do have an optical depth large enough to turn a photon 180 degrees are almost always well inside the cloud, so Beer's law extinction will kill this contribution before it leaves the cloud toward our eye. Crevices and cracks are an exception; they provide a window into the interior of the cloud volume where there are photon paths with relatively large optical depths, allowing a low-density shortcut for photons to escape, making the crevices brighter than the surrounding bulges.

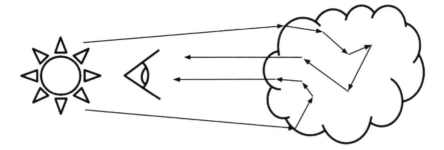

Figure 4.24. An illustration of in-scattering producing a 180-degree turn in the incoming light rays.

We chose to express this phenomenon as a probability. Imagine you are looking at one of these bulgy regions on a cloud at the same angle as a group of light rays coming from the sun behind you (Figure 4.25).

If we sample a point just below the surface on one of the bulges and compare it to a point at the same depth in one of the crevices, the point in the crevice will have more potential cloud material that can contribute to in-scattering (Figure 4.26). In terms of probability, the crease should be brighter.

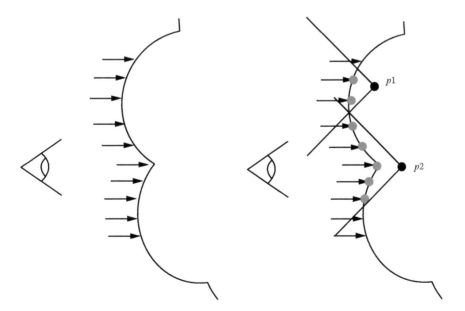

Figure 4.25. Light hitting bulges on a cloud.

Figure 4.26. Illustration showing higher in-scatter potential for the creases.

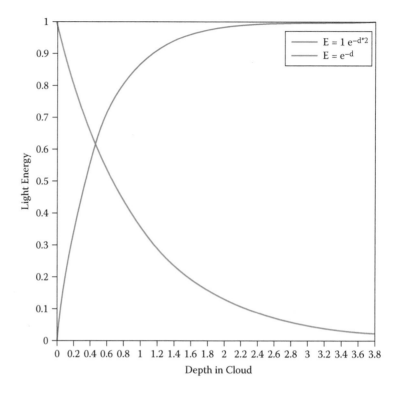

Figure 4.27. Beer's law compared to our approximation for the powdered sugar effect.

Using this thought experiment as a guide, we propose a new function to account for this effect. Because this result is effectively the opposite of Beer's law, we represent it as an inverse of the original function (Figure 4.27).

For our purposes this is an accurate enough approximation of this phenomenon, which does not require any additional sampling.

We combine the two functions into a new function: Beer's-Powder. Note that we multiply the entire result by 2, to bring it closer to the original normalized range (Figure 4.28).

Here is how it is implemented in code:

```
powder_sugar_effect  = 1.0 -  exp( - light_samples * 2.0 );
beers_law = exp( - light_samples );
light_energy = 2.0 * beers_law * powder_sugar_effect;
```

Some results both from an isolated test case and from our solution in-game are shown in Figure 4.29.

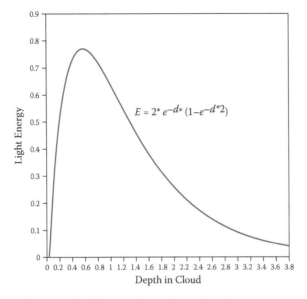

Figure 4.28. The combined Beer's-Powder function.

Figure 4.29. Lighting model without our function (top left) and with our function (top right). In-game results without our function (bottom left) and with our function (top right).

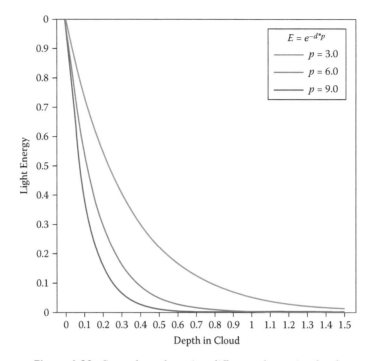

Figure 4.30. Several results using different absorption levels.

4.4.5 Rain Clouds

Our system also models the darker bases of rain clouds. Rain clouds are darker than other low-level clouds because the water droplets have condensed so much that most of the light gets absorbed before reaching our eye.

So, since we already have a precipitation attribute for the point that we are sampling, we can use it to artificially "thicken" the cloud material. This task is easily accomplished by increasing the sampled density that goes into the Beer's-Powder function; see Figure 4.30. The variable p stands for precipitation.

Figure 4.31 shows some results.

Figure 4.31. Rain clouds with (left) and without (right) increased light absorption.

4.4.6 Lighting Model Summary

In review, our lighting model is a combination of four components:

1. Beer's law (August Beer, 1852),

2. Henyey-Greenstein phase function (Henyey and Greenstein, 1941),

3. in-scattering probability function (powdered sugar effect),

4. rain cloud absorption gain.

With E as light energy, d as the density sampled for lighting, p as the absorption multiplier for rain, g as our eccentricity in light direction, and θ as the angle between the view and light rays, we can describe our lighting model in full:

$$E = 2.0 \times e^{-dp} \times \left(1 - e^{-2d}\right) \times \frac{1}{4\pi} \frac{1 - g^2}{1 + g^2 - 2g\cos(\theta)^{3/2}}.$$

4.5   Cloud Rendering

Choosing where to sample data to build the image is very important for performance and image quality. Our approach tries to limit expensive work to situations where it could potentially be required.

4.5.1   Spherical Atmosphere

The first part of rendering with a ray march is deciding where to start. When the viewer is located on a seemingly "flat" surface such as the ocean, the curvature of the Earth clearly causes clouds to descend into the horizon. This is because the Earth is round and cloud layers are spherical rather than planar. (See Figure 4.32.)

In order to reproduce this feature, our ray march takes place in a 3.5 km thick spherical shell starting at 1.5 km above the surface of the Earth. We use a sphere intersection test to determine the start and end points for our ray march. As we look toward the horizon, the ray length increases considerably, which requires that we increase the number of potential samples. Directly above the player, we take as many as 64 steps and at the horizon we take as many as 128 steps. There are several optimizations in our ray-march loop, allowing it to exit early, so the average sample count is much lower than this.

4.5.2   Ray March Optimizations

Instead of evaluating the full cloud density function every time, we only evaluate the low-frequency part of the cloud density function until we are close to a cloud. Recall that our density function uses low-detail Perlin-Worley noise to establish

Horizon line

Figure 4.32. Spherical atmosphere.

the base shape of our clouds and higher frequencies of Worley noise, which it applies as an erosion from the edges of this base cloud shape. Evaluating just the low-frequency part of the density function means one 3D texture is read instead of two, which is a substantial bandwidth and instruction count savings. Figure 4.33 illustrates the step through empty air using "cheap" samples and then the switch to expensive samples when close to a cloud. Once several samples return zero, we return to the "cheap" sample.

To implement this in code, we start with a `cloud_test` value of zero and accumulate density in a loop using a boolean value of `true` for our sampler. As long as the `cloud_test` is 0.0, we continue on our march searching for the cloud boundary. Once we get a nonzero value, we suppress the march integration for that step and proceed using the full cloud density sample. After six consecutive full cloud density samples that return 0.0, we switch back to the cloud boundary search. These steps ensure that we have exited the cloud boundary and do not trigger extra work.

Figure 4.33. Cloud boundary detection (left), and full samples inside of the cloud boundary (right).

```c
float density = 0.0;
float cloud_test = 0.0;
int zero_density_sample_count = 0;

// Start the main ray-march loop.
for (int i = 0; i <sample_count; i++)
{
    // cloud_test starts as zero so we always evaluate the
    // second case from the beginning.
    if(cloud_test > 0.0)
    {
        // Sample density the expensive way by setting the
        // last parameter to false, indicating a full sample.
        float sampled_density = SampleCloudDensity(p,
            weather_data, mip_level, false);

        // If we just samples a zero, increment the counter.
        if( sampled_density = 0.0)
        {
            zero_density_sample_count ++;
        }
        // If we are doing an expensive sample that is still
        // potentially in the cloud:
        if(zero_density_sample_count != 6)
        {
            density += sampled_density;
            p += step;
        } // If not, then set cloud_test to zero so that we go
          // back to the cheap sample case.
        else
        {
            cloud_test = 0.0;
            zero_density_sample_count = 0;
        }
    }
    else
    {
        // Sample density the cheap way, only using the
        // low-frequency noise.
```

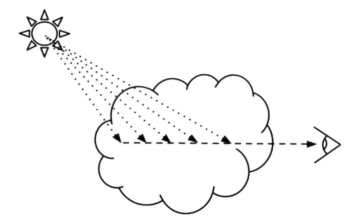

Figure 4.34. A light ray march for each view ray-march step.

```
cloud_test = SampleCloudDensity (p, weather_data,
                                 mip_level, true);
if ( cloud_test == 0.0)
{
    p += step;
}
    }
}
```

This algorithm cuts the number of 3D texture calls in half for the best case, where we are marching through empty sky.

To calculate the lighting, more samples need to be taken toward the light at each ray-march step. The sum of these samples is used in the lighting model and then attenuated by the current sum of density along the view ray for each view ray-march step. Figure 4.34 illustrates a basic light sample integration march within a ray march.

Because we are targeting for use in a game engine that is supporting many other GPU intensive tasks, we are limited to no more than six samples per ray-march step.

One way to reduce the number of light samples is to execute them only when the ray march steps inside of a cloud. This is an important optimization because light samples are extremely costly. There is no change in the visual result with this optimization.

```
...
        density += sampled_density;
        if ( sampled_density != 0.0)
        {
            // SampleCloudDensityAlongRay just walks in the
            // given direction from the start point and takes
```

```
              // X number of lighting samples.
          density_along_light_ray =
              SampleCloudDensityAlongRay(p)
    }
    p += step;
...
```

4.5.3 Cone-Sampled Lighting

The obvious way to find the amount of sun illumination is by measuring the transmittance of the cloud between the query point and the sun. However, the light at any point in a cloud is greatly affected by the light in regions around it in the direction of the light source. Think of it as a funnel of light energy that culminates at our sample position. To make sure that the Beer's law portion of our lighting model is being influenced in this way, we take our six light samples in a cone that spreads out toward the light source, thus weighting the Beer's law attenuation function by including neighboring regions of the cloud. See Figure 4.35.

Banding artifacts present themselves immediately because of the low number of samples. The cone sampling helps break up the banding a bit, but to smooth it out further, we sample our densities at a lower mip level.

To calculate the cone offset, we used a kernel of six noise results between $-(1, 1, 1)$ and $+(1, 1, 1)$ and gradually increased its magnitude as we march away from our sample position. If the accumulated density along the view march has surpassed a threshold value where its light contribution can be more generalized (we used 0.3), we switch our samples to the low-detail mode to further optimize the light march. There is very little visual difference at this threshold.

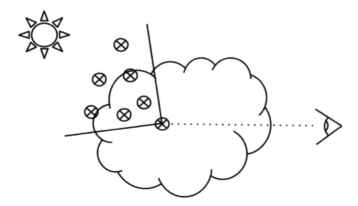

Figure 4.35. A cone-shaped sample area for the light ray-march samples.

```
static float3 noise_kernel [] =
{
    some noise vectors
}

// How wide to make the cone.
float cone_spread_multplier = length(light_step);

// A function to gather density in a cone for use with
// lighting clouds.
float SampleCloudDensityAlongCone(p, ray_direction)
{
    float density_along_cone = 0.0;

    // Lighting ray-march loop.
    for(int i=0; i<=6; i++)
    {
        // Add the current step offset to the sample position.
        p += light_step + ( cone_spread_multiplier *
                            noise_kernel[i] * float(i) );
        if( density_along_view_cone < 0.3)
        {
            // Sample cloud density the expensive way.
            density_along_cone += SampleCloudDensity(p,
                        weather_data, mip_level + 1, false);
        }
        else
        {
            // Sample cloud density the cheap way, using only
            // one level of noise.
            density_along_cone += SampleCloudDensity(p,
                        weather_data, mip_level + 1, true);
        }
    }
}
```

Additionally, to account for shadows cast from distant clouds onto the part of
the cloud for which we are calculating lighting, we take one long distance sample
at a distance of three times the length of the cone. (See Figure 4.36.)

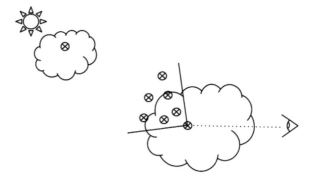

Figure 4.36. Long distance light sample combined with the cone samples.

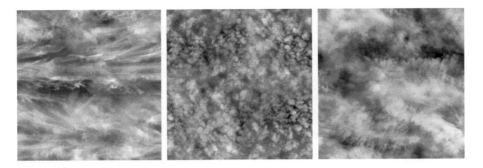

Figure 4.37. Several alto and cirrus cloud textures used instead of a ray march.

4.5.4 High Altitude Clouds

Our approach only renders low-level clouds volumetrically. High-altitude clouds are represented with scrolling textures. However, in order to integrate them with the volumetric clouds, they are sampled at the end of the ray march. The cost of this texture read is negligible for a 512^2 texture with three channels. We animate them in a wind direction that is different from the wind direction in our weather system to simulate different wind directions in different cloud layers. (See Figure 4.37.)

4.5.5 Results

A sequence of lighting results that illustrates a changing time of day is illustrated in Figure 4.38.

4.6 Conclusion and Future Work

This approach produces realistic, evolving cloudscapes for all times of day and completely replaces our asset-based approaches to clouds. It also means that the memory usage for our entire sky is limited to the cost of a few textures that total 20 MB instead of hundreds of megabytes for multiple sky domes and billboards for varying weather conditions and times of day. Performance on the GPU is roughly 20 ms, but when we build our image using temporal reprojection, that number reduces to 2 ms [Schneider 15, slide 91–93].

The in-scattering probability function was based on a thought experiment, but we are researching this further. We plan to use the brute-force approach used by Magnus Wrenninge [Wrenninge 15], which produces the dark edges naturally, to gather data points along the light ray and develop a function that fits these data more precisely.

Figure 4.38. Time lapse of a cloudscape, captured from the Playstation 4.

4.7 Acknowledgments

I would like to thank Nathan Vos, Michal Valient, Elco Vossers, and Hugh Malan for assistance with our development challenges. I would also like to thank Jan-Bart van Beek, Marijn Giesbertz, and Maarten van der Gaag for their assistance in accomplishing our look goals for this project.

Additionally, I would like to personally thank colleagues whose work has greatly influenced this: Trevor Thomson, Matthew Wilson, and Magnus Wren-ninge.

Bibliography

[Beer 52] A. Beer. "Bestimmung der Absorption des rothen Lichts in farbigen Flüssigkeiten" (Determination of the Absorption of Red Light in Colored Liquids). *Annalen der Physik und Chemie* 86 (1852), 78–88.

[Clausse and Facy 61] R. Clausse and L. Facy. *The Clouds*. London: Evergreen Books, LTD., 1961.

[Henyey and Greenstein 41] L. G. Henyey and J. L. Greenstein. "Diffuse Radiation in the Galaxy." *Astrophysical Journal* 93 (1941), pp. 78–83.

[Mandelbrot and van Ness 68] B. Mandelbrot and J. W. van Ness. "Fractional Brownian Motions, Fractional Noises and Applications." *SIAM Review* 10:4 (1968), 422–437.

[Perlin 85] K. Perlin. "An Image Synthesizer." In *Proceedings of the 12th Annual Conference on Computer Graphics and Interactive Techniques*, pp. 287–296. New York: ACM Press, 1985.

[Pharr and Humphreys 10] M. Pharr and G. Humphreys. *Physically Based Rendering: From Theory to Implementation.* Boston: Morgan Kaufmann, 2010.

[Quilez 13] I. Quilez. "Clouds." *Shadertoy.com*, https://www.shadertoy.com/view/xslgrr, 2013.

[Schneider 15] A. Schneider. "The Real-Time Volumetric Cloudscapes Of Horizon: Zero Dawn." Paper presented at ACM SIGGRAPH, Los Angeles, CA, August 26, 2015.

[Simul 13] Simul. "TrueSKY." http://simul.co/truesky/, 2013.

[Van De Hulst 57] H. Van De Hulst. *Light Scattering by Small Particles.* New York: Dover Publications, 1957.

[Worley 96] Steven S. Worley. "A Cellular Texture Basis Function." In *Proceedings of the 23rd Annual Conference on Computer Graphics and Interactive Techniques*, pp. 291–294. New York: ACM Press, 1996.

[Wrenninge 13] M. Wrenninge. *Production Volume Rendering: Design and Implementation.* Boca Raton, FL: CRC Press, 2013.

[Wrenninge 15] M. Wrenninge. "Art-Directable Multiple Volumetric Scattering." In *ACM SIGGRAPH 2015 Talks*, article no. 24. New York: ACM Press, 2015.

Rendering

Real-time rendering is an exciting field in part because of how rapidly it evolves and advances but also because of the graphics community's eagerness and willingness to share their new ideas, opening the door for others to learn and share in the fun! In this section we introduce three new rendering techniques that will be relevant to game developers, hobbyist, and anyone else interested in the world of graphics.

Our first chapter is "Adaptive Virtual Textures" by Ka Chen in which a technique for large, open world texturing is presented. This technique is able to achieve very high resolution textures and also supports dynamically composited decals that help create unique and complex-looking surfaces.

Next, we have "Deferred Coarse Pixel Shading" by Rahul P. Sathe and Tomasz Janczak. In this chapter the authors present an optimization technique in which regions of low visual complexity may be shaded at less than the pixel frequency. The performance benefits demonstrated by the authors are quite impressive!

Finally, we have "Progressive Rendering Using Multi-frame Sampling" by Daniel Limberger, Karsten Tausche, Johannes Linke, and Jürgen Döllner. In this chapter the authors present a framework for achieving very high quality rendered results by distributing sampling work across multiple frames. The authors demonstrate their framework in the context of antialiasing, depth of field, screen-space ambient occlusion, and order-independent transparency.

I would like to thank all our authors for sharing their exciting new work with the graphics community. We hope that these ideas encourage readers to further extend the state of the art in real-time rendering, and we look forward to the new advances that these ideas inspire!

—Christopher Oat

Adaptive Virtual Textures

Ka Chen

1.1 Introduction

Adaptive Virtual Textures (AVT) are an improvement upon Procedural Virtual Textures. This technique can be applied to a large open world and can achieve a much higher texture resolution when needed. With AVT, the artist can place thousands of projected decals with high-resolution textures on the terrain surface These decals will be baked together with terrain materials into virtual textures at runtime. Once baked, the rendering engine will directly display the virtual textures instead of rendering terrain materials and decals. Thus, the render performance is greatly improved.

1.2 Procedural Virtual Textures Basics

Procedural Virtual Textures are mipmapped texture caches that store the recent rendering result of terrain material blending and projected decals. In a deferred rendering engine, these virtual textures store the composite using the G-buffer's format, which can then be used directly when rendering subsequent frames. It is a powerful optimization technique because the rendering engine can simply skip the expensive terrain material blending once it has been cached in the virtual textures. (See [Widmark 12] for more details.)

1.3 Adaptive Virtual Textures

1.3.1 Goals

The standard virtual textures technique allocates a large mipmapped texture, which is then uniformly applied onto the whole terrain world. The actual texture resolution can be calculated as

$$\text{texel ratio} = \frac{\texttt{TextureSize.xy}}{\texttt{WorldSize.xy}}.$$

Although usually a very large virtual texture (such as $512K \times 512K$) is allocated, sometimes the texture resolution is not high enough when it is applied on a large open world such as a $10KM \times 10KM$ world. In this case the texel ratio is only 0.5 texels/cm. Such a low texture resolution limits the potential usage of procedural virtual textures in next-generation games. In order to prevent the look of low-resolution terrain, an additional detail material layer has to be applied on top of procedural virtual textured terrain.

In this chapter, we will present Adaptive Virtual Textures (AVT), which greatly improve the texture resolution in a very large world. We will discuss the practical implementation of AVT and how we overcame those challenges in our game.

1.3.2   Overview

By using a $512K \times 512K$ resolution virtual texture, we would like to achieve a high texture resolution such as 10 texels/cm in a $10KM \times 10KM$ world. Such a high texel ratio is only needed for terrain surfaces that may appear very close to the camera. For terrain surfaces that are a bit farther away, a lower texel ratio such as 5 texels/cm is sufficient. We would require even less texture resolution for surfaces that are much farther away. The key is to find a solution to apply the virtual texture based on the distance from the camera to the terrain surface.

We divide the game world into multiple sectors and each sector has a pre-defined size (such as 64×64 meters), as shown in Figure 1.1. Every sector is allocated with a virtual image inside the virtual texture. The size of the virtual image is calculated based on the distance from the camera. The closest sectors are allocated with the maximum virtual image size, for example $64K \times 64K$. Farther sectors are allocated with smaller sizes, such as $32K \times 32K$ or $16K \times 16K$. The minimum size can be $1K \times 1K$.

After allocating all the sectors in the world, our virtual texture becomes a texture atlas for all the virtual images with different sizes The closest sector has the maximum resolution of 10 texels/cm calculated as

$$\text{texel ratio} = \frac{64K}{64 \text{ meters}} = 10 \text{ texels/cm}.$$

Farther sectors have lower resolutions such as 5 texels/cm and so on. It is important to note that these virtual image sizes will be adjusted dynamically at runtime based on camera distance whenever the camera moves.

1.3.3   Allocate Virtual Texture Atlas

As mentioned at the end of Section 1.3.2, we need to adjust the size of each virtual image dynamically at runtime. It is important to have a good texture atlasing algorithm so that the performance of AVT is maximized and space fragmentation

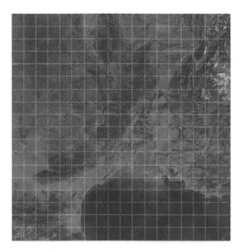

Figure 1.1. World divided into multiple sectors.

is kept to a minimum. We use a quad-tree scheme to allocate the virtual images. This scheme makes sure that the image is always allocated at the location where the UV address is aligned with image size. Figure 1.2 shows the allocation of three virtual images inside the virtual texture atlas.

1.3.4 Adjust Virtual Image Size at Runtime

In each frame we calculate a target virtual image size based on its distance from the camera. If the target size is different than the current size of the sector, we will insert a new image with the target size into the atlas and remove the old one. Listings 1.1 and 1.2 show the code to calculate and adjust, respectively, the size of virtual images for sectors in the world.

For example, as shown in Figure 1.3, when the camera moves and Sector B becomes farther away from the camera, it will be allocated using a smaller image size of 32K × 32K. Sector C becomes closer to the camera, so it will be allocated with a larger image size of 64K × 64K.

1.3.5 Remap the Indirection Texture

Indirection texture Our virtual texture system uses an indirection texture to translate from the virtual UV address to the physical UV address. (For the basic virtual texture technique and information about indirection textures, please refer to [Mittring 08].) When virtual image are moved and scaled, we have to update the indirection texture so that the new virtual UV address will reuse the existing pages in the physical texture caches. The format of our indirection texture is 32 bit and it is defined as in Figure 1.4.

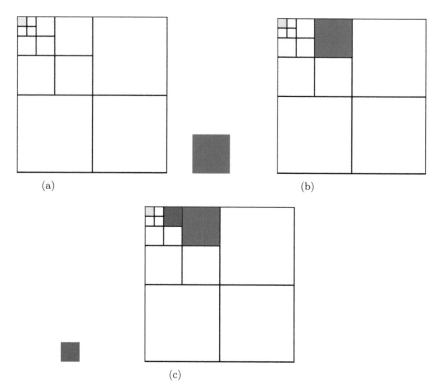

Figure 1.2. (a) First, insert a virtual image of size 16×16 for Sector A. (b) Then, insert a virtual image of size 64×64 for Sector B. (c) Then, insert a virtual image of size 32×32 for Sector C.

```
typedef unsigned int U32;
const U32 highestResolution = 64 * 1024;
U32 CalculateTargetImageSize(const SectorInfo& sectorInfo, const
Vector3& cameraPosition)
{
    //Get sectorPosition.
    ......
    // Distance between sector and camera in top-down view.
    float distance = -(sectorPosition - cameraPosition).GetLength2();
    U32 t = (U32)(distance / switchDistance);
    // Calculate the LOD of virtual image.
    U32 lodImage = 0;
    if(t >= 1)
    {
        lodImage = std::log2(t) + 1;
    }
    U32 virtualImageSize = highestResolution >> lodImage;
    return virtualImageSize;
}
```

Listing 1.1. Calculating the virtual image size.

```
std::vector<SectorInfo> delayedRemoveSectors;
for (auto& sectorInfo : m_AllSectors)
{
    virtualImageSize = CalculateTargetImageSize(sectorInfo,
                          cameraPosition);
    If (virtualImageSize != sectorInfo.m_VirtualImageSize)
    {
        m_Atlas.InsertImage(sectorInfo, virtualImageSize);
        delayedRemoveSectors.push_back(sectorInfo);
    }
}
for (auto& removingSector : delayedRemoveSectors)
{
    m_Atlas.RemoveImage(removingSector);
}
delayedRemoveSectors.clear();
```

Listing 1.2. Adjusting the virtual image size.

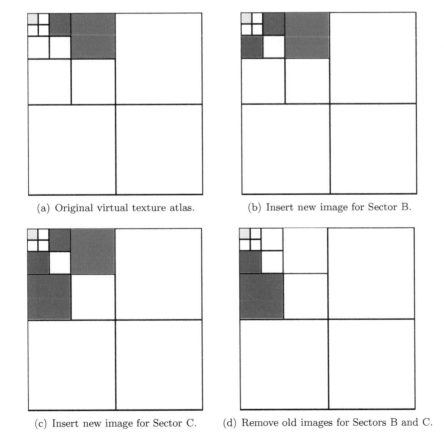

(a) Original virtual texture atlas.   (b) Insert new image for Sector B.

(c) Insert new image for Sector C.   (d) Remove old images for Sectors B and C.

Figure 1.3. Adjusting the size of two virtual images.

| PageOffsetX : 8 | PageOffsetY : 8 | Mip : 8 | Debug : 8 |

Figure 1.4. Indirection texture format.

```
scale = (virtual texture size / physical texture size) >> mip;
bias = physical page offset - virtual page offset * scale;
physical uv = virtual uv * scale + bias;
```

Listing 1.3. Calculating the physical texture UV address from the indirection texture and the virtual UV address.

`PageOffsetX` and `PageOffsetY` are the UV offsets of the physical page pointed to by the current virtual page. `Mip` describes the available mipmap level for the current virtual page. The final physical texture UV address is calculated as shown in Listing 1.3.

Remap the indirection texture when the image is up-scaled   The update of the indirection texture for Sector B is shown in Figure 1.5.

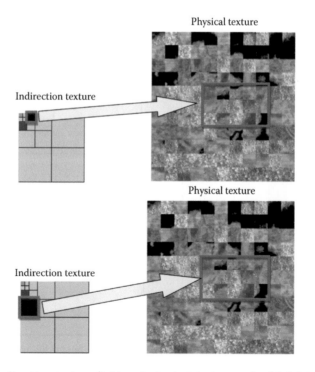

Figure 1.5. Indirection texture (left) and physical texture cache (right) before update (top) and after update (bottom).

```
For every mipmap level of the indirection texture ,
{
        //The following part is executed by a compute shader going
        //through all indirection texture entries , with the number of
        //threads set as the number of entries in the X and Y
        //dimensions .
        For every entry enclosed by new image in that mipmap level ,
        {
                If (current mipmap level is greater than 0)
                {
                        Copy the content from 1 mip level higher old image
                        (PageOffsetX , PageOffsetY , Mip) and increase Mip by 1
                        The new entry content becomes (PageOffsetX ,
                        PageOffsetY , Mip + 1);
                }
                else
                {
                        Copy the content from 1 mip level higher old image ,
                        The new entry content becomes (PageOffsetX ,
                        PageOffsetY , Mip);
                }
        }
}
```

Listing 1.4. Pseudocode to update the indirection texture for a newly allocated virtual image.

The work involved in updating the indirection texture is shown in Listing 1.4.

The remapping of an up-scaled virtual image can be viewed in Figure 1.6. In this case the image size is up-scaled from 32K to 64K. We can conclude that the indirection entries for the new image should point to the exact same entries of one mip level higher in the old image, as shown by the red arrows. As the mip level 0 of the new image doesn't exist in the old image, we will set the entries of mip level 0 in the new image to lower mip level physical texture pages to prevent visual popping in the current frame.

Remap the indirection texture when image is down-scaled   Remapping a down-scaled virtual image is just to reverse the steps of up-scaling a virtual image, as shown in Figure 1.7.

1.4   Virtual Texture Best Practices

In the previous section we discussed the key features of AVT and how to handle updating the virtual texture atlas and indirection texture when dynamic adjustments of the image size happens in real time. In this section we will talk about some practical implementation details of AVT.

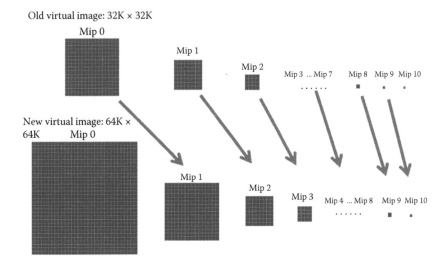

Figure 1.6. Remapping of an up-scaled virtual image.

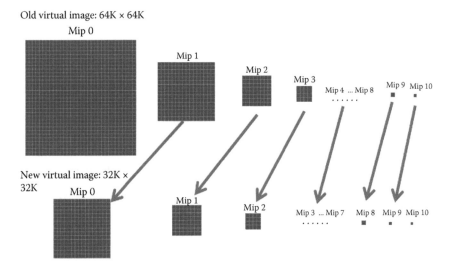

Figure 1.7. Remapping a down-scaled virtual image.

1.4.1 Output Page IDs

Virtual textures are divided into multiple 256×256 sized virtual pages. For every pixel on the screen, we calculate to which virtual page it is related and output the page information into a read/write buffer during the G-buffer rendering pass. We call this buffer the *Page ID buffer*.

PageID X : 12	PageID Y : 12	Mip : 4	Size : 4

Figure 1.8. The format of the page ID.

```
#define PAGEID_DOWNSCALE 8
void OutputPageID(VTextureArgs vArgs, float2 screenPos)
{
    //Write to page ID read/write buffer
    uint2 vpos = (uint2)screenPos;
    uint2 vpos2 = ((uint2) vpos) % PAGEID_DOWNSCALE;
    uint virtualPageID = pack_pageid(vArgs);
    if(vpos2.x == (uint)g_VirtualSectorsInfo.VirtualDither.x &&
        vpos2.y == (uint)g_VirtualSectorsInfo.VirtualDither.y)
            PageIDOutputTexture[((uint2) vpos) / PAGEID_DOWNSCALE] =
                virtualPageID;
}
```

Listing 1.5. Writing to $1/8 \times 1/8$ Page ID buffer in the G-buffer rendering shader.

The page information for every pixel is written as a 32-bit integer as shown in Figure 1.8.

`PageID` and `Size` are calculated as

$$\texttt{PageID.xy} = \frac{\texttt{Virtual UV.xy}}{\text{virtual page size}},$$

$$\texttt{Size} = \log_2(\text{virtual page size}).$$

The size of the Page ID buffer is $1/8$ of the G-buffer texture in both directions in order to reduce the memory overhead. Listing 1.5 is the fragment shader used to output the page ID to the small read/write buffer.

Note that `g_VirtualSectorsInfo.VirtualDither.xy` is the shader parameter passed in from the rendering engine, and its value ranges from 0 to 7 and changes according to a predefined pattern in every frame. Since we only pick one pixel out of 64 to output, if a page ID is missed in one frame, it will be processed during a subsequent frame.

1.4.2 Physical Textures and Compressing

We allocate three physical textures for deferred rendering purposes. These are the albedo texture, normal map texture, and specular texture. Table 1.1 provides the color channel information for these textures.

Every physical texture page is compressed at runtime by a compute shader on the GPU. We modified the sample code provided by Microsoft for the Xbox One to compress three different types of physical texture pages in one pass. For the normal map texture, we choose the BC5 format to compress only the X and Y

Physical Texture	Channels	Representation	Compress Format
Albedo Texture	RGB	Albedo Color	BC1
Normal Map Texture	RG	Tangent Space Normal	BC5
Specular Texture	RGB	Glossness, Specular Intensity, Normal Map Scale	BC1

Table 1.1. Physical textures' channel information.

```
//Output terrain G-buffer color by fetching physical texture cache.
gbuffer.albedo = DiffusePhysicalTexture.SampleGrad(
        TextureSampler, physical_uv, dx, dy).xyz;
gbuffer.normal.xy = NormalPhysicalTexture.SampleGrad(
        TextureSampler, physical_uv, dx, dy).xy;
gbuffer.normal.xy = gbuffer.normal.xy * 2 - 1;
gbuffer.normal.z = sqrt(saturate(1 - dot(gbuffer.normal.xy,
                gbuffer.normal.xy)));
float3 GlossnessSpecularIntensity =
    SpecularPhysicalTexture.SampleGrad(TextureSampler,
                physical_uv, dx, dy).xyz;
gbuffer.normal.xyz *= GlossnessSpecularIntensity.z;
gbuffer.glossness_specularIntensity =
    GlossnessSpecularIntensity.xy;
```

Listing 1.6. Calculating the final G-buffer colors from virtual textures.

channels of the normal map into a separated 4 bits-per-pixel block. This gives a much less blocky result than with the BC1 format. In some situations the normal vector saved in the virtual texture is not unit length. For example, when the pixel is on a big slope on the terrain surface, the final normal vector might be scaled by the slope angle or a mask texture. We save the scale of the normal vector in the Z channel of the Specular Physical Texture during compression. Later on, when we fetch the virtual textures, we reapply the scale to the normal vector coming from the physical texture. Listing 1.6 shows the HLSL shader for calculating the final G-buffer colors.

1.4.3   Improve Performance by Distributed Rendering

The performance of virtual texture rendering may vary depending on how many virtual pages are visible in a given frame. When the camera is moving or turning very fast, it could take significant time to cache the physical textures. We can spread the rendering of virtual pages into multiple frames to alleviate this problem. We call this method *distributed rendering*.

On the CPU we read the Page ID buffer that is output from the GPU, collect the visible virtual pages, and remove the duplicated pages. We then sort the

```
struct PageIDSortPredicate
{
    bool operator()(const unsigned id0, const unsigned id1) const
    {
        VTexturePageID key0(id0);
        VTexturePageID key1(id1);

        //key.size is saved in Log2 space, so it is in the same
        //space as the mipmap level.
        return (key0.size - key0.mip) < (key1.size - key1.mip);
    }
};

std::sort(pageIDs.Begin(),pageIDs.End(), PageKeySortPredicate());
```

Listing 1.7. Sorting the visible pages.

visible pages according to their image sizes scaled by mipmap level, as shown in Listing 1.7.

For each sorted virtual page starting from the first page, we first search for its physical page in the physical texture cache and allocate one if it is not already there; then, we render the fully composited terrain material into the page. At the same time we record the actual rendering time for virtual textures. If the accumulated rendering time for the current frame is longer than a threshold, we skip the rendering of the remaining pages in the list. The skipped pages will be rendered during the next frame.

We always sort the virtual pages such that we render the page with the smallest image size first. This guarantees that the terrain is always displayed on screen even if some pages have been skipped. Some parts of the image may appear blurry in the current frame if they have been skipped, but these areas will become sharper later, once they are updated. In practice this is generally not noticeable because it happens very quickly from one frame to the next.

1.4.4 Virtual Texture Filtering

Anisotropic filtering Our Adaptive Virtual Texutres support 8X anisotropic filtering. This means that the pixel shader may access neighboring pixels up to 4 pixels away If the shader accesses a pixel lying on the border of the page, its neighboring pixel could reside in another physical page and it might not be the correct neighboring pixel in the world space. This would cause color bleeding problems between pages.

To fix this problem, we allocate a 4-pixel-wide border on each side of the physical texture page. For a 256×256 virtual page, its physical page size becomes 264×264. When rendering into the physical page, the viewport is also enlarged to 264×264 so that the neighboring pixels at the border are rendered. (See Figure 1.9.)

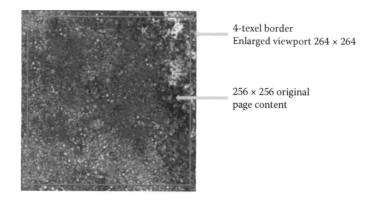

4-texel border
Enlarged viewport 264 × 264

256 × 256 original
page content

Figure 1.9. A 4-pixel border on a physical page.

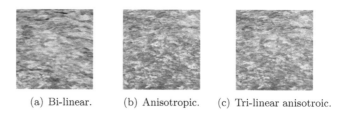

(a) Bi-linear.   (b) Anisotropic.   (c) Tri-linear anisotroic.

Figure 1.10. Comparison of three filtering methods.

Tri-linear filtering Software tri-linear filtering is also supported by simply fetching the indirection texture twice with a higher mipmap level and a lower mipmap level to get two sets of physical UV addresses, then fetching from the physical textures twice and blending between them according to the calculated ratio between the mipmap levels.

Another approach is to use hardware tri-linear filtering with virtual textures. For every physical texture we have, we can create an additional quarter size physical texture as mipmap level 1 and render into this mipmap level 1 page whenever the mipmap 0 page is rendered. This method requires 25% more video memory for the physical texture caches. It also increases the GPU overhead because the mipmap level 1 cache must be synced with the mipmap level 0 all the time.

Figure 1.10 shows a comparison between bi-linear filtering, anisotropic filtering, and tri-linear anisotropic filtering when looking at the ground with a sharp view angle. The image looks blurred with bi-linear filtering. With anisotropic filtering alone, the image looks much sharper but there is a visible seam where mipmap levels change. With tri-linear anisotropic filtering, both problems are solved.

(a) Render terrain materials.
(b) Render a decal on top
of terrain.
(c) Render next decal.
(d) Render the third decal.

Figure 1.11. Rendering terrain and decals into a virtual texture page.

1.4.5 Combine with Projected Decals

Adaptive Virtual Textures become very powerful when they are combined with projected decals on terrain. The G-buffer properties (albedo, normal, and specular) of the decals can be baked into the same virtual page where terrain surfaces are rendered. Thus rendering of projected decals becomes almost free with Adaptive Virtual Textures. Since AVT supports very high virtual texture resolutions (10 texels/cm), level artists can put thousands of high-detail projected decals on the ground, and this vastly improves the visual appearance for next-generation games.

The rendering pipeline for projected decals in adaptive virtual textures is quite straight forward:

For every visible page collected and sorted from the Page ID buffer,

1. find or allocate a physical texture page,

2. render terrain surface materials into the physical page,

3. find decals belonging to this page in the world space,

4. render decals into the physical page by projecting them into the virtual texture.

Figure 1.11 shows the steps to render terrain materials and decals into a virtual texture page.

1.5 Conclusion

This chapter described a new technique called Adaptive Virtual Textures for rendering terrain and decals with a high resolution in an open world. AVT is an improvement upon Procedural Virtual Textures. The main contribution of this technique is that it supports a very high virtual texture resolution at close range and can be used to render thousands of decals very efficiently.

Bibliography

[Mittring 08] Martin Mittring. "Advanced Virtual Texture Topics." In *ACM SIGGRAPH 2008 Games*, pp. 23–51. New York: ACM, 2008.

[Widmark 12] Mattias Widmark. "Terrain in Battlefield 3." Paper presented at Game Developers Conference, San Francisco, CA, March 5–9, 2012.

Deferred Coarse Pixel Shading

Rahul P. Sathe and Tomasz Janczak

2.1 Overview

Deferred shading has become a popular rendering technique in the games industry to avoid redundant shading of occluded pixels. With increasing screen resolutions and DPI, one can reduce the frequency of slowly varying components of the rendering equation to something lower than once per pixel without a perceivable difference in visual quality. Recent research addresses this issue and proposes hardware solutions like Coarse Pixel Shading [Vaidyanathan et al. 14]. Although an elegant solution, the Coarse Pixel Shader does not fit well into the deferred shading pipeline. Lauritzen proposed a solution for deferred shading engines that identifies the pixels where pixel rate shading is not enough and shades them at the sample rate using a compute shader [Lauritzen 10]. We extend the later idea further, but in the reverse direction by identifying the regions of the screen where one can reduce the shading to a rate lower than pixel frequency (e.g., 2×2 pixel sized blocks). With our technique we are able show about 40–50% reduction in shading time with a slight increase in the G-buffer generation time.

2.2 Introduction and Background

Shading calculations often involve multiple components, e.g., ambient occlusion, diffused lighting, and specular highlights. Some of these components have a lower spatial frequency than others. When these slowly changing components are evaluated at a rate lower than once per pixel, the image artifacts are hardly noticeable on a high DPI screen. A large percentage of the power consumed by the graphics processors is due to pixel shading [Pool 12]. As a result, reducing the pixel shader usage directly translates to a power savings. Vaidyanathan et al. proposed a solution that is well suited for the forward rendering pipeline [Vaidyanathan et al. 14]. In their approach, one shades primitives in screen space at different rates: coarse pixels (e.g., 2×2 block of pixels), pixels, and then samples. But this does not extend well to the deferred shading or postprocessing passes because at the time of deferred shading, the notion of primitive is not present. Moreover, the primitive might have been partly occluded with one or more additional primitives.

Lauretzen proposed a compute shader-based solution for deferred shading that works well with multisample antialiasing (MSAA) [Lauritzen 10]. In his approach, the G-buffer is rendered at the MSAA resolution and contains the view-space derivatives and the normal, in addition to other surface data used for shading. He then analyzes the G-buffer samples within a pixel to find if that pixel needs to be shaded at the sample frequency. He uses the triangle inequality of the view-space depth derivatives along with the normal variation to find out which pixels need to be shaded at the sample rate. We expand upon his idea, but in the opposite direction.

2.3   Algorithm

2.3.1   G-Buffer Generation

Just like in a normal deferred shading engine, our algorithm starts off by generating a G-buffer by writing out shading inputs at the pixel center. The G-buffer stores derivatives of the view-space Z values in addition to the other surface data (position, normal, UVs, TBN basis, etc.) required for evaluating the BRDF during the shading pass. View-space Z derivatives are calculated by first multiplying the position with the camera-world-view matrix and evaluating `ddx_coarse` and `ddy_coarse` instructions. We use the spherical encoding to encode the surface normal into `float2` to save some G-buffer space and bandwidth. Other types of encoding [Pranckevičius 09] are possible, but we chose a spherical encoding because that works well with the optimization discussed at the end of Section 2.3.2. We pack the specular intensity and the specular power in the other two components to occupy a full `float4`. The G-buffer layout is as follows:

```
struct GBuffer
{
    float4 normal_specular : SV_Target0;  // Encoded normal and
                                          // specular power/intensity.
    float4 albedo          : SV_Target1;  // Albedo.
    float4 biased_albedo   : SV_Target2;  // Albedo sampled with
                                          // the biased sampler.
    float2 positionZGrad   : SV_Target3;  // ddx, ddy of view-space Z.
    float  positionZ       : SV_Target4;  // View-space Z.
};
```

2.3.2   Shading Pass

For the shading pass, we use a tiled compute shader similar to the one proposed by Lauritzen [Lauritzen 10]. Our compute shader is launched such that one thread processes one coarse region of the screen (e.g., 2×2 or 4×4 pixels region, henceforth referred to as a *coarse pixel*). One thread group works on a larger screen-space region containing multiple coarse regions (henceforth referred to as a *tile*). Our compute shader is conceptually divided in multiple phases:

1. light tiling phase,

2. analysis phase,

3. coarse pixel shading phase,

4. pixel shading phase.

At the end of each phase, the threads within the thread group synchronize. Listing 2.1 shows the pseudocode for the shading pass. Figure 2.1 shows the flowchart for the same.

We will now describe each of the phases in detail.

Light tiling phase   When the renderer has a large number of lights to deal with, the bandwidth required to read the light data structures can be a substantial. To alleviate this problem, it is common practice to find the lights that intersect a particular tile. Once found, the indices to the lights that intersect a particular tile are maintained in the shared local memory. Subsequent portions of the shading pass deal with only the lights that hit at least one pixel in that tile. Further details about light culling can be found in [Lauritzen 10].

Analysis phase   The goal of this phase is to determine the coarse pixels at which the shading rate can be lowered. To that end, each thread reads the normals and the view-space depth derivatives for all the pixels within the coarse pixel. We then analyze the G-buffer data at each of the pixels in the coarse pixel with respect to a reference pixel (e.g., the top-left pixel in each region). During the analysis, similar to that of Lauritzen [Lauritzen 10], we use the triangle inequality to check if the shading rate can be reduced to once per coarse pixel. The underlying principle in using this criterion is to check if the entire region belongs to the same triangle. The maximum possible range of Z in a given region is calculated as the region's span (e.g., $\sqrt{2}N$ for $N \times N$ pixels) times the sum of the absolute values of the view-space derivatives of the reference sample. We use the triangle inequality to see if the absolute difference of the view-space Z is greater than the maximum possible Z range over that region. Alternatively, one could store a 3-tuple (`DrawcallId`, `InstanceId`, `PrimitiveId`) to identify if the coarse pixel belongs to a single primitive, but this consumes more memory and bandwidth.

Having the coarse pixel belong to one triangle is necessary, but it is not a sufficient condition for us to be able to reduce the shading rate. We also check if the maximum variation of the surface normal with respect to the reference pixel is under some predefined threshold (e.g., 2 degrees). If other G-buffer components contribute to BRDF in any meaningful way, we check to see if their variance from a reference sample is within the acceptable threshold.

```
#define GROUP_DIM   16
#define GROUP_SIZE (GROUP_DIM * GROUP_DIM)
groupshared uint sMinZ, sMaxZ; // Z-min and -max for the tile.

// Light list for the tile.
groupshared uint sTileLightIndices[MAX_LIGHTS];
groupshared uint sTileNumLights;

// List of coarse-pixels that require per-pixel shading.
// We encode two 16-bit x/y coordinates in one uint to save shared memory space.
groupshared uint sPerPixelCPs [GROUP_SIZE/(N*N)];
groupshared uint sNumPerPixelCPs;

[numthreads(GROUP_DIM/N,  GROUP_DIM/N, 1)] // Coarse pixel is NxN.
void ComputeShaderTileCS (...)

{
    // Load the surface data for all the pixels within NxN.
    // Calculate the Z-bounds within the coarse pixel.
    // Calculate min and max for the entire tile and store it in sMinZ, sMaxZ.

    // One thread processes one light.
    for (lightIndex = groupIndex..totalLights){
    // If the light intersects the tile, append it to sTileLightIndices[].
    }
    Groupsync ();

    // Read the lights that touch this tile from the groupshared memory.
    // Evaluate and accumulate the lighting for every light for the top-left pixel.
    // Check to see if per-pixel lighting is required.
    bool perPixelShading = IsPerPixelShading(surfaceSamples);
    if (perPixelShading) {
        // Atomically increment sNumPerPixelCPs with the read back.
        // Append the pixel to sPerPixelCPs[].
    } else {
        // Store the results in the intermediate buffer in groupshared or
        // global memory,
        // OR if no per-pixel component, splat the top-left pixel's color to other
        // pixels in NxN.
    }
    GroupSync ();

    uint globalSamples = sNumPerSamplePixels * (N*N -1);
    for (sample = groupIndex..globalSamples..sample += GROUP_SIZE/(N*N))
    {
        // Read the lights that touch this tile from the groupshared memory.
        // Accumulate the lighting for the sample.
        // Write out the results.
    }
    GroupSync ();

    // Process the per-pixel component for every pixel in NxN, and add the results
    // to the intermediate results calculated for the top-left pixel.
}
```

Listing 2.1. Pseudocode for the shading pass. It has four phases: light culling phase, analysis phase, coarse pixel shading phase, and pixel shading phase. Phases are separated by a groupsync().

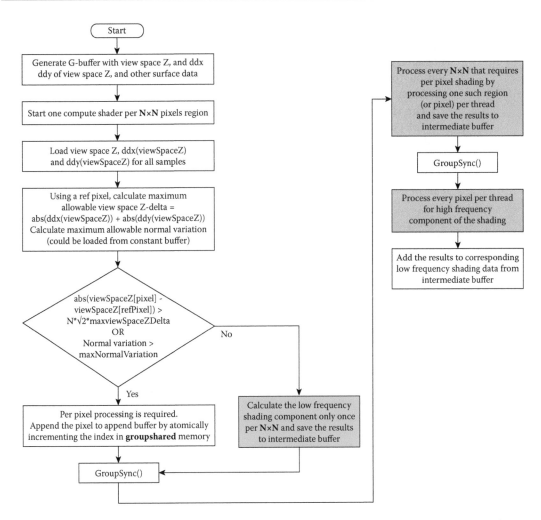

Figure 2.1. Overview of the shading pass. The items in green are evaluated at lower frequency (once per $N \times N$ pixels) and the items in orange are executed at once-per-pixel frequency.

Coarse pixel shading phase Regardless of whether we are able to reduce the shading frequency of the slowly varying shading term to the coarse rate or not, we evaluate it at the top-left pixel. Using the analysis described for the analysis phase, we find out where a shading term can be evaluated at the coarse rate and we store its results in memory (groupshared or global). If the DPI is high enough and there is no shading term that must be evaluated at the pixel rate, we can splat the intermediate results to the other pixels in that coarse pixel. For the other threads, we append their thread IDs to an append buffer in the groupshared memory, indicating that the shading term needs to be evaluated at the other pixels in that coarse pixel. All threads within the group wait at the synchronization point. By structuring the code this way, we have moved the shading term evaluation (often expensive) out of the control flow and reduced the control flow divergence.

For the regions where we could not lower the shading rate, we change the axis of parallelism from one thread per coarse pixel to one thread per pixel and evaluate the shading term. The threads that evaluated the shading term at the coarse rate wait at the group synchronization point. If the DPI is high enough, there may be no need to do per-pixel shading. In this situation, the next phase can be skipped altogether.

Pixel shading phase If there is a shading component that must be evaluated at the pixel rate (or if the DPI is not high enough), we change the axis of parallelism to one thread per coarse pixel again but now each thread processes all the pixels in that coarse pixel and adds the results to the ones calculated in the previous step.

2.3.3 Biasing the Sampler

Texturing is typically done in the forward passes and is not deferred. The G-buffer was generated at a pixel frequency (with the assumption that shading will be done once per pixel). However, we try to reduce the shading rate to once per coarse pixel wherever possible during the shading pass. This introduces temporal artifacts like shimmering. Possible solutions to this are

1. to sample the textures using a biased sampler (biased by $\log_2 N$) during the forward pass for the regions where the shading rate will be lowered;

2. to filter the texture data on the fly during the rendering pass.

The latter can increase the bandwidth significantly (depending on the size of N). So, we propose to introduce an additional G-buffer component per texture that uses a biased sampler. This does add some cost to the G-buffer generation.

The DirectX 11.2 Tier 2 specifications introduced minimum/maximum filtering along with tiled resources. One way to optimize this algorithm even further is to offload the minimum/maximum bounds calculation of the $N \times N$ region of the G-buffer to a texture sampling unit. This frees the shader cores from loading all the values and calculating the minimum/maximum. Shader cores reduce the shading rate when the difference in the minimum and maximum is less than some acceptable threshold. This technique might invoke some false positives because it is more conservative than the one proposed in the shader-based solution.

Loop Count	Power Plant			Sponza		
	Pixel (ms)	Coarse Pixel (ms)	Savings (%)	Pixel (ms)	Coarse Pixel (ms)	Savings (%)
0	22.7	11.2	50.7	12.5	9.4	24.9
100	50.3	21.1	58.1	26.8	17.6	34.3
500	87.7	34.9	60.2	43.6	27.7	36.5

Table 2.1. Shading time (ms) when shading was reduced to 2×2 pixel blocks wherever possible compared to when shading was performed every pixel.

2.4   Performance

We measured our performance on a system with Windows 8.1, running with an Intel HD 5500 integrated GPU. We used scenes that we felt were representative of game assets. We used two scenes, the power plant scene and the Sponza scene. Each scene was lit with 1024 colored point lights. Our rendering equation consists of the diffuse and the specular terms. We tried to reduce the frequency at which the entire rendering equation is evaluated to once per coarse pixel of the size 2×2 pixels. We could do that because our DPI was high enough at 1920×1080 pixels. At this DPI, we did not have a shading term that had to be evaluated at the pixel rate. To mimic how the performance would change for more expensive shaders, such as AO cone tracing, we added a dummy loop inside our shader to make it more compute intensive and varied the loop length as a parameter. In some cases, users may want to evaluate certain coefficients in the rendering equation at the lower rate, but the actual rendering equation could be evaluated at the higher rate. The algorithm proposed here is fully generic and one can lower the frequency of only some parts of the rendering equation.

Table 2.1 summarizes the performance benefits of reducing the shading rate as a function of shader length. We see anywhere from 25% to 60% improvement in the shading time depending upon the shader complexity. For a given scene, we see higher gains if the shader is more complex. However, sampling the albedo texture using a biased sampler and storing that as an extra G-buffer component increases the G-buffer generation time only by 2.2 ms and 1.9 ms for the power plant and the Sponza scenes, respectively. (See Figure 2.2.) As a result, we see this technique as a net win.

2.5   Conclusion

We have presented a technique to reduce the shading costs during deferred shading. The same technique is applicable to postprocessing passes, too. With this technique developers can apply their postprocessing effects at a reduced rate with minimal impact to image quality.

Figure 2.2. The power plant scene (left) and the Sponza scene (right). Coarse pixel size was 2×2 pixels. Top row images were rendered at the full pixel resolution. Middle row images were rendered with coarse pixel shading wherever possible. Bottom row shows in green the regions where shading was reduced to coarse pixel rate.

Demo

A real-time demo implemented using DirectX shader Model 5.0 will be available on the Intel Developer Zone (https://software.intel.com/en-us).

Bibliography

[Lauritzen 10] A. Lauritzen. "Deferred Rendering for Current and Future Rendering Pipelines." SIGGRAPH Course: Beyond Programmable Shading, Los Angeles, CA, July 29, 2010.

[Pool 12] J. Pool. "Energy-Precision Tradeoffs in the Graphics Pipeline." PhD thesis, Univeristy of North Carolina, Chapel Hill, NC, 2012.

[Pranckevičius 09] A. Pranckevičius. "Compact Normal Storage for Small G-Buffers." http://aras-p.info/texts/CompactNormalStorage.html, 2009.

[Vaidyanathan et al. 14] K. Vaidyanathan, M. Salvi, R. Toth, T. Foley, T. Akenine-Moller, J. Nilsson, J., et al. "Coarse Pixel Shading." Paper presented at High Performance Graphics, Lyon, France, June 23–25, 2014.

Progressive Rendering Using Multi-frame Sampling

Daniel Limberger, Karsten Tausche, Johannes Linke, and Jürgen Döllner

3.1 Introduction

This chapter presents an approach that distributes sampling over multiple, consecutive frames and, thereby, enables sampling-based, real-time rendering techniques to be implemented for most graphics hardware and systems in a less complex, straightforward way. This systematic, extensible schema allows developers to effectively handle the increasing implementation complexity of advanced, sophisticated, real-time rendering techniques, while improving responsiveness and reducing required hardware resources.

The approach is motivated by the following observations related to 3D system and application development:

- Creating advanced rendering techniques and computer graphics systems is intriguing in the case of target platforms equipped with the latest graphics hardware. Business and industry applications, however, are often strongly constrained in terms of both hardware and API support: software and hardware adapt slowly to new APIs and are often limited in terms of available processing power and video memory, e.g., with regards to high-resolution image generation. Thus, it sometimes takes years for state-of-the-art, real-time rendering techniques to become a core part of 3D systems and applications in business and industry.

- Many 3D systems and applications do not require a strictly continuous stream of high-quality images. For example, in interactive visualization of static data, which is common for digital-content-creation tools, the rendering process can be partially paused as user interactions and data changes occur less frequently. Thus, strict real-time, high-quality imaging constraints can sometimes be lessened.

- The adoption of the latest rendering techniques in 3D systems and applications is faced with increasing software complexity and increasing hardware requirements due to their single-frame design, e.g., designing, implementing, and testing complex, shader-based, multi-platform rendering techniques. In particular, this phenomenon increases financial and technical risks in system and application development.

The key idea of our approach, *multi-frame sampling*, is based on, technically speaking, the following idea: Instead of rendering a single frame in response to an update request, multiple frames are rendered and accumulated. Thereby, every accumulation result can be immediately displayed while the frame quality progressively increases. We demonstrate our approach for a variety of rendering techniques, i.e., antialiasing (AA), depth of field (DoF), soft shadows, and screen-space ambient occlusion (SSAO), as well as order-independent transparency (OIT). Progressive rendering using multi-frame sampling allows us to use rather simple implementations of rendering techniques to produce state-of-the-art effects. Furthermore, the multi-frame approach usually reduces memory usage, decreases rendering cost per frame (lower response time), allows for better maintainable implementations, and provides more comprehensible parameterizations.

3.2   Approach

An integral part of today's hardware-accelerated, real-time rendering technologies is built on *sampling*, as the "process of rendering images is inherently a sampling task" [Akenine-Möller et al. 08]. Sampling is generally used to approximate continuous characteristics and signals, e.g., reducing aliasing artifacts caused by insufficient depictions of continuous domains. For single-frame rendering, sampling is limited to a single frame. Increasing the number of samples improves the resulting image quality but also increases the rendering costs per frame in terms of time and memory.

Our multi-frame sampling approach distributes samples over a well-defined number n_{MF} of consecutive frames. With each frame we progressively increase image quality while having reduced cost per frame and still being able to process massive amounts of samples. Each frame generated during multi-frame sampling uses a unique subset of samples of a well-defined set of samples called the *kernel*. Consecutive frames are accumulated until n_{MF} frames are generated and the rendering finally pauses. On any update request, the accumulation process is restarted.

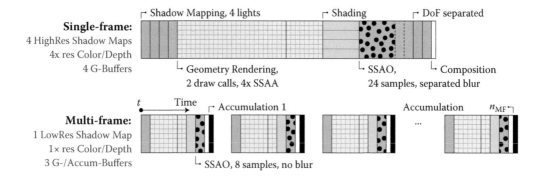

Figure 3.1. Conceptual illustration of a typical single-frame rendering structure transformed into a multi-frame rendering structure: Only one shadow pass instead of four, and 8 SSAO samples instead of 24, are used. DoF and AA are inherently available due to camera and NDC (normalized device coordinate) space shifting. The required resources are reduced, and to increase quality, more frames can be rendered and accumulated.

Assumptions The application of multi-frame sampling in 3D systems and applications is based on the following assumptions:

- The underlying rendering uses sampling as one of its elements.

- Rendering update requests are less frequent, and responsiveness in terms of frames per second is favored over intermediate frame quality.

- The converging image quality is not disruptive to the use cases or usability of 3D systems and applications.

Implementation To transform a given single-frame, sampling-based technique into a multi-frame technique, we proceed as follows:

1. We identify segments within the technique that are processed repeatedly. A parameterization that controls an iteration per frame (e.g., number of samples) often indicates such segments. These iterations are unrolled, which causes samples to be distributed over consecutive frames (Figure 3.1).

2. We have to verify that (a) an increase in number of executions of a segment results in better quality and (b) each segment's result can be accumulated throughout multiple consecutive frames.

3. We adapt the original technique such that it supports an appropriate sampling characteristic: the sampling type (single or multiple samples per frame) and the spatio-temporal distribution of samples.

When multi-frame sampling is used with multiple techniques simultaneously, depending on their assembly, there might be combinations that require special attention, for example, stochastic per-fragment discarding combined with screen-space ambient occlusion.

The remainder of this chapter describes sampling strategies and frame accumulation. For a variety of rendering techniques, associated multi-frame approaches are discussed (Section 3.3). Within each of these sections, results are discussed and brief performance remarks are given. All code snippets are based on GLSL and C++ using the OpenGL API.

3.2.1 Sampling Strategies

For multi-frame sampling we distinguish between techniques processing either one or multiple samples per frame. A single sample per frame is taken from a kernel, which is precomputed on the CPU and provided as a *uniform* (usually `float`, `vec2`, or `vec3`). For every subsequent frame, the uniform is updated (per technique). When using multiple samples per frame, the kernel is precomputed on the CPU as well but then uploaded to the GPU encoded as a uniform buffer, texture, or buffer (depending on kernel's size and shader capability). Since the rendering can unfold over multiple frames, most rendering techniques can be reduced to their core concept. Neither performance-related caching nor other optimization strategies are required. Furthermore, some techniques are virtually for free because they are inherent to multi-frame rendering (e.g., AA, DoF).

Nevertheless, the final rendering quality and especially the convergence speed and its "temporal tranquility" strongly depend on a well-designed kernel. The kernel's characteristics include

- required number of samples for targeted quality,

- spatial distribution or value-based distribution,

- sample regularity and completeness for finite accumulation,

- temporal convergence constraints regarding the sequence of samples,

- additional per-fragment randomization.

Since we do not use GPU-based pseudo-randomness and all samples are typically precomputed and designed for a specific multi-frame number n_{MF}, accumulating additional frames on top of that is futile. Especially when passing low multi-frame numbers, this may lead to temporal clustering. The presented techniques have been implemented based on the open-source, header-only libraries `glm` [Riccio 15] and `glkernel` [Limberger 15] used for dynamic computation of kernels of required characteristics at runtime.

```
1  // weight = 1.0 / n, with n enumerating the current multi-frame.
2  uniform float weight;
3  ...
4  {
5     ...
6     vec3 a = texture(accumBuffer, v_uv).rgb;
7     vec3 c = texture(frameBuffer, v_uv).rgb;

9     // average is pointing to the accumulation target.
10    average = mix(a, c, weight);
11 }
```

Listing 3.1. Example of an accumulation GLSL fragment shader adding the last frame to the overall average; `frameBuffer` contains the nth frame's color and `accumBuffer` the last average. Texture filtering is set to nearest filtering for both texture objects.

3.2.2 Frame Accumulation

The accumulation of consecutive frames can be implemented using hardware-accelerated blending. Alternatively, the accumulation can be executed as an additional postprocessing pass. Either a screen-aligned triangle with a fragment shader or, if available, a compute shader can be used to average all existing frames. For this, the accumulation buffer is set up as an input texture and a color attachment of the target framebuffer object simultaneously. The current frame is provided as a second input texture. The color c of the nth frame is read and added to the previous average a: $a = c/n + a(1 - 1/n)$. This works with a single accumulation buffer (no ping pong; reduced memory footprint) as long as no adjacent fragments are processed (Listing 3.1).

On update requests, multi-frame rendering is reset to a multi-frame number of 1 and accumulation is just blitting this frame; accumulation is skipped and the frame is rendered into the accumulation buffer directly. The accumulation buffer's texture format should support sufficient accuracy (16I or 32F) because the weight for frame averaging gets subsequently smaller (Figure 3.2).

Since the scene and its underlying data is assumed to be static during accumulation, the time per frame is roughly constant for subsequent frames. Thus, individual sampling characteristics can be adapted ad hoc for the second and all subsequent frames to approach the constrained frame time (e.g., decrease or increase number of samples per frame). Alternatively, vertical synchronization can be turned off during accumulation. In our tests we experienced no tearing artifacts because the expected, consecutive differences converge to zero. Apart from that, extensions for application-controlled synchronization could be used to exclude artifacts entirely.

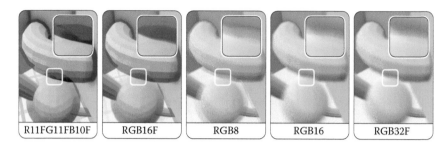

Figure 3.2. Accumulation results (test scene, AA and DoF) for 1024 frames using various texture formats. From left to right, the quality is (obviously) increasing.

3.3   Multi-frame Rendering Techniques

One motivation for multi-frame sampling is to have better control of the adjustment of the rendering quality, while implementing against older, limited APIs and conserving as many GPU resources as possible. Even though the techniques discussed in this section do not always reflect state-of-the-art techniques, they have been picked to express the required (re)thinking when creating multi-frame rendering techniques. They are intended as blueprints for the transformation of other sampling-based techniques.

3.3.1   Multi-frame Antialiasing

Without taking specific countermeasures, image synthesis based on rasterization depicts a continuous domain and, thus, usually contains aliasing artifacts like jagged edges and moiré patterns. Antialiasing is commonly applied to mitigate these artifacts, e.g., super-sampling and multi-sampling: Color or depth buffers are rendered at a higher resolution than the output resolution. While these buffers provide good results for single-frame-constrained applications, they use a lot of processing power and memory. Alternatively, several sampling strategies for post-processing have been created, e.g., AMD's MLAA, NVIDIA's FXAA, and Intel's CMAA. Varying in their performance and quality, these all provide a comparably low memory footprint. With temporal antialiasing, another type of antialiasing was introduced recently: NVIDIA's TXAA and subsequently MFAA [NVIDIA 15] claim to result in better quality and increased performance in comparison to MSAA. Temporal antialiasing already uses varying sampling patterns and information from multiple consecutive frames, albeit limited (two subsequent frames) as they are still designed for single-frame rendering.

Approach   For our implementation, a sampling offset in $[-0.5, +0.5]$ is semi-randomly chosen per frame. The offset is then transformed into a subpixel off-set and added to the vertices' xy-coordinates in normalized device coordinates

```
1  in vec3 a_vertex;
2  uniform mat4 mvp; // Model view projection
3  // Per-frame offset in [-0.5,+0.5], pre-multiplied by
4  // 1.0 / viewport size.
5  uniform vec2 ndcOffset;
6    ...
7      vec4 ndcVertex = mvp * vec4(a_vertex, 1.0);

9      // Shift the view frustum within the subpixel extent.
10     ndcVertex.xy += ndcOffset * ndcVertex.w;
11     gl_Position = ndcVertex;
```

Listing 3.2. A GLSL vertex shader for progressive multi-frame antialiasing.

(NDC), effectively shifting the complete NDC space (Listing 3.2). Note that shifting the camera's position and center in world space does not work due to the parallax effect.

Sampling characteristics Pseudo-randomly chosen offsets within a square work surprisingly well. The convergence can be speed up by using uniform, shuffled samples or common sampling patterns [Akenine-Möller et al. 08]. For our implementation we use shuffled Poisson-disk sampling to generate a uniform distribution of offsets for a specific number of frames (Listing 3.3). This prevents clustering of "pure" random sampling and provides better convergence than regular patterns for a large number of samples (e.g., eight or more), which are nontrivial to calculate for an arbitrary number of samples. Due to the random distance between consecutive offsets, the image tends to shift noticeably by up to one pixel during the first few frames. This can be almost eliminated by constraining the first sample to the center of the pixel (offset $[0.0, 0.0]$). Sorting all offsets by their length (i.e., the distance to the pixel center) is not recommended: Although it reduces the subtle shifting further, it also results in temporal clustering. Finally, to avoid clustering at pixel edges and corners of adjacent pixels, we use a tile-based Poisson-disk sampling (Figure 3.3).

Performance and remarks Accumulation of only a few frames usually results in decent antialiasing. With Poisson-disk sampling, it takes about 16 frames for a result that appears optimal and about 64 frames until subsequent frames yield no visual improvements anymore. In comparison, pseudo-random sampling takes about 1.3 times longer to yield comparable quality and, additionally, is less predictable due to clustering. As an addition, blurring can be applied by increasing the offsets and using an appropriate distribution.

```
1  // 3D array of glm::vec2 values with extent: 64x1x1 (glkernel)
2  auto aaSamples = glkernel::kernel2{ 64 };
3  glkernel::sample::poisson_square(aaSamples, -.5f, .5f);
4  glkernel::shuffle::random(aaSamples, 1); // From index 1 to last

6  while(rendering)
7  {
8      ...
9      const auto ndcOffset = aaSamples[accumCount] / viewport;
10     program.setUniform("ndcOffset", ndcOffset);
11     ...
12 }
```

Listing 3.3. C++ example for an AA sample computation using `glkernel`.

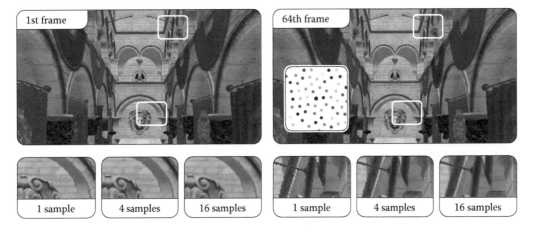

Figure 3.3. Sponza scene rendered with multi-frame AA (shuffled Poisson). The dots depict a 64-sample kernel, encoding its sequence from dark to light gray, starting at the center (big circle).

3.3.2 Multi-frame Depth of Field

Depth of field is an effect that can be used to guide a users attention to a certain region within a scene. The effect blurs objects depending on their distance to a chosen focal plane or point, which usually lies on an object or region of interest. DoF is often implemented at postprocessing, mixing the sharp focus field with one or two (near and far field) blurry color buffers per fragment, based on the fragment's distance to the focal point or plane [Bukowski et al. 13]. More advanced techniques are also available, usually reducing boundary discontinuities and intensity leakage artifacts as well as accounting for partial occlusion by using

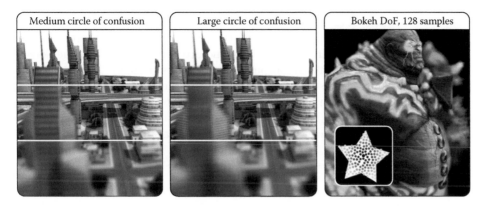

Figure 3.4. Multi-frame DoF with (top to bottom) 4, 16, and 64 samples for medium and large CoC. The sequence of 128 samples is depicted from dark to light gray.

multiple focus layers [Schedl and Michael 13, Selgrad et al. 15]. Even though multi-layer approaches can be adapted to multi-frame rendering, we present a minimal approach favoring rendering speed over convergence time and enabling high-quality DoF.

Approach For DoF we use a random two-dimensional vector on a unit disc as per-frame sample. This vector indicates for each point in a scene, where on its circle of confusion (CoC) it should be rendered on the image plane. With subsequent sampling, each point gradually covers its circle of confusion. Similar to our AA approach, the sample vector is added to the vertices' xy-coordinates in a vertex shader, this time, however, in view space before applying the projection matrix. It is scaled with the vertices' z-distance to the chosen focal plane. Additional postprocessing passes per frame, e.g., separated blurring, are not required. (See Figure 3.4.)

```
1  // z−distance to the camera at which objects are sharp
2  uniform float focalDist;
3  // Point in circle of confusion (opt. pre−multiplied by scale)
4  uniform vec2 cocPoint;
5  ...
6  {
7      ...
8      vec4 viewVertex = modelView * vec4(a_vertex, 1.0);
9      viewVertex.xy += cocPoint * (viewVertex.z + focalDist);
10     gl_Position = projection * viewVertex;
11 }
```

Sampling characteristics Similar to multi-frame antialiasing, random sampling works but results in comparatively long convergence times. Furthermore, fragments of points distant from the focal plane are spread widely on the screen, causing substantially unsteady output in the first few frames. To prevent this, Poisson-disk samples are sorted by the distance to the center. The center is used as the initial sample again, omitting shifting for consecutive update requests. By that, the effect gradually increases until all samples have been processed. Arbitrary Bokeh shapes can be easily accounted for by masking the samples with the desired shape:

```
1  auto dofSamples = glkernel::kernel2{ 128 };
2  glkernel::sample::poisson_square(dofSamples, -1.f, 1.f);
3  // Opt. mask every sample by its position using a bitfield
4  glkernel::mask::by_value(dofSamples, bitmask);
5  // Sort by dist to ref
6  glkernel::sort::distance(dofSamples, 0.f, 0.f);
```

Performance and remarks The number of required samples to produce an "artifact-free" image depends on the largest CoC any point in the scene has, which in turn is proportional to the desired effect scale as well as the point's distance to the focal plane. Although it may seem counterintuitive, scaling the number of required samples linearly with the CoC's radius, at least for reasonably large CoCs, results in sufficient image quality. We found a sample count (and thus, frame count) about ten times the radius in pixels to be sufficient. While this can mean a few seconds to full convergence in extreme cases, keep in mind that the effect's strength gradually increases over time.

For implementing a focal point instead of a focal area, one can scale the sample by the vertices' distance to that point. If a strong blurriness for out-of-focus objects in combination with a large focal area is desired, the vertex shader could be extended accordingly.

3.3.3 Multi-frame Soft Shadows

Shadow mapping is an omnipresent technique in real-time computer graphics. The original approach renders distances as seen from a light. Advanced variations improve on problems like heavy aliasing and hard edges at the cost of additional texture lookups per fragment, more computations, or additional passes. While soft shadows cast by occluders of large distance to the receiver can be handled well, correctly and efficiently modeling shadow casting of area lights is still a problem for single-frame techniques.

Approach For our approach, we use the most-basic shadow mapping and take only a small number of lights into account per frame. For multi-frame shadow mapping, the lights' surfaces are randomly sampled: For each frame, a random position on each of the selected lights is used for shadow map rendering as well as scene lighting and shading. Accumulating multiple frames results in realistic and aliasing-free soft shadows with large penumbras.

Sampling characteristics Good convergence is achieved by uniformly sampling the surfaces of all lights. For very large area or volumetric lights, we used an approach similar to the previously described multi-frame DoF, starting with sampling the light in its center and slowly progressing toward its edges, gradually increasing the penumbras. If multiple light sources of various areas/volumes are used, each light should be accounted for at least once per frame. Lights of larger surfaces should be sampled preferentially.

Performance and remarks The convergence time depends on the maximum penumbra width, which in turn depends on the size of the area lights and their relation to occluding and receiving scene objects. Similar to DoF, we experienced that the number of samples required for a completely banding-free result correlates to the largest penumbra width in the screen space. Convergence can be greatly improved, e.g., by applying variance shadow mapping [Donnelly and Lauritzen 06] combined with perspective shadow maps [Stamminger and Drettakis 02]. We also found that surprisingly low shadow map resolutions can provide visually pleasing shadows: A resolution of 128×128 pixels, for example, does not result in any distracting artifacts, although smaller objects and scene details were not captured and contact shadows were inadequate (Figure 3.5).

Since our approach relies on sampling light surfaces, all lights should show at least a certain surface (larger for lower shadow map resolutions). Even for hard cases (imagine a large TV illuminating a room with nearby occluders), the presented approach is able to provide correct shadows of high quality, albeit with increased convergence times. For a correct illumination induced by large numbers of local lights, our basic frame accumulation of non-HDR lights currently conflicts with partial light sampling.

3.3.4 Multi-frame Screen-Space Ambient Occlusion

The complex interactions of real-world objects and lights pose a significant challenge even for today's most sophisticated real-time rendering engines. SSAO is typically used to capture local effects of real-world lighting. Since Crytek's initial concept, numerous variants and enhancements have been proposed (e.g., HBAO+, SSDO). Due to the performance-intensive nature of these effects, they use different optimizations at the cost of quality: e.g., blurring the occlusion map to mask the noise (and its resulting shower-door artifacts) is usually suggested. Multi-frame approaches can also be found: For example, using reverse reprojection provides higher temporal coherence but introduces additional complexity and resource requirements (history buffers) and utilizes only the previous frame.

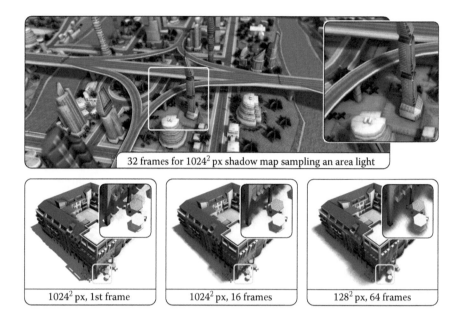

Figure 3.5. Soft shadows using area light sampling and basic shadow mapping.

Approach We use the original SSAO as the basis for our multi-frame approach. In order to mitigate banding artifacts produced by using the same sampling kernel for all pixels, the original implementation randomly rotates the kernel per pixel. This in turn introduces noise to the image, which is masked by blurring. When using multi-frame sampling, the noise is mitigated within a few frames even without blurring. In fact, removing the blur pass results in a better final image quality. The random rotation can also be removed, although the banding artifacts are more noticeable and result in a more unsteady image during the first few frames.

Sampling characteristics We use Poisson-disk sampling with best-candidate optimization to uniformly distribute points in a unit sphere that are used as sampling offsets. Compared to a single-frame approach, a lower sample count per frame can be used to accommodate for low-end devices. If desired, all samples can be assigned a random length within the unit sphere and can be sorted by this to account for local ambient occlusion effects for early frames. As for DoF, this reduces noise and banding artifacts resulting in a less disruptive effect.

Performance and remarks For this effect the number of frames required for a converging image is again dependent on its desired parameters, more specifically its radius. For moderate settings we found that about 480 samples provided a nearly artifact-free result, i.e., 60 frames when using 8 samples per frame. For small radii, removing the random rotation actually improves convergence times, reducing the adequate number of samples by two thirds. Since the more recent screen-space ambient occlusion and obscurance approaches rely on sampling the depth buffer multiple times per frame as well, they should be similarly easy to adapt to multi-frame sampling.

3.3.5 Multi-frame Transparency

Rendering transparent objects is often avoided in real-time rendering systems. Most approaches either achieve high performance by neglecting correctness and thus quality, or produce credible results by using many rendering passes or super-sampling while lowering rendering performance. Additionally, they are hard to integrate into deferred rendering systems (except that k-buffer rendering is available).

Screen-door transparency [Mulder et al. 98] applies a threshold pattern to small groups of fragments; within each group, fragments with an opacity value lower than their threshold are discarded. Drawbacks comprise highly visible patterns and insufficient accuracy. Stochastic transparency [Enderton et al. 10] improves on that by applying random patterns per pixel using multi-sampling, but still produces slightly noisy output for a single frame. The suggested multiple passes per frame can be transformed to a 1:1 frame mapping for multi-frame rendering of fast converging transparency.

Approach We discard super-sampling (color and coverage sampling) due to the heavy resource implications. Instead, transparent fragments are discarded based on a single random opacity threshold per fragment or object at a time. (See Figure 3.6.) Thus, using per-fragment thresholding with back-face culling disabled, we achieve correct order-independent transparency.

Sampling characteristics The technique's implementation is straightforward, but special care must be taken to generate "good" per-fragment randomness. Based on stochastic transparency, a mapping of n distinct opacity values in the range $[0, 1]$ to associated bitmasks is precomputed on the CPU and provided to the GPU (Figure 3.7). For example, for an opacity of 0.8 and bitmask size of 1024, a bitmask of about $0.8 \cdot 1024 = 819$ uniformly distributed (avoiding clusters) bits is computed. Additionally, random, fragment-specific offsets can be used to shuffle the threshold access between adjacent fragments over time. For object-based transparency, no objects should be discarded within the first frame. Thus, all objects are initially opaque and gradually converge toward their individual opacity (limiting minimal opacity to $1/n$ for n frames). For all consecutive frames, the object-based bit masking skips the draw call or discards fragments based on an object ID (Figure 3.7).

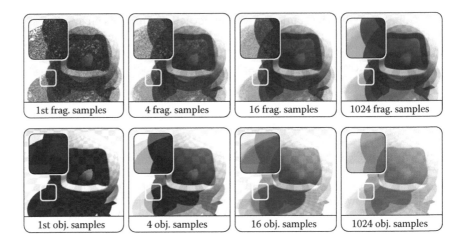

Figure 3.6. Convergence for per-fragment (top row) and per-object (bottom row) transparency thresholding. For per-fragment thresholding, back-face culling is on. Note the two distinct shadows resulting from the inner and out sphere.

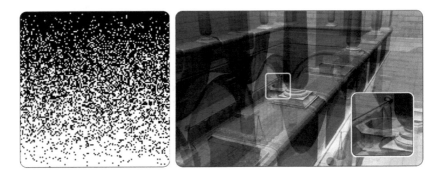

Figure 3.7. Kernel used for transparency masking. Left: For 128 opacity values from 0 (top) to 1 (bottom), 128 uniformly distributed bits (left to right) are computed. Right: This kernel can be used for per-fragment as well as per-object discarding, the latter shown here, but with 1024 instead of 128 bits per mask.

Performance and remarks Stochastic transparency usually requires full multi-sampling within a single pass with up to 16 coverage samples per fragment, requiring extreme amounts of memory. In contrast, multi-frame transparency requires no additional memory at all. The amount of frames required for a low-noise transparency is dependent on the depth complexity of the current scene and camera angle. While direct use of more advanced techniques like stochastic transparency might lead to shorter convergence times, we prefer the more basic

 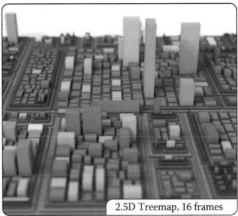

Sponza, 16 frames   2.5D Treemap, 16 frames

Figure 3.8. Multi-frame sampling applying the presented techniques all together.

approach for its low memory footprint, minimal performance overhead per frame, and implementation simplicity.

A major drawback for pixel-based transparency is that it can hardly be combined with some postprocessing techniques, e.g., SSAO, as the G-buffers of individual frames are highly noisy and do not show coherent surfaces. In contrast, though still not completely accurate, object-based transparency shows SSAO results on transparent objects and even on objects overlaid by them; this is usually difficult to achieve in conventional real-time rendering. Using object-based transparency, however, (1) opacity cannot be determined via texturing anymore, and (2) back-faces as well as concave objects cannot be rendered adequately (at least, not without additional draw calls) and might result in inaccuracies.

3.4 Conclusion and Future Work

We have presented an approach to transform and integrate sampling-based rendering techniques into a progressive multi-frame rendering system (Figure 3.8). It allows us to focus on sampling and its characteristics instead of optimizations necessary for satisfying single-frame limitations. It favors low response times and low-level APIs over per-frame quality. Furthermore, at least for the discussed techniques, a better maintainability and simpler, easy-to-understand parameterization in terms of target quality and effect characteristics is derived. From a software-engineering perspective, our approach reduces the implementation complexity of 3D systems and applications that need to combine independent, real-time rendering techniques.

The current limitations and future challenges include the following topics: When using multiple multi-frame techniques simultaneously, sampling parameterization of all effects is to be coordinated for the targeted number of frames. In addition, some techniques might not be used in combination (e.g., pixel-based transparency with SSAO), and interaction issues arise for, e.g., picking or coordinate retrieval because depth and ID buffers cannot be accumulated in a meaningful way.

For future work, automatically adapting kernel parameterization to hardware and frame rendering times is desirable. Additional research comprises strategies for optimal convergence, a generic multi-frame rendering template for sampling-based rendering techniques, and finally, the evaluation of other techniques' applicability (e.g., image-based reflections, translucency, massive lighting, subsurface scattering).

3.5 Acknowledgment

This work was funded by the Federal Ministry of Education and Research (BMBF), Germany, within the InnoProfile Transfer research group "4DnDVis" (www.4dndvis.de).

Bibliography

[Akenine-Möller et al. 08] Tomas Akenine-Möller, Eric Heines, and Naty Hoffman. *Real-Time Rendering*, Third edition. Natick, MA: A K Peters, Ltd., 2008.

[Bukowski et al. 13] Mike Bukowski, Padraic Hennessy, Brian Osman, and Morgan McGuire. "The Skylanders SWAP Force Depth-of-Field Shader." In *GPU Pro 4*, edited by Wolfgang Engel, pp. 175–184. Boca Raton, FL: A K Peters/CRC Press, 2013.

[Donnelly and Lauritzen 06] William Donnelly and Andrew Lauritzen. "Variance Shadow Maps." In *Proceedings of the 2006 Symposium on Interactive 3D Graphics and Games, I3D '06*, pp. 161–165. New York: ACM, 2006.

[Enderton et al. 10] Eric Enderton, Erik Sintorn, Peter Shirley, and David Luebke. "Stochastic Transparency." In *Proc. of the 2010 ACM SIGGRAPH Symposium on Interactive 3D Graphics and Games, I3D '10*, pp. 157–164. ACM, 2010.

[Limberger 15] Daniel Limberger. "Kernel Utilities for OpenGL (glkernel)." https://github.com/cginternals/glkernel, 2015.

[Mulder et al. 98] Jurriaan D. Mulder, Frans C. A. Groen, and Jarke J. van Wijk. "Pixel Masks for Screen-Door Transparency." In *Proceedings of the Conference on Visualization '98, VIS '98*, pp. 351–358. Los Alamitos, CA: IEEE Computer Society Press, 1998.

[NVIDIA 15] NVIDIA. "Multi-frame Sampled Anti-aliasing (MFAA)." http://www.geforce.com/hardware/technology/mfaa/technology, 2015.

[Riccio 15] Christophe Riccio. "OpenGL Mathematics (GLM)." http://glm.g-truc.net/, 2015.

[Schedl and Michael 13] David Schedl and Wimmer Michael. "Simulating Partial Occlusion in Post-Processing Depth-of-Field Methods." In *GPU Pro 4*, edited by Wolfgang Engel, pp. 187–200. Boca Raton, FL: A K Peters/CRC Press, 2013.

[Selgrad et al. 15] Kai Selgrad, Christian Reintges, Dominik Penk, Pascal Wagner, and Marc Stamminger. "Real-time Depth of Field Using Multi-layer Filtering." In *Proceedings of the 19th Symposium on Interactive 3D Graphics and Games, i3D '15*, pp. 121–127. New York: ACM, 2015.

[Stamminger and Drettakis 02] Marc Stamminger and George Drettakis. "Perspective Shadow Maps." In *Proceedings of the 29th Annual Conference on Computer Graphics and Interactive Techniques, SIGGRAPH '02*, pp. 557–562. New York: ACM, 2002.

IV

Mobile Devices

The latest mobile GPUs have feature parity with most of the desktop GPUs, but occupy only fractional parts of the silicon area. Implementing advanced graphics on mobile devices often requires rethinking existing graphics methodology. This section will talk about a new mobile-friendly soft shadows technique as well as about how physically based deferred rendering can be implemented on mobile.

In "Efficient Soft Shadows Based on Static Local Cubemap," Sylwester Bala and Roberto Lopez Mendes introduce a novel soft shadow technique that makes use of local cubemaps. The technique allows for very nice looking smooth shadows at minimal performance cost.

In "Physically Based Deferred Shading on Mobile," Ashely Vaughan Smith and Mathieu Einig describe how to implement physically based deferred shading on a power-constrained mobile device using extensions such as pixel local storage and framebuffer fetch. The chapter also explains how these extensions can be used to implement deferred decal rendering very easily on mobile GPUs.

Lastly, I would like to thank all the contributors in this section for their great work and excellent chapters.

—Marius Bjørge

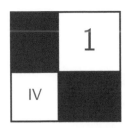

Efficient Soft Shadows
Based on Static Local Cubemap
Sylwester Bala and Roberto Lopez Mendez

1.1 Overview

Contemporary mobile GPUs are very powerful and rich in features that make game and application content shine while preserving high performance. As developers want to make use of the latest features, we cannot forget about two very important factors. First, for a game to be successful, it must target as many people as possible around the world. This can be achieved only when using a lower set of features of the GPU because not everyone has a high-specification mobile device. Second, how can you make the player engage with your game for as long as possible? On mobile devices in particular it becomes a challenge because energy source is coming from a battery. Even though ARM's technology is designed for low energy consumption, developers cannot forget that a battery has finite energy capacity. In this chapter we address this problem and help developers to deliver even better quality, higher performance, and longer battery life when playing games. As the subject is very wide and could be addressed to many areas of real-time graphics software development, we want to narrow the scope to one visual effect: soft shadows. We introduce a novel technique of rendering semi-dynamic soft shadows. Although the technique is robust, it cannot be applied for all use cases, and we also explain in which cases you may make the most of this technique.

1.2 Introduction

In this chapter you will learn about a novel soft shadows technique based on local cubemaps. (See the example in Figure 1.1.) We believe that with this you will be able to develop high-quality semi-dynamic shadows of your local environment and at the same time preserve high performance and allow for longer battery life.

Figure 1.1. Our soft shadows technique has been implemented in the Ice Cave project.

What makes this really interesting is that it can save a lot of bandwidth because it uses a static cubemap texture. The cubemap texture size can be lower than the screen resolution and the quality still will be really good. On top of that, the texture can be compressed, for instance by using ASTC, and can use even less bandwidth. In the next section you will find out more about the technique.

1.3   Algorithm Overview

The overall algorithm is very simple and consists of two steps. The first step is to create a static local cubemap texture, and it is recommended to do this offline as then you can compress the texture and achieve even better performance. The second step is to apply shadows in a scene. In this step most of the work is done in the fragment shader. Having information about light(s) and the bounding volume, you can calculate a vector to the light; then, having this vector, you can calculate the intersection with the bounding volume. Once the intersection point is known, you need to build a vector from the cubemap's position to the

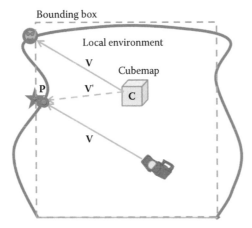

Figure 1.2. Using a proxy geometry to apply the local correction.

intersection point and use this vector to fetch the texel from the cubemap texture. The alpha channel of the texel determines how much shadow needs to be applied to the current fragment.

The two steps are explained in detail later in the chapter.

1.4 What Is a Local Cubemap?

Before we dive further into the explanation of this technique, it would be good to understand what we mean by "local cubemap." A local cubemap is more than the cubemap texture type, which is supported by most GPUs today. You can hardly find a device with a GPU that does not support the cubemap texture type. The cubemap texture has been supported since early versions of OpenGL, even before shaders were introduced. The local cubemap technique has been known in the industry for while [Bjork 04, Czuba 10, Lagarde and Zanuttini 12, Lopez 14].

If we render a cubemap in a local environment and intend to use it in the conventional way, it will not produce the desired results. In Figure 1.2 the camera is looking in the direction of $\mathbf{V}$ to the star. If we use this vector to retrieve the texture from the cubemap, what we really get will be a texel with the smiley face instead of the star.

In order to obtain the star instead of the smiley face, we need to use a new vector $\mathbf{V'} = \mathbf{CP}$ from the cubemap to the intersection point $\mathbf{P}$ of the view vector $\mathbf{V}$ with the boundary. As the boundary can be arbitrary, we simplify the problem of finding the intersection point by using a proxy geometry. The simplest proxy geometry is the bounding box.

The bounding volume describes the boundaries of the local environment where the cubemap is valid and in which the shadows from the cubemap should be applied. In other words, the bounding volume is a geometric approximation of your local environment that must be created in such a way that the cube faces of the volume are as close to the geometry as possible. For instance, in a four-walled room with floor and ceiling, it is fairly easy to create a bounding volume (local environment) because the bounding box describes perfectly the geometry. If you take another example with uneven walls, unlike the room, such as a cave, then an artist needs to compromise the undulated walls and create an approximated cube bounding volume for this geometry.

We come this way to the concept of the local cubemap. The *local cubemap* consists of

- a cubemap texture;

- two extra data, which are position and bounding volume (bounding box);

- the local correction procedure.

Fetching texels from the local cubemap is done with the same shader function that is used for fetching texels from the cubemap textures. The only difference is that the vector used to point out which texel should be fetched needs to be local corrected according to the cubemap's generation position and the bounding volume.

1.5   Creating a Shadow Cubemap

It has already been mentioned that a local cubemap contains a cubemap texture, a world position, and a bounding volume in the world space of the local environment. Now, you need to decide from which point of your scene the cubemap texture should be rendered. Most of the time, the most suitable position is the center of the room, but it does not have to be exactly in the center.

Now you are ready to render your local environment to the cubemap texture. You need to render your scene six times, once for each face. The main idea of this technique is to store the transparency (or, in other words, occlusion) in the alpha channel of your local environment into the cubemap texture. (See Figure 1.3.) An individual texel of the cubemap determines how much light can reach the local environment from outside of the bounding volume.

Along with the alpha value you can also store color values, as you may want to make color-tinted shadows. The color-tinted shadow may give you really interesting results, for example, a stained glass window in the room casting different colors of shadows. You can also reuse the color for reflections, refractions, and other effects, but the main component will be transparency.

It is important to mention that at this stage you are not storing any information related to the lights.

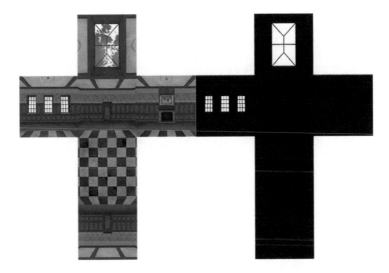

Figure 1.3. An example of a generated cubemap with alpha channel.

1.6 Applying Shadows

Once you have created the local shadow cubemap, it is time to apply shadows to your local environment. Applying shadows is fairly easy and straightforward. It requires fetching a texel from the cubemap texture using the fragment-to-light vector and applying the amount of shadow based on the texel alpha value.

The procedure to render the shadows is practically the same for point and directional light sources.

In the case of a point light source, the fragment-to-light vector can be built directly in the fragment shader or can be obtained by the interpolation of the vertex-to-light vector.

In the case of a directional light source, we just need to replace the vertex-to-light vector (or the fragment-to-light vector) with the light direction vector.

Having the to-light vector—for either type of light, directional or point—you need to apply local correction on this vector before fetching the texel from the cubemap. The vector correction can be done in the following way (see also Figure 1.4):

Input parameters:

> EnviCubeMapPos—the cubemap origin position
>
> BBoxMax—the bounding volume (bounding box) of the environment
>
> BBoxMin—the bounding volume (bounding box) of the environment
>
> V—the vertex/fragment position in world space
>
> L—the normalized vertex-to-light vector in world space

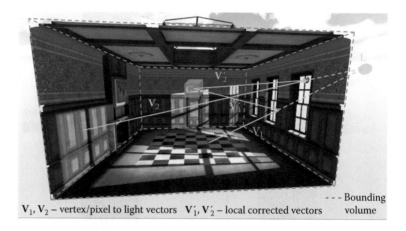

$\mathbf{V}_1, \mathbf{V}_2$ – vertex/pixel to light vectors $\mathbf{V}_1', \mathbf{V}_2'$ – local corrected vectors   - - - Bounding volume

Figure 1.4. Representation of local correction of a vector according to the cubemap position and the bounding volume.

Output value:

> Lp—the corrected vertex-to-light vector which needs to be used to fetch a texel from the shadow cubemap.

There may be many other methods of correcting the vector. The one that we used is listed in Listing 1.1.

```
// Working in the world coordinate system
vec3 intersectMaxPointPlanes = (BBoxMax − V) / L;
vec3 intersectMinPointPlanes = (BBoxMin − V) / L;

// Find only intersections in the forward direction of the ray.
vec3 largestRayParams = max(intersectMaxPointPlanes,
                            intersectMinPointPlanes);

// The smallest value of the ray parameters is the distance
// to the intersection point.
float dist = min(min(largestRayParams.x, largestRayParams.y),
                 largestRayParams.z);

// Find the position of the intersection point.
vec3 intersectPositionWS = V + L * dist;

// Get the local corrected vector.
Lp = intersectPositionWS − EnviCubeMapPos;
```

Listing 1.1. A vector local correction.

```
float shadow = texture(cubemap, Lp).a;
```

Listing 1.2. Fetching a texel from the shadow cubemap.

All the code in Listing 1.1 is executed in the fragment shader. Now, having the Lp corrected vector from the fragment to the light position, you can fetch the texel from the cubemap texture as shown in Listing 1.2.

The alpha channel from the texel represents how much shadow (intensity of the shadow) to apply on the currently processing fragment. At this moment, once you have completed this stage and run your application, you can set the light position in an arbitrary place and see the semi-dynamic shadows change according to the light position. (See Figure 1.5.)

You can have more than one light in the scene, but you need to implement the vector correction individually per light. However, the texel fetching should be from the same cubemap texture. For other improvements of this technique, see the next sections.

Figure 1.5. The hard shadows from the static cubemap.

```
float texLod = length(IntersectPositionWS - V);
```

Listing 1.3. The distance calculation from the fragment to the intersection point.

1.7   Smoothness

This section is the most interesting section of this chapter because once you do what is described here, you will make your shadows look amazing! In the real world you can observe nonuniform shadow penumbra. The farther away the object that is casting shadows, the more blurred the edge of the shadow becomes and the less intense it gets. There are many factors causing this phenomenon, but the main factor is the area size of the light source. This also indirectly implies light bouncing (radiosity) in the real world. This technique allows you to achieve similar, if not the same, shadows effects in your scene. On top of that, you will achieve even better performance as the softness effect requires lower mipmap levels, which requires less bandwidth.

All you need to do is make sure you enabled trilinear filtering to your cubemap texture. Then, in the rendering process you need to calculate a distance from the fragment position to the intersection point of the light vector against the bounding volume. This distance has already been calculated in the local correction process (Listing 1.1), and you can reuse it here. Use the distance to fetch a texel from the cubemap texture accordingly. The distance should be normalized to the maximum distance within your local environment and the number of mipmaps in the cubemap texture. But there is an even simpler approach. You can expose a single float parameter that is a multiplier of the distance and help to fine tune the shadows effect to the desired quality level that fits to the local environment. Listings 1.3–1.5 show step by step what you need to code in order to achieve desired results:

1. Calculate the distance from the fragment position to the intersection point (Listing 1.3).

2. Normalize the distance to the number of mipmap levels of your cubemap texture. The easiest approach we found ourselves is to expose a single float parameter that then is multiplied by the distance (Listing 1.4).

```
texLod *= distanceNormalizer;
```

Listing 1.4. Normalize the distance to the cubemap level of detail.

```
shadow = textureLod(cubemap, Lp, texLod).a;
```

Listing 1.5. Fetching a texel from the shadow cubemap with level of detail.

3. At this stage, fetch the right texel with the right mipmap level by reusing the above calculation results (Listing 1.5).

After implementing the above, you should be able to see pretty dynamic smooth shadows in your project, as in Figure 1.6.

1.8 Combining the Shadow Technique with Others

As mentioned earlier, the bounding volume needs to be approximated to the local environment. The closer the bounding volume is defined to the real geometry, the less error-prone is the technique. This technique will work for geometry that is near the boundaries of the local environment (bounding volume). For instance,

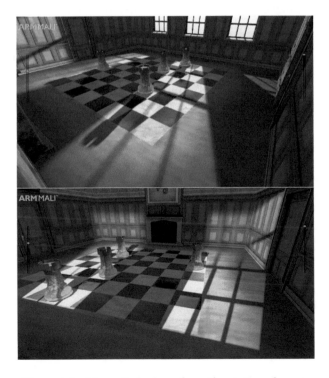

Figure 1.6. The soft shadows from the static cubemap.

Figure 1.7. The cubemap technique combined with shadowmap: with no shadowmap (left) and with the shadowmap producing shadows for the chesspieces (right).

the room in Figure 1.6 is the most suitable environment for this technique as each wall is defined on the boundaries of the volume.

Dynamic objects may also be problematic. Producing shadows of dynamic objects using this technique is not suitable because it would require updating all six faces of the cubemap texture every frame. However, dynamic objects can still receive shadows from the cubemap though they cannot cast shadows. If you require dynamic objects that cast shadows, we recommend using other techniques. The main idea behind this technique is to make the cubemap texture static, containing pre-baked intensity of all static geometries and the surroundings. Other objects within the scene such as dynamic objects need to be rendered with another technique for the instance shadowmap. Whichever technique is chosen for rendering shadows from dynamic objects, there is an easy mathematical calculation involved in merging the results into one final result, as in Figure 1.7.

1.9   Performance and Quality

Our soft shadows technique, unlike other shadow techniques, does not require writing to memory whether rendering to a depth texture, stencil, or color of the framebuffer object.

In comparison, when shadowmaps are used, very often, if not at every frame, the depth texture needs to be updated. When updating the depth texture, data must be flushed from the GPU to the memory. Then, when applying shadows, data needs to be transferred back from the main memory to the GPU as a texture. Also, updating the depth texture often requires extra CPU-side work such as culling and resubmitting occluder geometry for rendering the shadow map. Another disadvantage of using shadowmaps is that you cannot use ASTC texture compression, which is designed to reduce bandwidth traffic.

The technique requires reading memory as many times as the number of lights per frame. On top of that, when using lower mipmap levels for the softness effect, there is even less data to be transferred. Therefore, the technique won't cause

Figure 1.8. Quality comparison of shadows produced with 512×512 texture resolution: the local cubemap shadows technique (left) and a shadowmap (right).

"unstable texel" artifacts. This is due to the cubemap texture being static and the content not changing from frame to frame, which is not the case when using shadowmap. (See Figure 1.8.)

1.10   Future Work

As you may have noticed, in this chapter we focus mainly on one environment with one local cubemap texture. We have not covered how to deal with more-complex environments that would require more than one cubemap. However, while we have not done any work in this area, we are rather confident that it is very possible to blend multiple cubemap shadows in order to achieve an even more complex shadowing system in a scene.

Another important thing to note here is that we assume the light is always outside of the bounding volume in order to do the calculations in the fragment shader in the most efficient way. We have not covered in this chapter what to do when a light moves from the outside of a bounding volume to the inside. This is a subject for more research.

1.11   Conclusion

What makes the technique described here really interesting is that while it produces high-quality shadows and saves a lot of bandwidth, it does not require any extra GPU features. All it requires is at least OpenGL ES 2.0, and it can be implemented on almost any platform available on the market.

You may find some restrictions with this technique, which were mentioned above, such as that the technique might not be applicable to your current work, but certainly there are many other applications where the technique is suitable. When we first came up with this idea, we thought that it would be applicable only for specific use cases and that we might have not been able to use it for the Ice Cave project. In the end we found that the technique really worked well for the project even though the uneven walls of the cave were far from the approximated bounding volume in some places.

Bibliography

[Bjork 04] Kevin Bjork. "Image-Based Lighting." In *GPU Gems*, edited by Randima Fernando, Chapter 19. Reading, MA: Addison-Wesley, 2004.

[Czuba 10] Bartosz Czuba. "Box Projected Cubemap Environment Mapping." *Gamedev.net*, http://www.gamedev.net/topic/568829-box-projected -cubemap-environment-mapping/?&p=4637262, 2010.

[Lagarde and Zanuttini 12] Sebastien Lagarde and Antoine Zanuttini. "Local Image-Based Lighting with Parallax-Corrected Cubemap." In *ACM SIG-GRAPH 2012 Talks,* article no. 36. New York: ACM, 2012.

[Lopez 14] Roberto Mendez Lopez. "Implementing Reflections in Unity Using Local Cubemaps." http://malideveloper.arm.com/downloads/ ImplementingReflectionsinUnityUsingLocalCubemaps.pdf, 2014.

Physically Based Deferred Shading on Mobile

Ashley Vaughan Smith and Mathieu Einig

2.1 Introduction

In order for graphical applications to achieve maximum performance and therefore maximum graphical quality, they need to utilize memory bandwidth as best as possible. This is especially true on mobile devices without large, fast DDR RAM, like discrete GPUs have, and where power is limited through battery life.

This bandwidth bottleneck is even more tangible in the context of deferred shading renderers, where large G-buffers need to be stored and retrieved multiple times during the rendering process. It is possible to take advantage of the fast on-chip memory that exists on tile-based GPUs to prevent unnecessary data transfers, which improves power consumption and increases performance.

This chapter discusses how to achieve minimum main memory bandwidth utilization along with the tradeoffs and benefits to doing so, including power usage. Also discussed is how to take advantage of the savings in time spent reading and writing to main memory by implementing a physically based deferred rendering pipeline. (See the example in Figure 2.1.)

2.2 Physically Based Shading

One key aspect of rendering is trying to reproduce real-world materials in a convincing way. This is a problem that has to be solved both on the engineering side (how do I render shiny metals?) but also on the art side (what colors do I need for a gold material in this specific renderer?), usually leading to either the creation of an impractical number of material shaders that have their own sets of constraints or to simpler shaders that cannot approximate most common materials.

Figure 2.1. An efficient deferred shading renderer.

Physically based shading (PBS) is an attempt at solving the rendering equation [Kajiya 86], but with a more unified shading model than its ad-hoc predecessors [Pharr and Humphreys 04]. While there has been an increasing amount of attention on PBS in the past few years, it should be noted that it does not involve any fundamentally new concept. It should instead be seen as a set of criteria and constraints (for both the developers and artists) that, if respected, should produce an image with plausible materials in most scenarios. Some of the key concepts are as follows:

- Energy conservation: you cannot reflect more light than you receive. This means that the specular intensity is inversely proportional to its size.

- Everything has Fresnel reflections.

- Lighting calculations need to be done in linear space to achieve correct output.

It also formalizes the material parameters:

- Albedo: Formerly known as the diffuse map, with a few notable differences: lighting information should not be present, and this texture is mostly uniform. Metals do not have an albedo color.

- Reflectance: Formerly known as the specular map, expect that in PBS, this is mostly a material constant. Only metals have color information in their reflectance.

Figure 2.2. Specular workflow: albedo (left) and reflectance (right).

Figure 2.3. Metallicness workflow: albedo/reflectance texture (left) and metallicness texture (right).

- Roughness: This is the micro surface data (i.e., the bumps that are too high frequency to be stored in a normal map). It defines the "blurriness" of the specular highlights. This is where artists should focus most of the details. It should also be noted that the roughness textures' mipmap levels should be generated from the original texture and the normal map.

Figure 2.2 shows an example of albedo and reflectance textures for a material with stone and gold.

The albedo and reflectance textures are nearly mutually exclusive: Metals do not have a diffuse component, and insulators can be assumed to have the same constant specular color. This means that they can both be merged into a single texture. An extra mask, representing which areas are to be treated as specular, has to be created. But this saves memory and could be stored as the alpha channel for convenience. See Figure 2.3 for the same material represented using the metallicness workflow.

Using a metallicness workflow requires less memory; however, it also introduces visual artifacts due to texture compression and filtering. The metallicness map should normally be a nearly binary texture, but because of bilinear filtering or mipmapping, sharp transitions between metal and dielectric will become

Figure 2.4. Bright halos caused by the transition between the gold and stone materials.

smooth gradients. This causes the renderer to interpret the color texture as both an albedo and specular map, which may then lead to unnaturally shiny or matte halos, as shown in Figure 2.4.

These issues can generally be fixed by eroding or dilating the metallicness mask around the problematic areas.

2.3 An Efficient Physically Based Deferred Renderer

With the ever-increasing computing power available on mobile chips, state-of-the-art rendering techniques and paradigms such as physically based shading are becoming increasingly feasible on mobile. A deferred renderer is a common way to achieve detailed dynamic lighting [Smith 14]. In the next section we detail how to create an efficient deferred physically based renderer.

2.3.1 A Bandwidth Friendly G-Buffer Setup

Standard deferred shading renderers use multiple passes, each rendering to their own framebuffer, as shown in Figure 2.5. At the end of each render, the content of the on-chip memory is transferred to the main memory, which consumes a prohibitive amount of bandwidth for a mobile GPU.

However, given that each pass relies solely on the previous output and only requires data from the same pixel, it is possible to merge them all into a single large pass and to use the Framebuffer Fetch mechanism [Khronos 13] to bypass the intermediary data transfer. The OpenGL ES Framebuffer Fetch extension

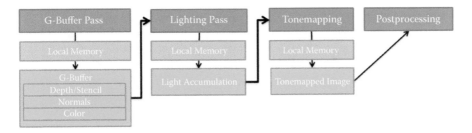

Figure 2.5. Standard deferred shading pipeline.

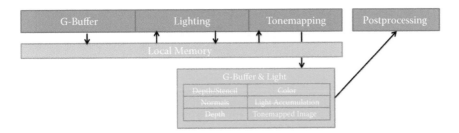

Figure 2.6. Bandwidth-friendly pipeline using Framebuffer Fetch.

allows the shader to treat what is traditionally the output as an input/output register.

Figure 2.6 shows how the pipeline can be modified to limit the amount of data transfer for the G-buffer, lighting, and tonemapping passes. These three passes are merged into one, which has several implications on the G-buffer layout: The HDR light accumulation buffer and tonemapped output are both added to the G-buffer. Furthermore, in order to access the geometry depth in the lighting stage, we pass the current depth through in local memory. Because only the tonemapped output is needed in the subsequent passes, all other attachments should be explicitly discarded to avoid unnecessary data transfer using `glInvalidateFramebuffer()`. It is also possible to reduce the G-buffer size by recycling the normal or color attachments into the tonemapped output.

This pipeline can be improved further: A whole G-buffer is allocated, even though it is never actually written to since its attachments are discarded. Its main use is only to define the data layout to be used for the render pass. The Pixel Local Storage (PLS) extension [Khronos 14] fixes this issue by letting the developer define the data layout in the shaders and write arbitrary data to the on-chip pixel memory. Figure 2.7 shows the same pipeline, improved with PLS: The G-buffer storage is no longer needed, and only one simple RGB color attachment is created for the whole deferred shading renderer.

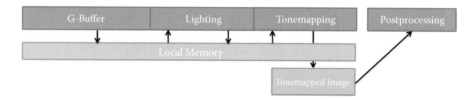

Figure 2.7. Optimal pipeline with Pixel Local Storage.

```
layout(rgb10a2) highp vec4 lightAccumulation_padding;
layout(r32f) highp float depth;
layout(rgba8) highp vec4 normals_roughness;
layout(rgba8) highp vec4 baseColour_padding;
layout(rgba8) highp vec4 specularColour_padding;
```

Listing 2.1. Specular G-buffer setup (160 bits, 142 bits actually used).

PowerVR Rogue series 6 GPUs have 128 bits of per-pixel on-chip memory. It is possible to access up to 256 bits per pixel, at the cost of performance: The spilled data will be transferred back to the main memory, unless it is small enough to fit in a cache. This means that ideally the whole G-buffer and light accumulation buffer would need to fit in 128 bits for a bandwidth-efficient renderer.

Using the specular workflow leads to the data layout in Listing 2.1. Although it is the most flexible and straightforward in terms of assets, and best in terms of quality, it requires 160 bits of storage per pixel, which makes it suboptimal for the hardware because 32 bits may be spilled to main memory per pixel.

Using the metallicness workflow allows us to pack the whole pixel data into 128 bits (see Listing 2.2), which fits nicely in the per-pixel on-chip memory without spilling.

2.3.2   Fast Gamma Approximation

The albedo and reflectance channels of the G-buffer should be stored in gamma space to prevent banding issues. This conversion to and from gamma space is

```
layout(rgb10a2) highp vec4 lightAccumulation_padding;
layout(r32f) highp float depth;
layout(rgba8) highp vec4 normals_roughness;
layout(rgba8) highp vec4 albedoOrReflectance_metallicness;
```

Listing 2.2. Metallicness G-buffer setup (128 bits, 126 bits used).

```
vec3 toGamma(vec3 linearValue) {
  return pow(linearValue, vec3(2.2));
}
vec3 toLinear(vec3 gammaValue) {
  return pow(gammaValue, vec3(1.0/2.2));
}
```

Listing 2.3. Manual gamma correction.

```
vec3 toGamma(vec3 linearValue) {
  return linearValue*linearValue;
}
vec3 toLinear(vec3 gammaValue) {
  return sqrt(gammaValue);
}
```

Listing 2.4. Pseudo-gamma correction.

usually done for free by the hardware as long as the G-buffer relevant attachments are set up as sRGB. However, because the optimized pipeline does not write to a physical G-buffer, this has to be done manually by simply raising to the power of 2.2 (see Listing 2.3).

This can be optimized by assuming a gamma of 2.0, which simplifies the gamma conversion and can be a good compromise between visual quality and speed (see Listing 2.4).

2.3.3 Lighting

We have defined how to input the material parameters to the rendering system. We now define how to input the lighting information. We use and extend physically based rendering techniques from different sources [Lagarde 12]. The types of information we need to include are static diffuse lighting, static specular lighting, and dynamic specular lighting.

An offline renderer is used to generate HDR lightmaps that are used to represent static diffuse lighting information such as shadows and radiosity. As these textures can take up a large memory footprint, they should be compressed to reduce memory usage and improve texture throughput. One such compression format is ASTC, which supports HDR data; however, not all devices currently support HDR ASTC. Non-HDR compression formats such as PVRTC can be used along with an encoding method, RGBM [Karis 09], in which a second texture is used as a scale factor to enable HDR output. The RGB channels should be compressed, but the scale factor channel should be left uncompressed to prevent serious block artifacts. See Listing 2.5 on how to decode this value. Diffuse

```
const float RGBM_SCALE = 6.0;
vec3 RGBMSqrtDecode(vec4 rgbm) {
  vec3 c = (rgbm.a * RGBM_SCALE) * rgbm.rgb;
  return c*c;
}

dualRGBM.rgb = texture(LightmapTexture, uv).rgb;
dualRGBM.a = texture(LightmapTextureScale, uv).r;
vec3 diffuseLight = RGBMDecode(dualRGBM);
diffuseLight *= surfaceColour * (1.0 - surfaceMetallicness);
```

Listing 2.5. Code for calculating the static diffuse lighting information.

lighting can be output into the light accumulation buffer in the geometry pass of the technique. Note that metallic materials do not reflect diffuse lighting.

We use image-based lighting as the input to the static specular lighting. An offline renderer is used to produce a cubemap that represents the lighting from a certain point in space. These cubemaps are converted to Prefiltered mipmaped radiance environment maps (PMREM) using the modified AMD cubemap gen tool [Lagarde 12]. A PMREM is a cubemap filtered by integrating the radiance over a range of solid angles of the hemisphere depending on the mipmap level. During the lighting stage, the surface roughness is used to select which mipmap levels of the cubemap should be sampled (see Listing 2.6). As with the lightmaps, the environment maps are stored in RGBM HDR. Listing 2.6 shows how the static specular lighting is computed, including the implementation of Shlick's approximation of Fresnel [Lagarde 12].

These static specular lights can be rendered in the same way as other dynamic lights in a deferred renderer, with a transparent mesh encompassing the light bounds.

```
// From seblagarde.wordpress.com/2011/08/17/hello-world
vec3 fresRough(vec3 specCol, vec3 E, vec3 N, float smoothness) {
  float factor = 1.0 - clamp(dot(E, N), 0.0, 1.0);
  return specCol + (max(vec3(smoothness), specCol) - specCol) *
    pow(factor, 5.0);
}
vec3 iblSpec(float roughness, vec3 specCol, vec3 N, vec3 V) {
  vec3 iblFresnel = fresRough(specCol, V, N, 1.0 - roughness);
  vec3 refDir = reflect(-V, N);
  float mipLevel = 8.0 * roughness; // 8 mips total
  vec3 envMapResult = RGBMDecode(
    textureLod(SpecularProbe, refDir, mipLevel));
  return envMapResult * iblFresnel;
}
```

Listing 2.6. Code for computing the image-based specular contribution.

For dynamic specular lighting we use the GGX equation [Walter et al. 07]. This takes into account roughness and is designed for a physically based pipeline.

2.3.4 Decals Made Easy

Decals are a popular method for adding extra details to the scene by adding layers of textured transparent geometry. However, this is often limited by the use of fixed function blending, meaning that the decal will be composited to the scene with either an addition or an interpolation.

The Framebuffer Fetch and Pixel local Storage mechanisms allow developers to do programmable blending, meaning complete freedom in how the decals will affect the G-buffer. More importantly, some G-buffer attachments are packed in ways that would prevent naive blending to work properly [Pranckevičius 10], but would be trivial with programmable blending.

It also makes environmental awareness (i.e., knowing what is behind the decal) completely free in terms of bandwidth because the G-buffer no longer needs to be flushed to VRAM before being sampled as a texture.

Finally, programmable blending makes it easy for developers to write selectively to specific outputs (e.g., a decal that only modifies the normals). Writing selectively to framebuffer attachments has always been possible, but with programmable blending, it is no longer defined in the renderer itself but in the shader. This makes it completely transparent to the application, which is convenient and slightly more efficient. With the Pixel Local Storage extension, this goes even further as there is no concept of framebuffer attachment, giving a very fine-grained control over what gets written to what.

2.4 Experiments

Tests were performed on a consumer-available device with a PowerVR series 6 GPU. An analysis of the application using the PowerVR SDK shows that the optimized renderers (Framebuffer Fetch and PLS) execute fewer rendering tasks— meaning that the G-buffer generation, lighting, and tonemapping stages are properly merged into one task. It also shows a clear reduction in memory bandwidth usage between the on-chip and the main memory: a 53% decrease in reads and a 54% decrease in writes (see Figure 2.8). All these optimizations result in a slightly lower frame time but in much lower power consumption, as shown in Figure 2.9. This means longer battery life on mobile devices.

2.5 Conclusion and Future Work

In this chapter, we presented an efficient physically based deferred shading renderer targeted at mobile devices. We have shown how the traditional deferred

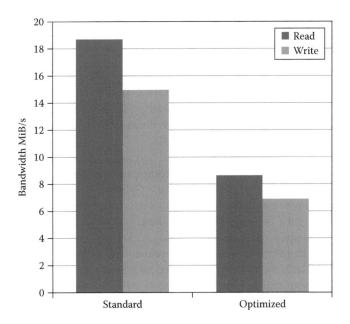

Figure 2.8. Bandwidth comparison.

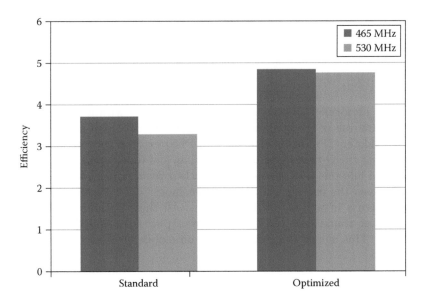

Figure 2.9. Efficiency in FPS (frames per second) per Watt of total system power.

```
layout(r32f)  highp  float  posx;
layout(r32f)  highp  float  posy;
layout(r32f)  highp  float  posz;
layout(rg16f)  highp  vec2  lightAccumRG;
layout(rg16f)  highp  vec2  lightAccumB_normalsX;
layout(rg16f)  highp  vec2  normalsYZ;
layout(rg16f)  highp  vec2  roughness_metallicness;
layout(r11f_g11f_b10f)  highp  vec3  albedoOrReflectance;
```

Listing 2.7. Future metallicness workflow PLS G-buffer setup (256 bits).

```
layout(r32f)  highp  float  posx;
layout(r32f)  highp  float  posy;
layout(r32f)  highp  float  posz;
layout(rg16f)  highp  vec2  lightAccumRG;
layout(rg16f)  highp  vec2  lightAccumB_roughness;
layout(r11f_g11f_b10f)  highp  vec3  normals;
layout(r11f_g11f_b10f)  highp  vec3  albedo;
layout(r11f_g11f_b10f)  highp  vec3  reflectance;
```

Listing 2.8. Future specular workflow PLS G-buffer setup (256 bits).

shading pipeline could be improved using OpenGL ES extensions such as Framebuffer Fetch and Pixel Local Storage to significantly reduce the amount of necessary bandwidth and therefore power and battery usage. We have proposed an efficient 128-bit G-buffer for PLS that allows state-of-the-art physically based shading, shown how to integrate high-quality static and dynamic lighting, and explained how decals could be made more complex at a lower performance cost.

In the next series of PowerVR GPUs, the available fast storage will increase from 128 to 256 bits per pixel. This gives application developers a wider variety of techniques and optimizations they can take advantage of.

Two examples of possible future G-buffer layouts using 256 bits per pixel are shown in Listings 2.7 and 2.8. Instead of storing depth, the world position is stored, which saves an expensive operation in the lighting stage. All the surface parameters are stored with higher precision, meaning they can all be stored in linear space. This saves an expensive conversion during both the geometry and lighting passes. Normals are also stored in higher precision for better quality. Finally, these G-buffer layouts are also very efficient in terms of ALU usage due to the fact that they are composed mostly of FP16 and FP32 registers, which do not require any packing and unpacking on PowerVR GPUs.

Such a large local storage could also be used for advanced effects such as Order Independent Transparency [Bjørge et al. 14], which could easily be integrated into our proposed deferred pipeline. Transparent objects would be rendered between the lighting and tonemapping stages, reusing the same PLS storage and overwriting it, keeping only the light accumulation data from the previous stage.

Bibliography

[Bjørge et al. 14] Marius Bjørge, Sam Martin, Sandeep Kakarlapudi, and Jan-Harald Fredriksen. "Efficient Rendering with Tile Local Storage." In *ACM SIGGRAPH 2014 Talks*, SIGGRAPH '14, pp. 51:1–51:1. New York: ACM, 2014.

[Kajiya 86] James T. Kajiya. "The Rendering Equation." *SIGGRAPH Comput. Graph.* 20:4 (1986), 143–150.

[Karis 09] Brian Karis. "RGBM Color Encoding." http://graphicrants.blogspot. co.uk/2009/04/rgbm-color-encoding.html, 2009.

[Khronos 13] Khronos. "Framebfufer Fetch." https://www.khronos.org/registry/ gles/extensions/EXT/EXT_shader_framebuffer_fetch.txt, 2013.

[Khronos 14] Khronos. "Pixel Local Storage." https://www.khronos.org/ registry/gles/extensions/EXT/EXT_shader_pixel_local_storage.txt, 2014.

[Lagarde 12] Sébastien Lagarde. "AMD Cubemapgen for Physically Based Rendering." https://seblagarde.wordpress.com/2012/06/10/amd-cubemapgen -for-physically-based-rendering, 2012.

[Pharr and Humphreys 04] Matt Pharr and Greg Humphreys. *Physically Based Rendering: From Theory to Implementation.* San Francisco: Morgan Kaufmann Publishers, Inc., 2004.

[Pranckevičius 10] Aras Pranckevičius. "Compact Normal Storage for Small G-Buffers." http://aras-p.info/texts/CompactNormalStorage.html, 2010.

[Smith 14] Ashley Vaughan Smith. "Deferred Rendering Techniques on Mobile Devices." In *GPU Pro 5*, edited by Wolfgang Engel, pp. 263–272. Boca Raton, FL: A K Peters/CRC Press, 2014.

[Walter et al. 07] Bruce Walter, Stephen R. Marschner, Hongsong Li, and Kenneth E. Torrance. "Microfacet Models for Refraction Through Rough Surfaces." In *Proceedings of the 18th Eurographics Conference on Rendering Techniques*, EGSR'07, pp. 195–206. Aire-la-Ville, Switzerland: Eurographics Association, 2007.

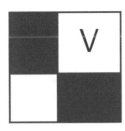

3D Engine Design

Welcome to the "3D Engine Design" section of this seventh iteration of *GPU Pro*. I always feel excited editing chapters for this section because it covers a big spectrum of challenges and concerns involved in bringing our 3D engines up to the state of the art. Without further ado, here is a short introduction to each of the four chapters you will find in this edition.

First, Homam and Wessam Bahnassi describe a new real-time particle simulation method that works by capturing simulation results from DCC tools and then replaying them in real time on the GPU at a low cost while maintaining the flexibility of adding interactive elements to those simulations. Their technique "Interactive Cinematic Particles" has been applied successfully in the game *Hyper Void*, which runs at 60 fps even on the Playstation 3 console.

Second, Krzysztof Narkowicz presents the chapter "Real-Time BC6H Compression on GPU." The chapter describes a simple real-time BC6H compression algorithm, one which can be implemented on GPU entirely with practical performance figures. Such a technique can be very useful for optimizing rendering of dynamic HDR textures such as environment cubemaps.

The third chapter by Gustavo Bastos Nunes is "A 3D Visualization Tool Used for Test Automation in the Forza Series." The tool introduced automatically analyzes a mesh for bad holes and normal data and gives the manual tester an easy semantic view of what are likely to be bugs and what is by-design data. The tool was used during the entire production cycle of *Forza Motorsport 5* and *Forza: Horizon 2* by Turn 10 Studios and Playground Games, saving several hundred hours of manual testing and increasing trust in shipping the game with collision meshes in a perfect state.

Finally, Takahiro Harada presents the chapter "Semi-static Load Balancing for Low-Latency Ray Tracing on Heterogeneous Multiple GPUs," which describes a low-latency ray tracing system for multiple GPUs with nonuniform compute powers. To realize the goal, a semi-static load balancing method is proposed that uses rendering statistics of the previous frame to compute work distribution for the next frame. The proposed method does not assume uniform sampling density on the framebuffer, thus it is applicable for a problem with an irregular sampling pattern. The method is not only applicable for a multi-GPU environment, but it can be used to distribute compute workload on GPUs and a CPU as well.

I hope you enjoy this edition's selection, and I hope you find these chapters inspiring and enlightening to your rendering and engine development work. Welcome!

—Wessam Bahnassi

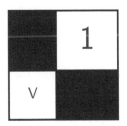

1
V

Interactive Cinematic Particles
Homam Bahnassi and Wessam Bahnassi

1.1 Introduction

In this chapter, we describe a new real-time particle simulation method that works by capturing simulation results from Digital Content Creation (DCC) tools and then replaying them in real time on the GPU at a low cost while maintaining the flexibility of adding interactive elements to those simulations.

This technique we call *Interactive Cinematic Particles* (ICP) has been applied successfully in the game *Hyper Void*, which runs at 60 FPS on the Playstation 3 console. Figure 1.1 shows one of the enemies in the game modeled using a large number of particles. The enemy moves and attacks the player interactively while retaining the cinematic animation aspects by conveying an angry liquid face designed and simulated using Autodesk Softimage's ICE environment.

1.2 Background

In a lot of games—including new AAA titles on the latest generation of gaming consoles—particles have been limited in their uses (mainly to represent fire, explosions, and smoke). While there has been quite some investment in the ren-

Figure 1.1. An enemy from *Hyper Void* modeled using a large number of particles.

dering and display techniques of these particles to make them look realistic, their simulation techniques remain rather simplistic and limited. One possible source of this limitation is due to the tools used to design those particle simulations—which in themselves shaped a mindset that confines using particles to smoke and explosion effects only. The result is that there is much unexplored potential in this freeform method of visualization.

Interestingly, one does not have to look too far to see the state-of-the-art tools for authoring particle simulations. Major DCC tools have long offered advanced simulation capabilities and a rich library of operators to drive simulations in the way the artist envisions. Admittedly, some of these operators can be quite expensive to evaluate at runtime in a game scenario, which is one reason why DCC tools are capable of introducing more interesting results. The question here is, how can we leverage the powerful simulation authoring capabilities of those DCC tools and port their results to real-time scenarios? We bring up ICP as a step toward this goal.

Please note that the focus of this chapter is on the simulation aspect rather than the rendering aspect, which is a different area of study in 3D particle effects.

1.3   Challenges and Previous Work

In the following we highlight some of the research areas that have contributed toward this highly demanded aspect of 3D game rendering.

1.3.1   Particle Simulations on the GPU

The GPU's capability to execute general computations has attracted developers for solving particle simulation on the GPU instead of the CPU [Drone 07, Thomas 14]. As a result, games are able to simulate higher particle counts with more complex operators. However, with the performance boost, the tools for authoring simulations for games are still limited.

1.3.2   Solving Fluids in Games

Solving physical and specifically fluid simulations in games has been the focus of the industry in the recent years [Stam 03, Hegeman et al. 06]. With the impressive and realistic results of these solvers, they are still not applicable on a large scale due to the high memory and performance costs. In addition to that, they are still limited when it comes to creating fantasy simulation scenes due to the limitations of authoring tools in game engines. DCC tools offer higher flexibility when combining different operators and solvers (including fluid solvers), which allows artists to apply any art style to the effects. (See the example in Figure 1.2.)

Figure 1.2. Fluid smoke simulated in real time [Macklin et al. 14].

1.3.3 Dedicated Particle Editors for Games

There are very few particles editors dedicated for games [PopcornFX 15, Fork 15]. The main advantage of these tools is providing better authoring tools than most of the out-of-the-box particle editors in game engines. Also, they provide more simulation operators, allowing artists to create more interesting effects. However, editors are still not as powerful as DCC tools and artists need to learn new tools. The particle editors also require integration in the game editor, especially for in-house engines. Performance is heavily affected by the optimization of the simulation operators provided by the middleware tool and the complexity of the effect (operator count, particle count, etc.).

With all the advancement in particle simulation, we can summarize the main challenges in three main points:

- performance,

- artist friendly workflow,

- cinematic quality operators.

1.3.4 Streaming Presimulated Data per Frame

While not particularly built for particle simulations, the work of Gneiting was used to drive geometric animations exported frame by frame in the game *Ryze* developed by Crytek [Gneiting 14]. The feature was driven by the need to achieve next-generation mesh animations. Some of the concepts in [Gneiting 14] are similar and useable in the system outlined in this chapter. However, that technique does not include any support for real-time interactivity.

1.4   Interactive Cinematic Particles (ICP) System Outline

The ICP system handles particle simulations in a similar way to how a modern game handles animations for a character. In this example, the character has a bank of animation clips authored by animators; those clips are loaded at runtime and are played back and blended together according to character actions. Furthermore, additional procedural animation operators can be executed on the final pose to add detail (e.g., head-tracking, breathing, etc.).

The ICP system works in a similar way. First, particle simulation clips are exported from a DCC tool. Those clips are loaded or streamed at game runtime and are selectively blended and processed according to interactive game logic. Runtime operators can additionally be applied to the blended simulation to add further detail. The final output is the location, rotation, size, color, etc. of each particle each frame. This information is then used to render the particle system using any rendering technique needed to achieve the final look.

There are three main aspects to ICP:

1. Data authoring workflow: This aspect covers the process of designing and exporting particle simulation clips out of the DCC tool.

2. Offline build process: The data exported from DCC tools is passed through a build process that transforms it into a representation suitable for runtime streaming and playback on the GPU. This involves a GPU-friendly compression scheme that reduces disk size for storing the simulation clips as well as reducing runtime memory requirements.

3. Runtime execution: This describes how to load and execute the particle simulation clips efficiently on the GPU. With this building block, a system is designed to take those clips and process them in the context of a larger graph that can apply further operators to support interactivity and response to real-time conditions. The implementation of some operators used in *Hyper Void* is described (e.g., blend, local shatter, and deformation to bullets).

The high-level flowchart in Figure 1.3 explains the pipeline.

1.5   Data Authoring Workflow

The goal of the data authoring workflow is to start from the concept of an interactive particle simulation and to break it down into elements that can be represented by one or more particle simulation clips. Then, each of those clips is

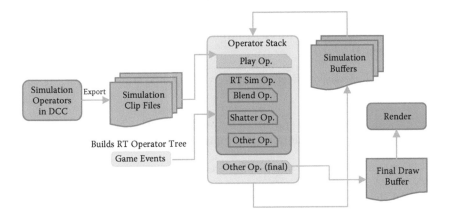

Figure 1.3. Interactive Cinematic Particles pipeline.

authored and exported using some intermediary file format that will be further processed to prepare it for runtime execution.

This section will delve into the details of each of the above mentioned steps. A case study from our game *Hyper Void* will be used as an example.

1.5.1 Authoring Interactive Particle Simulations

Adding interactivity to an offline-authored particle simulation requires considering how this simulation is to be used in the game. Here is a simple example scenario: A water flood starts by a break in a barrier, then water continues to pour in for a time determined by varying game conditions, and finally the flood stops and the water stream reduces to drips before it completely stops. In this example, three major components can be identified:

1. an intro clip (flood breaking in),

2. a looping section (water pouring),

3. an outro clip (water drying out).

When these three simulation clips are made available to the game, the game can then play the intro once, then loop on the looping section until the event to stop the flood is triggered, at which time the outro clip is played once.

Breaking down a particle simulation depends on the user story behind the effect. Since it is impossible to cover all user story possibilities, here are a few questions that can be asked to determine a good simulation breakdown:

1. Does the effect have interactivity elements to it?

2. What parts of the effect need to be done via authored simulation clips versus being achieved using runtime operators? (Real-time operators will be covered later.)

3. For an interactive effect, what are the possible states in which it can end up?

4. How do these states transition between each other? Are special transition clips needed, or would a simple runtime cross-blend work?

5. Does the effect have any looping parts?

Based on the answers to these questions, it is possible to plan and identify what parts need to be authored and how they should be authored. Later, this plan is used to put the effect together in the game engine.

With this information, artists can now use whatever DCC tool they see fit to author those simulation clips. They can use all available features in the tool in the way with which they are familiar.

1.5.2   Exporting Simulation Clips

Once simulation clips are authored, they must be exported to a file format for the game engine build process to handle.

DCC tools offer the capability to store particle simulations in *cache files*. Those caches are used to accelerate simulation playback and scrubbing through time. But, they can also be parsed by the game engine build process to extract the simulation state every frame, provided that the file format specification is well documented.

When caching particle simulations, DCC tools are capable of storing many simulation attributes per particle. This includes basic data such as ID, position, rotation, color, and velocity as well as more-specific data such as age, heat, and glow.

It is important to note that the data attributes stored will have a big impact on the cache file size. Remember that this data is multiplied per particle per simulation frame. Thus, it is of big importance to plan ahead about what attributes are needed for the runtime effect and to only store those in the files.

1.5.3   Case Study

In the case of *Hyper Void*, effects were authored using Softimage ICE. ICE is a multi-threaded visual programming language designed for creating cinematic effects. (See Figure 1.4.)

The tool was liberally used in the same manner as in full motion-picture production. Simulation clips were cached to disk using the `.icecache` file format,

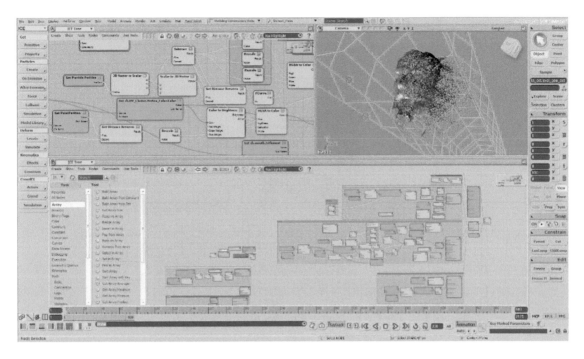

Figure 1.4. ICE visual programming language graphs.

which is the built-in format for caching particles in Softimage. There are numerous advantages to using this file format. First, it is readily available and its specifications are documented. Second, it is capable of storing any selected set of particle attributes (e.g., ID, position, color, and velocity) to save disk space as well as time spent processing those files in the game engine build process.

Another great advantage is the ability to import the simulation cached files back to Softimage and reassemble the effect the same way it is going to be assembled in the game, using the Cache Manager (shown in Figure 1.5). In Softimage, imported simulation caches are edited similar to how video clips are edited in a nonlinear video editing software. Artists can re-time, loop, and mix multiple simulations together and see the final result in the 3D viewport. (See Figure 1.6.) This allows artists to experiment with different breakdowns for the effect before building the final logic in the game.

To streamline the process of breaking down simulation states, exporting packages, and importing them in the game engine and/or DCC tool, a set of tools were implemented. These include tools for defining different states of the effect, batch-exporting simulation clips with proper settings, and importing previously exported simulation clips. (See Figure 1.7.)

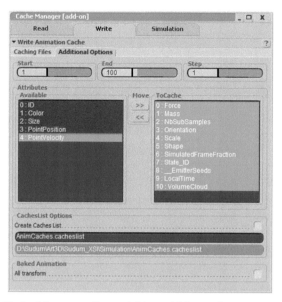

Figure 1.5. The Cache Manager allows picking which attributes to store in a file cache.

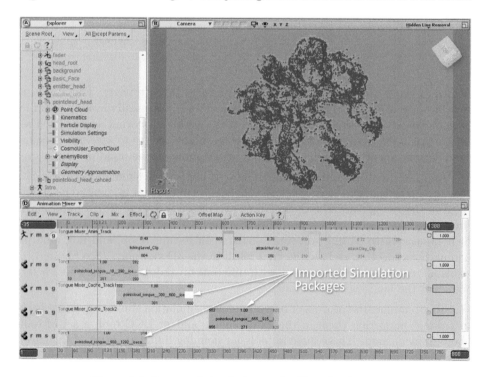

Figure 1.6. Imported simulation cache files edited as clips.

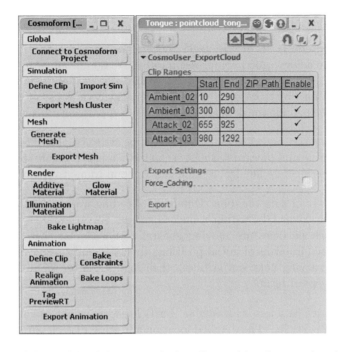

Figure 1.7. Tool for defining simulation clips and batch-exporting them.

1.6   Offline Build Process

The particle simulation clips generated from the DCC tool contain all the simulation information at full precision. This raw representation will result in large clip sizes on disk. For example, consider an exported clip of 300 frames made of 100,000 particles. Each particle contains the following:

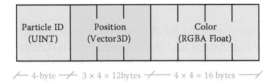

1. Particle ID: 4-byte integer.

2. Position: 3D vector of 32-bit floats.

3. Color: 4D vector of 32-bit floats.

The resulting disk size for the above clip would be roughly 915.5 MB. Even streaming such a file at runtime to play at 30 FPS would be problematic for disk access (reading ca. 90 MB per second). Therefore, it is important to compress these clips for efficient runtime access.

1.6.1   Data Compression

Data compression is an art by itself. Leveraging on the nature of compressed data is key to achieve good compression rates. We do not advocate for a specific compression scheme. Instead, it is advisable that this part of the ICP system gets reconsidered for every project's needs. The following is a list of considerations that should help guide the decision for a certain compression scheme for a project:

1. The playback mode used at runtime: If clips are to be played back from their first frame and onward without seeking, then it is possible to avoid storing any intermediate key frames and rely only on frame-to-frame differences.

2. The range of data variation: Difference encoding works best if the variation in data values falls within a limited range. For example, a particle effect in which particles are moving generally at a similar speed could be re-expressed in terms of initial position, direction, and speed. Since the speed is not varying between particles, then higher compression can be utilized on the speed term.

3. How much data loss is acceptable: Particle effects usually involve large numbers of particles. The detailed location and state of each particle might not be that noticeable as long as the overall effect maintains its general shape and properties. It is thus possible to accept a window of error for each individual particle.

4. Amount and frequency of animation detail: If the animation of the particle effect does not involve a lot of detail, then it is possible to drop frames entirely and regenerate them at runtime as the interpolation between two more-distant frames. For example, it might be acceptable to export the simulation clip at 15 FPS but play it back at 60 FPS in runtime, using smooth interpolation between frames to maintain the same timing.

5. Processing power budgeted for the ICP system: The nature of the processor executing the simulation and its capabilities can dictate how elaborate the compression scheme can be. GPUs can efficiently process disjoint data, whereas CPUs can be a better option for schemes like LZ4.

1.6.2   Case Study

Since *Hyper Void* had to run on the older Playstation 3 console, the technical capabilities of the hardware had a big impact on the choice of compression scheme for the game's particle simulation clips.

The particle effects in the game needed only two pieces of information: position and color. Other properties were constant and thus needed not be stored for every particle every frame (e.g., size, orientation, glow amount, and illumination). Thus, the files exported from the DCC tool included only the following information: ID, position, and color.

The particle ID was needed by the .icecache file representation because the particles are not always guaranteed to be listed in the same order across all frames of the simulation clip. In the build process, those IDs are only used to identify the particle throughout the .icecache. The output of the build process is an ordered list of particles for every frame. The ordering does not change across frames; therefore, storing the IDs was not necessary in the final output.

Compressing position is the interesting part. The particle effects in *Hyper Void* did not have a large variation in movement speed between particles. Moreover, simulation clips needed only to play forward without seeking. Thus, difference encoding over position was chosen. The first frame of the clip records the initial absolute 3D position of each particle as three 16-bit floating point values. Each subsequent frame is expressed as the difference against its predecessor. Then, the difference values for all particles within a single frame are normalized to $[0, 1]$, and each value is stored as a single 8-bit integer $[0, 255]$. The frame stores the numbers needed to denormalize the difference values during decompression. In conclusion, the first frame consumes 6 bytes per particle, while subsequent frames consume only 3 bytes per particle for storing position information.

The last piece of data remaining is color information. After determining that the position consumes 3 bytes per particle, it was highly desired to reserve only 1 byte for color information, leading to a total of 4 bytes per particle. To achieve this, a color palette of 256 entries was used. The color palette is generated from all colors across the entire simulation clip. It is also possible to generate a palette for each frame, but the particle effects in *Hyper Void* did not have a lot of variety across frames, hence a single color palette for the entire simulation clip was quite sufficient. Each particle searches for the palette entry closest to its color and takes the palette entry ID.

The final output format thus is as follows:

1. Color palette: made of 256 entries of 4-channels; each channel is 1-byte.

2. First frame: 8 bytes per particle (6 bytes for position, 1 byte for color, and the final byte was left unused).

3. All other frames: 4 bytes per particle (3 bytes for position and 1 byte for color), as in the following graph:

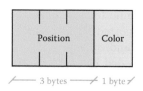

Back to the example of the 300 frames simulation clip with 100,000 particles, the new compressed size will come close to 115 MB, down from 915.5 MB of uncompressed data (streaming at ca. 11 MB per second). The size can further be cut in half should the simulation clip be processed in 15 FPS instead of 30 FPS (by dropping every other frame and interpolating it at runtime), thus resulting in streaming at ca. 5.5 MB per second. This is yet without any additional compression schemes such as LZ4. (See Table 1.1.)

1.7   Runtime Execution

In this section, the runtime aspects of the ICP system are described. With the particle simulation clips exported and compressed, the only part remaining is to stream clip data at runtime and incorporate it into the simulator that will generate the final particle simulation state at every frame ready for rendering.

1.7.1   Streaming Particle Simulation Clips

With the clip's runtime data format fully specified, the runtime must stream and decode the exported data. Again, there are a number of decisions to be made depending on the game's needs.

One major consideration is CPU access. If the particle effect must interact with other game entities that are simulated on the CPU, then the data must be made available to the CPU. However, it is advisable that such interactions are carried on the GPU instead since the processing involves possibly thousands of particles.

The case study compression scheme described in the previous section allowed streaming of the compressed particle data directly to VRAM resident textures.

Data Layout (100,000 particles)	Particle Size	Average Frame Size	Average Data Rate
ICE Cache (30 FPS)	32 bytes	3 MB	90 MB/s
Hyper Void (30 FPS)	4 bytes	0.38 MB	11.4 MB/s
Hyper Void (15 FPS interpolated to 30 FPS)	4 bytes	0.38 MB	5.7 MB/s

Table 1.1. Data size and streaming data rate comparison.

The CPU did not do any work besides driving the memory flow from the simulation clip file to VRAM. All the details of decoding and interpolating frames to update the state of the particle effect were done on the GPU using pixel shaders. The streaming code reads the first frame and instructs the GPU to use it as a key frame. Then, it reads subsequent frames as time advances, while keeping a look-ahead buffer of some size. This was possible because the clips were only meant to be played from start to finish without seeking.

1.7.2 Decoding Frames

In *Hyper Void*, the textures receiving the streamed clip data were as follows:

1. Color palette: A 1D texture of 256 texels in ARGB8 format.

2. Key frame: A 2D texture with powers-of-two dimensions aiming for a square aspect ratio where possible. The total number of texels in this texture must be equal to or greater than the total number of particles in the effect. The format is ARGB16.

3. Difference frame: Same as the key-frame texture except that the format is ARGB8.

The data streamed to all these textures was pre-swizzled in the offline build process so that the GPU could access these textures with optimal performance.

The last resource needed in the decoder is the *state render target texture*. This is a double-buffered texture that will hold the state of all particles in the effect. The goal of the decoding process is to fill this texture. Once this texture is updated, it can be used for actually rendering the particle effect on screen.

This texture is of the same dimensions as the key-frame and difference-frame textures mentioned above, but its format is RGBA32F because it will hold decompressed 3D positions.

The graph in Figure 1.8 illustrates how the data flows for a single particle simulation clip.

The high-level decoding process proceeds as follows:

1. Upon opening the clip file, read the palette texture.

2. Read the first frame texture.

3. Directly populate the double-buffered state texture with contents from the first frame texture. Only one of the buffers (the current) needs to be populated.

   By now, the first frame has been decoded and the particle effect can be rendered from the contents of the current state texture.

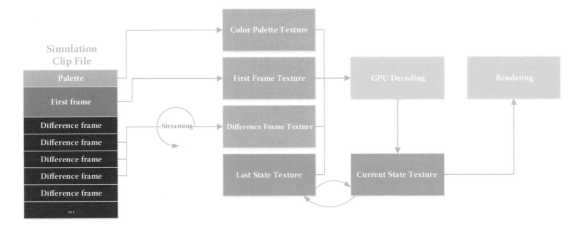

Figure 1.8. Data flow for a single particle simulation clip.

4. Time advances by a certain amount (t), and the updated clip time now falls in the frame after the current one.[1]

5. The double-buffered state texture is flipped, and what was "current" will be used as input to update the new "current."

6. A difference frame is streamed into the difference texture.

7. The GPU uses both the input state texture and the difference texture to compute the new state texture according to the following formula:

$$\texttt{newPos} = \texttt{oldPos} + \texttt{decode}(\texttt{posDifference}),$$

where `decode()` is a function that denormalizes the compressed position difference values as described in Section 1.6.2.

8. The color index is carried over from the difference texture to the state texture. Only at render time is this color index looked up from the color palette.

1.7.3 Particle Effect Graph

So far, the system is able to stream-in and playback a single particle simulation clip exported from a DCC tool in which an artist has authored the particle effect to his desire. The only remaining part of the system is to add interactivity.

---

[1]To keep the system description simple, assume no interpolation between particle simulation frames for now. Section 1.8.1 will show the additional operations needed to support smooth playback.

Interactivity means that the effect played back in runtime is capable of responding to interactions ultimately instigated by player actions.

Perhaps the most basic shape of responding to interactivity is the ability to play a certain particle simulation clip in response to a certain player action. However, a sudden switch between clips breaks continuity and is rejected aesthetically in most cases. Thus, the ability to *blend* between two different clips is required. Additionally, various particle operators could be executed at runtime to further modify the final effect in interesting and interactive ways. Those will be described in Section 1.7.4.

Taking clip playback as a basic building block, it is possible to include it under a larger framework that can hold multiple clips, play them back, blend between them, and do various effects as well according to game conditions.

In *Hyper Void*, clip playback logic was encompassed in what we call "Goal-Source," and the framework under which various clips can exist is called "Simulation." Those entities were exposed in the engine's logic builder, allowing the game designer to take full control of which clips to play, as well as when and how to blend between them. (See Figure 1.9.)

Underneath, the framework code keeps track of clip playback, as well as doing further processing after the active clips update their state. For example, the blend operator takes the final state of two different clips and simply does a linear interpolation between them to a separate render target texture that will be used for rendering.

1.7.4 Procedural Operators

Depending on the project's needs, further procedural operators could be added to the framework and exposed for triggering by game design. For *Hyper Void*, major enemy bosses were expressed using particle effects that shape up in monstrous forms and attack the player. To serve this purpose, a number of special procedural operators were added. The following list shows some of those operators:

1. Full shatter: When the enemy is destroyed, all of its particles are shattered away in random directions from a central point. To implement this, the framework takes the state texture and pushes each particle in a direction determined by a random value (originating from a noise texture). Additionally, it fades away the particle color with time.

2. Local shatter: The player can explode a bomb near the enemy boss, taking off a portion of its surface. The boss can heal again and restore the missing portion.

   The framework keeps track of explosion spheres. For each explosion sphere, all particles that fall in that sphere at a certain frame are marked to be affected by the local shatter logic, which pushes the marked particles away

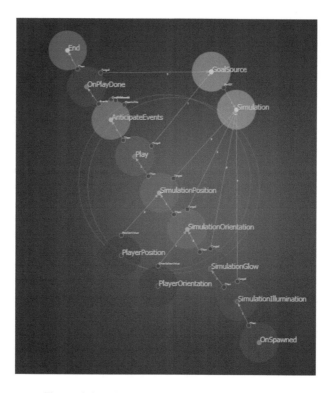

Figure 1.9. The graph tool in the game editor.

from the sphere's center. The push amount goes from 0 to the maximum then back to 0 when restoration is done.

3. Deformation to bullets: The framework sends bullet information to the GPU simulation update shader, which evaluates if a particle falls close to a bullet and pushes that particle away from the bullet until the bullet passes by a certain amount. The final effect is as if the particles forming the enemy boss are being disturbed by the player's bullets but regain formation when the bullets pass by.

1.7.5 Rendering

The final output of the entire system is a texture holding each particle's location. Other properties may come in more textures as well (such as color). It is up to the game to decide what to show using these locations and properties.

For *Hyper Void*, the textures were fed into a simple vertex shader that transformed each particle to the clip space and then handed it to the hardware for point-sprite expansion. The result was a very efficient rendering system capable of handling hundreds of thousands of particles in a few milliseconds. The game even had to draw the same particle effect more than once in a frame due to multiple passes being needed for some postprocess effects. Still, even the Playstation 3 was capable of handling the entire operation in less than 3.5 ms of GPU time.

1.8 Additional Notes

1.8.1 Variable Time Step

The decoding process in Section 1.7.2 accumulated full decoded frames, which resulted in playback at discreet time steps without possible interpolation between frames. To support variable time steps, one additional parameter is needed in the formula used to update the new position:

$$\texttt{newPos} = \texttt{oldPos} + \texttt{decode}(\texttt{posDifference}) \times \texttt{timeRatio},$$

where $\texttt{timeRatio}$ is a weight $[0, 1]$ determined from the time step and the clip's playback speed. This way, only a portion of the next frame is accumulated to the state at each system tick. The accumulated amount is proportional to how much time has passed since the last system tick. It is necessary to ensure that the decoded frame is fully accumulated before moving to the next one.

1.8.2 Preloading Clip Files

In addition to large bosses in *Hyper Void*, some smaller enemies where also modeled using ICP. However, they only had a few thousand particles and rather short clips, but multiple enemies could appear together. In that case, reading the clip data for each enemy put unnecessary stress on disk access. Thus, an additional feature was added to allow reading the entire clip file to memory first, and the rest of the ICP system would read from this in-memory file instead of reading from disk.

The implementation details of the two notes above should be easy to figure out and are left as an exercise to the reader.

1.9 Conclusion

The Interactive Cinematic Particles (ICP) system is a full pipeline that supports authoring particle effects using DCC tools, compressing them and loading them at runtime, and simulating those effects while adding interactivity to the simulation using procedural operators. The system was developed and used in the game *Hyper Void*, which shipped at a constant 60 FPS on multiple platforms including old-generation consoles.

1.10   Acknowledgment

We would like to thank Nicolas Lopez for his help and time reviewing this chapter.

Bibliography

[Drone 07] Shannon Drone. "Real-Time Particle Systems on the GPU in Dynamic Environments." In *ACM SIGGRAPH 2007 Courses*, pp. 80–96. New York: ACM, 2007.

[Fork 15] Fork Particle: Effects editor and particle system middleware, http://www.forkparticle.com/, 2015.

[Gneiting 14] Axel Gneiting. "Realtime Geometry Caches." In *ACM SIGGRAPH 2014 Talks*, article no. 49. New York: ACM, 2014.

[Hegeman et al. 06] Kyle Hegeman, Nathan A. Carr, and Gavin S. P. Miller. "Particle-Based Fluid Simulation on the GPU." In *Computational Science— ICCS 2006*, Lecture Notes in Computer Science vol. 3994, pp. 228–235. Berlin: Springer, 2006.

[Macklin et al. 14] Miles Macklin, Matthias Müller, Nuttapong Chentanez, and Tae-Yong Kim. "Unified Particle Physics for Real-Time Applications." *ACM Transactions on Graphics (TOG): Proceedings of ACM SIGGRAPH 2014* 33:4 (2014), article no. 153.

[PopcornFX 15] PopcornFX: Real-time particle FX solution, https://www.popcornfx.com/, 2015.

[Stam 03] Jos Stam. "Real-Time Fluid Dynamics for Games." Paper presented at Game Developers Conference, San Jose, CA, March 4–8, 2003.

[Thomas 14] Gareth Thomas. "Compute-Based GPU Particle Systems." Paper presented at Game Developers Conference, San Francisco, CA, March 17–21, 2014.

Real-Time BC6H Compression on GPU

Krzysztof Narkowicz

2.1 Introduction

BC6H texture compression is a lossy block compression designed for compressing high-dynamic range (HDR) images; it is also widely supported by modern GPUs. It drastically decreases memory usage and improves runtime performance, as it also decreases required GPU bandwidth.

Real-time HDR compression is needed in certain applications—e.g., when HDR data is generated at runtime or when offline compression is too slow. It is usually desirable for real-time compression to entirely bypass the CPU and run the compression algorithm on the GPU. This way, resource expensive CPU-GPU synchronization is avoided and data transfer between CPU and GPU is not required at all.

This chapter describes a simple real-time BC6H compression algorithm, one which can be implemented on GPU entirely.

2.1.1 Real-Time Environment Map Compression

A typical BC6H compression application is HDR environment maps, commonly used in physically-based lighting. Open-world games often require separate environment maps for every location, time of day, or weather condition. The resulting combinatorial explosion of possibilities makes it impractical to generate and store them offline. In those cases games have to generate environment maps dynamically. Some games use simplified scene representation to render a single global environment map every frame [Courrèges 15]. This environment map is attached to the camera and used for all reflections. Another possible option is to store G-buffer data for every environment map and dynamically relight it when lighting conditions change [McAuley 15].

Generating dynamic environment maps is not limited to open world games only. It also allows dynamic scenes to be lit—procedurally generated scenes, scenes containing geometry destruction, or ones containing dynamic object movement.

Furthermore, when using dynamic environment map generation, only the environment maps in the viewer's proximity have to be kept in memory. This allows a greater density of environment maps and better lighting quality. Environment maps are pre-convolved for a given single point—usually the center of capture. Lighting quality degrades further from that center because of the changing filter shape, occlusion, and limited resolution [Pesce 15]. The simplest way to alleviate those artifacts is to increase the number of environment maps by generating them at runtime.

2.1.2   BC6H Alternatives

Before BC6H was introduced, HDR images were usually stored in BC3 compressed textures with special encoding. These encodings could also be used to compress in real time as suitable BC3 compression algorithms exist [Waveren 06]. Such encodings either separate chrominance and luminance and store luminance in two channels (LogLuv, YCoCg) or store normalized color and some kind of multiplier (RGBE, RGBM, RGBD, RGBK) [Guertault 13]. The compression ratio is on a par with BC6H and runtime performance is usually better for LDR formats. However, those approaches will result in inferior image quality, as the mentioned methods result in various encoding and compression artifacts. Encoding only individual channels causes a hue shift, while encoding all the channels together increases luminance errors. BC3 compression was designed for LDR images, where small value changes resulting from compression are acceptable. In the case of encoded HDR data, the consequence of such small changes can be magnitude differences in the decoded results. Finally, current hardware does not support native texture filtering for these kinds of encodings, so either additional filtering artifacts will appear or manual texture filtering is required.

2.2   BC6H Details

BC6H block compression was introduced together with Direct3D 11. It is designed for compressing signed and unsigned HDR images with 16-bit half-precision float for each color channel. The alpha channel is not supported, and sampling alpha always returns 1. BC6H has an 6:1 compression ratio and stores the texture data in separate 4×4 texel blocks. Every block is compressed separately. It is convenient for native GPU decompression, as the required blocks can be located and decompressed without the need to process other data. The basic idea is the same as for BC1, BC2, or BC3. Two endpoints and 16 indices are stored per block. A line segment in RGB space is defined by endpoints, and indices define

Bits	Value
[0;4]	Header – 0x03
[5;14]	First endpoint red channel
[15;24]	First endpoint green channel
[25;34]	First endpoint blue channel
[35;44]	Second endpoint red channel
[45;54]	Second endpoint blue channel
[55;64]	Second endpoint green channel
[65;67]	First index without MSB
[68;71]	Second index
[72;75]	Third index
...	...
[124;127]	Last index

Table 2.1. Mode 11 block details [MSDN n.d.].

a location of every texel on this segment. The entire format features 14 different compression modes with different tradeoffs between endpoint, index precision, and palette size. Additionally, some modes use endpoint delta encoding and partitioning. Delta encoding stores the first endpoint more precisely, and instead of storing the second endpoint, it stores the delta between endpoints. Partitioning allows defining two line segments per block and storing four endpoints in total. Using one of 32 predefined partitions, texels are assigned to one of the two segments.

BC6H was designed to alleviate compression quality issues of BC1, BC2, and BC3: "green shift" and limited color palette per block. "Green shift" is caused by different endpoint channel precision. BC1 uses 5:6:5 precision—this is why many grayscale colors cannot be represented and are shifted toward green (e.g., 5:6:5 encodes the grayscale color RGB 15:15:15 as RGB 8:12:8). In order to prevent a hue shift, BC6H encodes every channel with the same precision. Another prominent compression issue occurs when a block contains a large color variation—a variation that cannot be well approximated by a single segment in RGB space. In order to fix this, BC6H has introduced compression modes with two independent endpoint pairs.

2.2.1 Mode 11

The proposed real-time compression algorithm uses only mode 11. This specific mode was chosen because it is simple, universal, and, in most cases, has the best quality-to-performance ratio. Mode 11 does not use partitioning or delta encoding. It uses two endpoints and 16 indices per 4×4 block (see Table 2.1). Endpoints are stored as half-precision floats, which are quantized to 10-bit integers by dropping last 6 bits and rescaling. Indices are stored as 4-bit integers indexed into a palette endpoint interpolation weight table (Table 2.2).

Index	0	1	2	3	4	5	6	7	8	9	10	11	12	13	14	15
Weight	0	4	9	13	17	21	26	30	34	38	43	47	51	55	60	64

Table 2.2. Index interpolation weight table.

Weight 0 corresponds to the first endpoint and weight 64 to the second endpoint. The values in between are calculated by interpolating quantized integers and converting the results to half-precision floats. They are interpolated as 16-bit integers instead of as floats, thus allowing efficient hardware implementation. Due to IEEE floating point specification, this method actually works reasonably well, as the integer representation of a float is a piecewise linear approximation of its base-2 logarithm [Dawson 12]. In this case, interpolation does not have to handle special cases because BC6H does not support NAN or infinities.

There is one final twist. The MSB (most significant bit) of the first index (the upper-left texel in the current block) is not stored at all. It is implicitly assumed to be zero, and the compressor has to ensure this property by swapping endpoints if the first index is too large.

2.3   Compression Algorithm

The compression algorithm consists of two steps:

1. Compute two endpoints per block.

2. Compute indices for every texel located in this block.

2.3.1   Endpoints

The classic endpoint algorithm for real-time BC1 compression computes a color-space bounding box of the block's texels and uses its minimum and maximum values as endpoints [Waveren 06]. This algorithm is very fast, as it requires only 16 minimum and 16 maximum instructions. J. M. P. van Waveren additionally decreases the size of the calculated bounding box by 1/16th. In most cases, this lowers the encoding error because most colors will be located inside the new bounding box, but it also tends to cause visible blocky artifacts when colors in a block are clustered near the edges of the bounding box. To solve this, it is better to refine the bounding box by rebuilding it without the outliers—minimum and maximum RGB values. The resulting bounding box decreases encoding error and removes mentioned artifacts (Figure 2.1).

The final step of the endpoint calculation algorithm is to convert the resulting endpoints to half-precision floats and quantize them to 10-bit integers. The presented algorithm does not form an optimal palette, but it is a good and fast approximation.

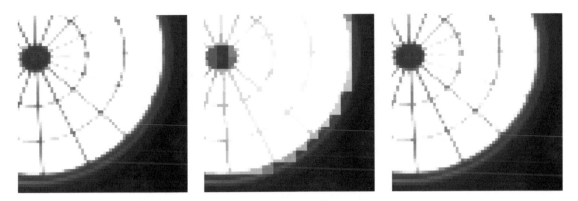

Figure 2.1. Endpoint algorithm: reference (left), compressed using bounding box inset (center), and compressed using bounding box refine (right).

2.3.2 Indices

Index computation requires picking the closest color from a palette that consists of 16 interpolated colors located on the segment between endpoints. A straightforward approach is to compute the squared distance between the texel's color and each of the palette entries and to choose the one that is closest to the texel's color. Due to a relatively large palette, this approach is not practical for real-time compression. A faster approach is to project the texel's color on a segment between the endpoints and pick the nearest palette entry. Unfortunately, endpoint interpolation weights are not evenly distributed (see Table 2.2). The first and last indices have the smallest range of best weights, and the remaining indices have similar ranges. A simple approximation is to fit the equation for smallest error—which is the same as solving the equation for the first and last bucket:

$$\text{index}_i = \text{Clamp}\left[\left(\frac{\text{texelPos}_i - \text{endpointPos}_0}{\text{endpointPos}_1 - \text{endpointPos}_0}\right) \times \frac{14}{15} + \frac{1}{30}, 0, 15\right].$$

The above equation wrongly assumes that the distance between middle indices is equal, but in practice this error is negligible. The final step is to swap endpoints if the MSB of the first index is set, as it is assumed to be zero and, thus, is not stored.

2.3.3 Implementation

The algorithm can be entirely implemented using a pixel shader, but if required, it could also be implemented using a compute shader or CPU code.

In the case of pixel shader implementation in DirectX 11, two resources are required: temporary intermediate R32G32B32A32_UInt render target and the destination BC6H texture. The first step is to bind that temporary render target and output compressed blocks from the pixel shader. The render target should be 16 times smaller than the source texture, so one texel corresponds to one BC6H block (16 source texels). The final step is to copy the results from the temporary render target to the destination BC6H texture using the `CopyResource` function.

To achieve optimal performance, the algorithm requires a native float to half conversion instructions, which are available in Shader Model 5. Additionally, it is preferable to avoid integer operations altogether (especially 32-bit divides and multiplies), as they are very costly on modern GPUs. For example, the popular Graphics Core Next (GCN) architecture does not natively support integer division, and it has to be emulated with multiple instructions [Persson 14]. The floating point number consists of a 24-bit integer (1-bit sign and 23-bit mantissa) and an 8-bit exponent. The algorithm uses only 16-bit integers, so all of the calculations can be done using floating point numbers without any loss of precision. Fetching a source 4×4 texel block can be done efficiently using 12 gather instructions instead of sampling a texture 16 times, as the alpha channel is ignored. Finally, `CopyResource` can be skipped entirely, when using low-level APIs that support resource aliasing of different formats.

The HLSL code in Listing 2.1 shows an implementation of the presented algorithm.

```
float Quantize( float x )
{
    return ( f32tof16( x ) << 10 ) / ( 0x7bff + 1.0f );
}

float3 Quantize( float3 x )
{
    return ( f32tof16( x ) << 10 ) / ( 0x7bff + 1.0f );
}

uint ComputeIndex( float texelPos, float endpoint0Pos,
                   float endpoint1Pos )
{
    float endpointDelta = endpoint1Pos - endpoint0Pos;
    float r = ( texelPos - endpoint0Pos ) / endpointDelta;
    return clamp( r * 14.933f + 0.0333f + 0.5f, 0.0f, 15.0f );
}

// Compute endpoints (min/max RGB bbox).
float3 blockMin = texels[0];
float3 blockMax = texels[0];
for ( uint i = 1; i < 16; ++i )
{
    blockMin = min( blockMin, texels[i] );
    blockMax = max( blockMax, texels[i] );
}

// Refine endpoints.
float3 refinedBlockMin = blockMax;
float3 refinedBlockMax = blockMin;
for ( uint i = 0; i < 16; ++i )
{
```

```
        refinedBlockMin = min( refinedBlockMin,
            texels[i] == blockMin ? refinedBlockMin : texels[i] );
        refinedBlockMax = max( refinedBlockMax,
            texels[i] == blockMax ? refinedBlockMax : texels[i] );
    }

    float3 deltaMax = ( blockMax - blockMin ) * ( 1.0f / 16.0f );
    blockMin += min( refinedBlockMin - blockMin, deltaMax );
    blockMax -= min( blockMax - refinedBlockMax, deltaMax );

    float3 blockDir = blockMax - blockMin;
    blockDir = blockDir / ( blockDir.x + blockDir.y + blockDir.z );

    float3 endpoint0    = Quantize( blockMin );
    float3 endpoint1    = Quantize( blockMax );
    float  endpoint0Pos = f32tof16( dot( blockMin, blockDir ) );
    float  endpoint1Pos = f32tof16( dot( blockMax, blockDir ) );

    // Check if endpoint swap is required.
    float texelPos = f32tof16( dot( texels[0], blockDir ) );
    indices[0] = ComputeIndex( texelPos, endpoint0Pos,
    endpoint1Pos );
    if ( indices[0] > 7 )
    {
        Swap( endpoint0Pos, endpoint1Pos );
        Swap( endpoint0, endpoint1 );
        indices[0] = 15 - indices[0];
    }

    // Compute indices.
    for ( uint j = 1; j < 16; ++j )
    {
        float texelPos = f32tof16( dot( texels[j], blockDir ) );
        indices[j] = ComputeIndex( texelPos, endpoint0Pos,
                                   endpoint1Pos );
    }
```

Listing 2.1. BCH6 compression algorithm.

2.4 Results

The proposed algorithm was compared with two offline BC6H compressors: Intel's BCH6 CPU-based compressor and the DirectXTex BC6H GPU-based compressor.

2.4.1 Quality

Root mean square error (RMSE) was used for measuring quality. RMSE is a generic measure of signal distortion, where lower values are better:

$$RMSE = \sqrt{\frac{1}{3n} \sum_{i=1}^{n} \left[(\hat{r}_i - r_i)^2 + (\hat{g}_i - g)^2 + (\hat{b}_i - b_i)^2 \right]}.$$

Based on the results shown in Table 2.3, the proposed algorithm has similar quality to Intel's "veryfast" preset. Intel's "veryfast" has a smaller error

	Proposed Algorithm	Intel BC6H "veryfast"	Intel BC6H "basic"	Intel BC6H "veryslow"	DirectXTex BC6H
Atrium	0.122	0.112	0.1	0.099	0.084
Backyard	0.032	0.027	0.024	0.024	0.025
Desk	0.992	1.198	0.984	0.975	0.829
Memorial	0.25	0.278	0.241	0.237	0.216
Yucca	0.086	0.083	0.065	0.064	0.063
Average	0.296	0.340	0.283	0.280	0.243
Average of relative errors	22%	22%	10%	7%	0%

Table 2.3. Quality comparison (RMSE).

for images with a low RMSE, where 10-bit mode 11 quantization becomes a limiting factor. This is due to the delta encoding that is implemented even in the "veryfast" preset. For harder-to-compress images ("desk" and "memorial"), however, the proposed algorithm has error similar to Intel's "basic" preset. (See Figure 2.2.)

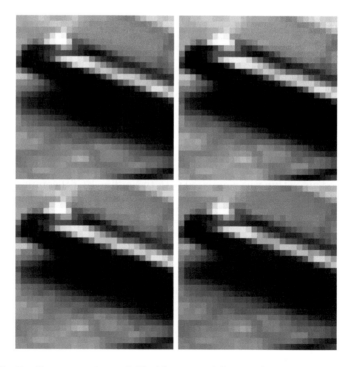

Figure 2.2. Quality comparison of "desk": original (top left), proposed algorithm (top right), Intel "veryfast" (bottom left), and Intel "basic" (bottom right).

	Image Size	Proposed Algorithm	DirectXTex BC6H
Atrium	760×1016	0.094 ms	1230 ms
Backyard	768×1024	0.095 ms	1240 ms
Desk	644×872	0.074 ms	860 ms
Memorial	512×768	0.057 ms	840 ms
Yucca	1296×972	0.143 ms	1730 ms
Average		7957.8 MP/s	0.6 MP/s

Table 2.4. Performance comparison.

2.4.2 Performance

Performance was measured using AMD PerfStudio. Results were verified by comparing timings obtained from DirectX performance queries. Tests were run on AMD Radeon R9 270 (mid-range GPU). The timings presented in Table 2.4 do not include `CopyResource` time, so the measured times should be increased by ~15% for APIs that require a redundant copy in order to modify the destination BC6H texture.

A standard $256 \times 256 \times 6$ environment map with a full mipmap chain has almost the same number of texels as the "Desk" image, which can be compressed in about 0.07 ms on the mentioned GPU. This performance level is fast enough to compress dynamically generated environment maps or other content without a noticeable impact on performance.

2.5 Possible Extensions

A straightforward way to enhance quality is to use other compression modes. There are two possibilities:

1. to add delta encoding,

2. to use partitioning.

2.5.1 Delta Encoding

The first possible approach is to add modes 12, 13, and 14. These modes extend mode 11 with delta encoding by storing the first endpoint in higher precision (respectively 11, 12, and 16 bits) and storing the delta instead of a second endpoint in the unused bits (respectively 9, 8, and 4 bits). Delta encoding implementation is not too resource expensive. Its impact on quality is also limited, as in the best case delta encoding cancels the 10-bit quantization artifacts.

The delta encoding algorithm starts by computing the endpoints using the proposed endpoint algorithm. Endpoints are encoded with various formats, and the encoding precision is compared in order to select the best mode. Next, the indices are computed with the same algorithm as for mode 11. Finally, the appropriate block is encoded in a rather non-obvious way. First, 10 bits of the first endpoint are stored just as in mode 11. Next, the bits are stored together with the delta instead of the second endpoint. Both have their bits reversed.

2.5.2   Partitioning

The second approach is to add mode 10 (supporting partitioning). Partitioning adds a second palette (endpoint pair). This greatly improves the worst-case result—when colors in a block cannot be well approximated by a single segment in RGB space. Unfortunately, it is slow due to a large search space.

The partitioning algorithm starts with the selection of the best partition. This requires calculating all possible endpoints for partitions. There are 32 possible partition sets, so it means computing 32 combinations of endpoints. The partition with the smallest sum of bounding-box volumes is selected. Indices are computed just as for mode 11. Finally, the block is encoded using the computed endpoints, indices, and selected partition index.

2.6   Conclusion

The presented algorithm allows real-time BC6H compression on GPU with quality similar to fast offline solution presets. The quality can be improved further by using other compression modes—at the cost of lower performance. The algorithm proved to be efficient enough in the terms of both quality and performance for compressing runtime generated environment maps in *Shadow Warrior 2*—a game by Flying Wild Hog. The full source code for a simple application that implements the presented algorithm and the HDR images used for the tests can be found in the book's supplemental materials or on GitHub (https://github.com/knarkowicz/GPURealTimeBC6H).

2.7   Acknowledgements

Big thanks for proofreading to Przemysław Witkowski, Bartłomiej Wronski, Michał Iwanicki, and Artur Maksara.

Bibliography

[Courrèges 15] Adrian Courrèges. "GTA V—Graphics Study." http://www.adriancourreges.com/blog/2015/11/02/gta-v-graphics-study, November 2, 2015.

[Dawson 12] Bruce Dawson. "Stupid Float Tricks." https://randomascii. wordpress.com/2012/01/23/stupid-float-tricks-2/, January 23, 2012.

[Guertault 13] Julien Guertault. "Gamma Correct and HDR Rendering in a 32 Bits Buffer." http://lousodrome.net/blog/light/2013/05/26/ gamma-correct-and-hdr-rendering-in-a-32-bits-buffer/, May 26, 2013.

[McAuley 15] Stephen McAuley. "Rendering the World of Far Cry 4." Presented at Game Developers Conference, San Francisco, CA, March 2–6, 2015.

[MSDN n.d.] MSDN. "BC6H Format." https://msdn.microsoft.com/en-us/ library/windows/desktop/hh308952, no date.

[Persson 14] Emil Persson. "Low-level Shader Optimization for Next-Gen and DX11." Presented at Game Developers Conference, San Francisco, CA, March 17–21, 2014.

[Pesce 15] Angelo Pesce. "Being More Wrong: Parallax Corrected Environment Maps." http://c0de517e.blogspot.com/2015/03/being-more-wrong -parallax-corrected.html, March 28, 2015.

[Waveren 06] J. M. P. van Waveren. "Real-Time DXT Compression." http: //mrelusive.com/publications/papers/Real-Time-Dxt-Compression.pdf, 2006.

3

V

A 3D Visualization Tool Used for Test Automation in the Forza Series

Gustavo Bastos Nunes

3.1 Introduction

Physics engines usually rely on a collision mesh that is hand-crafted by artists. This meshes may have holes, bad normals, or other wrong data that might cause weird behavior at runtime. Testing those wrong behaviors manually has an extremely high cost in regards to manual testing. One small hole or bad normal can cause a character or vehicle to behave in a completely wrong manner, and those bugs are seldom reproduced because it might depend on many variables such as engine time step, character speed, and angle.

Finding issues like open edges in a mesh is not a complex problem in the polygon mesh processing area, and this feature is available in some 3D content creation packages. However, topology-wise for non-closed meshes, there is no difference from a boundary of a mesh and a hole. Therefore, visualizing what is by design and what is a bug requires filtering and semantic analysis of such a given mesh, which is simply impractical at those tools, particularly for multiscale collision meshes. Thus, this yields a myriad of hard-to-find bugs.

This chapter will introduce a 3D visualization tool that automatically analyzes a mesh for bad holes and normal data and gives the manual tester an easy semantic view of what are likely to be bugs and what is by-design data. It will also go through a quick review of the algorithmic implementation of topics in polygon mesh processing such as mesh traversal, half-edge acceleration data structures, detection of holes, open edges, and other issues. This tool was used during the entire production cycle of *Forza Motorsport 5* and *Forza: Horizon 2* by Turn 10 Studios and Playground Games. At previous releases of the *Forza* series, without this tool, the test team used to spend several hundred hours manual-testing the game to find collision mesh issues and finished without a guarantee that there were none, since it was basically a brute-force approach. With this tool, an entire mesh of a track can now be analyzed and all collision bugs can be found in less than 500 milliseconds. Moreover, this provides us the trust that we are shipping the game with collision meshes in a perfect state.

3.2   Collision Mesh Issues

The tool was originally crafted to detect only holes at the collision mesh; later on it was expanded to also detect flipped/skewed normal and malformed triangles. Those are the main issues that causes problems with the physics engine at runtime.

3.2.1   Holes

Holes in the collision mesh was a great problem to us. Big holes were usually not a problem because they end up being caught by the testers and their behaviors are typically very deterministic and clear: e.g., the car goes through a wall that it is not supposed to or it falls through the world. Although it was not fast to detect those issues and sometimes it was costly, they wind up being detected and fixed. The real problems were the small/tiny holes where it would cause the car to behave oddly and in a non-natural way; such a bug would only reproduce with a specific car, in a specific speed, and if hit at a specific angle. Moreover, when the bug was filed, it usually only had a video with the odd behavior happening at that specific part of the track, so the artist that would be responsible to fix it usually would not know what specific triangle was causing that. Figures 3.1 and 3.2 show a tiny hole being detected by the tool.

3.2.2   Wrong Normals

Normals in the collision mesh are responsible for determining the force that is applied to the car at each particular vertex. Thus, if a particular piece of road is flat, the normal at those vertices should be straight up. If the normal was flipped, the user would see the car being dragged into the ground. As with small holes, a single skewed or flipped normal could cause a completely wrong behavior at runtime, and it may also be very hard to detect by only reproducing in very specific scenarios. In this chapter I will call a *flipped normal* any normal where the angle with the Y-up vector is greater than 90°. A flipped normal is always a wrong normal; however, we can have by-design skewed normals, which is how we simulate the physics effects of the tires hitting the rumble strips. Therefore, it is particular hard to detect when a skewed normal is by design or not.

Artists do not usually author the normals by hand; they are created by the 3D digital content creation tool. The reason why the normals get skewed or flipped

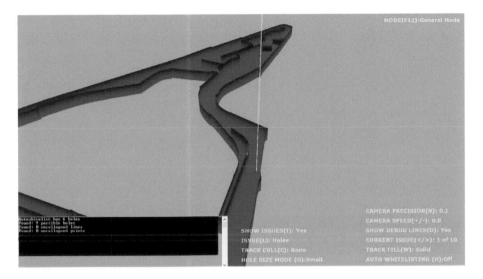

Figure 3.1. A small hole highlighted by the tool in green.

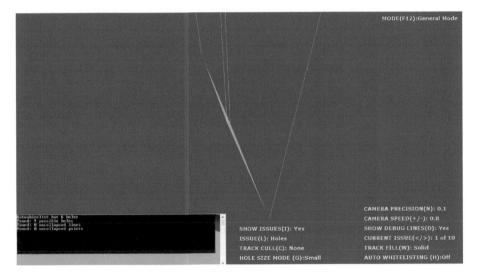

Figure 3.2. Same hole from Figure 3.1 on a very close-up view.

is because they might weld vertices and create really small triangles. Those small triangles together yield precision issues on the calculation of normals by the 3D DCC tool, and the collision mesh ends up with bad normals. Figure 3.3 shows a flipped normal detected by the tool. Note how every normal is following a good

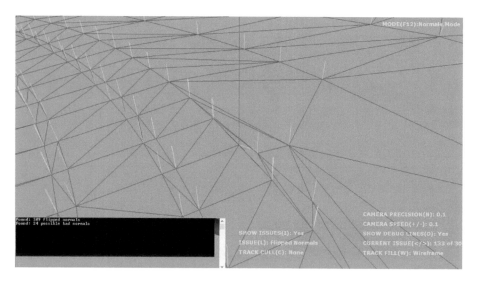

Figure 3.3. A flipped normal flagged by the tool in red.

pattern of being aligned with the Y-up vector while the flagged normal clearly disturbs this pattern.

3.2.3   Malformed Triangles

Triangles that are malformed, such as triangles that are lines (i.e., two vertices are collinear) or triangles where the three vertices are the same, are also detected by the tool. Usually they are not sources of very bad behaviors like holes or bad normals, but they are definitely wrong data that should not be there to begin with.

3.3   Detecting the Issues

This section will cover the details of building the data structure needed to query and traverse the mesh and how we detect each of the issues described in the previous section.

3.3.1   Building the Data Structure

To be able to detect holes, we need to add the mesh to an easy queryable data structure. We used a half-edge data structure [Mäntylä 88, pp. 161–174; Kettner 99]. Half-edge data structures are easy to implement and are able to represent arbitrary orientable 2-manifold polygonal meshes with no complex edges or vertices.

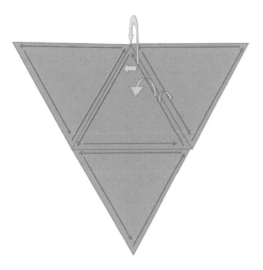

Figure 3.4. Half-edges in red and its references in yellow to the face, vertex, next half-edge, and opposite half-edge.

The data structure is stored in such a way that each triangle face has three half-edges in the same winding order and each of those edges references the next half-edge, the opposite half edge of its neighbor face, and a vertex like it is shown in Figure 3.4. The members of our mesh are detailed in the following pseudocode snippet:

```
class Mesh
{
    List<Face> faces; //List of all faces of this mesh.
}

class HalfEdge
{
    Face face; //Reference to the face this half-edge belongs to.
    HalfEdge next; //Reference to the next half-edge.
    HalfEdge opposite; //Reference to the opposite half-edge.
    Vertex v; //Reference to the tail vertex of this half-edge.
}

class Face
{
    HalfEdge edge; //Reference to one half-edge of this face.
    Vertex v1, v2, v3; //Reference to the three vertices of this face.
}
class Vertex
{
    Vector3 Position; //Position of the vertex.
    Vector3 Normal; //Normal of the vertex.
}
```

By parsing the vertex and index buffer of a mesh and filling into a data structured like the above one, it is really easy to start doing queries on the mesh. For instance, the following snippet finds all neighboring faces of a given face:

```
List<Face> GetNeighbors (Face face)
{
    List<Face> neighbors = new List<Face>();

    if (face.edge.opposite != null)
    {
        neighbors.Add(face.edge.opposite.face);
    }
    if (face.edge.next.opposite != null)
    {
        neighbors.Add(face.edge.next.opposite.face);
    }
    if (face.edge.next.next.opposite != null)
    {
        neighbors.Add(face.edge.next.next.opposite.face);
    }

    return neighbors;
}
```

For more information on half-edge data structures, we suggest the following references to the reader: [McGuire 00, Botsch et al. 10].

3.3.2   Detecting Holes

After storing the mesh in the half-edge data structure, we iterate on the mesh by first looking for holes. To do that, we treat the mesh as if it is an undirected graph where each triangle face is a node and each triangle edge is an edge of the graph. This is illustrated in Figure 3.5.

Next, we conduct a breadth-first search (BFS) looking for any half-edge that does not have an opposite half-edge; this would be an open edge as shown on Figure 3.5. Any open edge is always part of a hole, and we store this open edge on a list of open edges. This process is shown in the following pseudo-code snippet:

```
List<Hole> FindHoles ()
{
    //All open edges.
    List<HalfEdgeIdxs> holesEdges = new List<HalfEdgeIdxs>();

    //List of holes to return.
    List<Hole> meshHoleList = new List<Hole>();

    //A set that contains all visited faces.
    Hashset<Face> visitedFaces = new Hashset<Face>();
    //Start by visiting the first face of the mesh.
    Face currFace = meshFacesList[0];
    //A set that contains the non-visited faces.
    HashSet<Face> allFacesHashSet
```

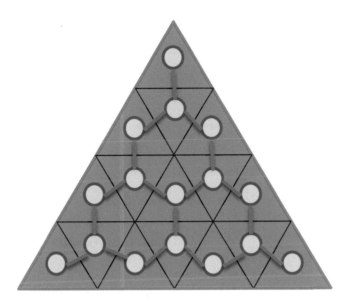

Figure 3.5. Each face is a node, and each triangle edge is an edge of the undirected graph. All the red edges are open edges.

```
           = new HashSet<Face>(meshFacesList );
   //Initialize the BFS queue.
   Queue<Face> bfsQueue = new Queue<Face >();
   bfsQueue.Enqueue(currFace);
   visitedFaces.Add(currFace);
   //Only quit if we have visited all faces
   while (bfsQueue.Count > 0 || visitedFaces.Count
                              != meshFacesList.Count)
   {
       //If the BFS queue is empty and we are still in the
       //loop, it means that this mesh is a disjoint mesh;
       //we leave this set and go to the next set by
       //re-feeding the queue.
       if (bfsQueue.Count == 0)
       {
           Face face = allFacesHashSet.Next();
           visitedFaces.Add(face);
           bfsQueue.Enqueue(face);
       }
       //Remove from the queue and from the non-visited faces.
       currFace = bfsQueue.Dequeue();
       allFacesHashSet.Remove(currFace);

       //Visit the neighbors of the face.
       List<Face> neighbors = currFace.GetNeighbors();
       foreach (Face neighbor in neighbors)
       {
           if (!visitedFaces.ContainsKey(neighbor))
           {
               visitedFaces.Add(neighbor, true);
               bfsQueue.Enqueue(neighbor);
```

```
            }
        }
        //If the number of neighbors of this face is 3,
        //it has no open edges; continue.
        if (neighbors.Count == 3)
        {
            continue;
        }

        HalfEdge currHalfEdge = currFace.Edge;
        int i = 0;
        //This face has open edges; loop through the edges of
        //the face and add to the open edges list.
        while (i < 3)
        {
            if (currHalfEdge.Opposite == null)
            {   //Add the half edge to the hole;
                //V1 and V2 are the indices of the vertices
                //on the vertex buffer.
                HalfEdgeIdxs holeEdge
                    = new HalfEdgeIdxs(currHalfEdge.V1,
                                        currHalfEdge.V2);

                holesEdges.Add(holeEdge);
            }

            currHalfEdge = currHalfEdge.Next;
            i++;
        }
    }
    //If there are no open edges, return an empty hole list.
    if (holesEdges.Count == 0)
    {
        return meshHoleList;//No holes.
    }
    //Method continues in the next code snippet.
```

The last step is to create a hole based on the open edge information. To do that, we get the first open edge from the list, and let the vertices of this edge be V1 and V2. Next, we assign the open edge to a hole and remove that edge from the open edge list. Also, we mark V1 as the first vertex of the hole; this is the vertex where the hole has to end when the hole cycle is completed. In other words, there must be an edge on the mesh with vertices (Vn, V1) that completes this hole. Now, we loop through all the open edges to find an edge where the first vertex is V2; this is the next edge of our hole, and we add it to the hole and remove it from the list of open edges. We continue this search until we find the edge (Vn, V1); this edge completes the hole, and we move on to the next hole. The loop finishes when there are no more edges in the open edges list. The following snippet illustrates this last step:

```
//Get the first open edge and add it to a new hole.
HalfEdgeIdxs currEdge = holesEdges[0];
Hole hole = new Hole();
hole.HoleHalfEdges.Add(currEdge);
//Mark the first vertex of the hole.
```

```
int firstVertexOfHole = currEdge.V1;
//Remove the open edge added to the hole from the list of open edges.
holesEdges.Remove(currEdge);
while (true)
{
    //Find the next edge of this hole, where the first vertex is
    //equal to the second one of the current edge.
    HalfEdgeIdxs currEdgeNext = holesEdges.Find(x => x.V1
                                        == currEdge.V2);
    //Add the found edge to the hole and remove it from the list
    //of open edges.
    hole.HoleHalfEdges.Add(currEdgeNext);
    holesEdges.Remove(currEdgeNext);

    //Test if we found the edge that ends the hole cycle.
    if (currEdgeNext.V2 == firstVertexOfHole)
    {
        meshHoleList.Add(hole);
        //No more open edges; finish loop; all holes found.
        if (holesEdges.Count == 0) break;

        //If there are still open edges, get the next one from
        //the list and start a new hole.
        currEdge = holesEdges[0];
        holesEdges.Remove(currEdge);
        firstVertexOfHole = currEdge.V1;
        hole = new Hole();
        hole.HoleHalfEdges.Add(currEdge.GetName(), currEdge);
    }
    else
    {
        //If we did not find the end of the hole, just go to
        //the next edge.
        currEdge = currEdgeNext;
    }
}
//Return the mesh list with all holes.
return meshHoleList;
}
```

This algorithm identifies mesh boundaries as a hole, which is explained in the next subsection.

3.3.3 Hole Classification

Topology-wise, for an open mesh, there is no difference between a hole and a boundary of a mesh. This can be easily visualized by making a sector of a circle with a piece of paper and building a cone with this circle, leaving the bottom of the cone open. The bottom of the cone is a hole in the mesh, but it is also the boundary of it. By flattening the cone and making it a circle again, you can again visualize that there is no topology difference between a boundary and a hole; see Figure 3.6.

In our collision meshes there are a great number of boundaries that are by design, and flagging them all as possible issues to be filtered out by the tester would generate too much noise and false positives, making the usage of the tool

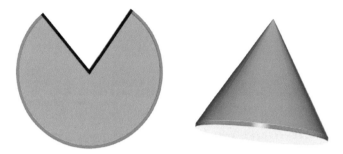

Figure 3.6. The boundary of our flattened cone is highlighted in red (left). The cone is assembled with its hole/boundary highlighted in red (right).

unpractical. To address this issue, we came up with two rules to whitelist holes that are highly likely to be by design. First, our collision meshes have very high vertical walls to prevent cars from falling out of the world, and the vast majority of the by-design boundaries are at the tops of those walls. We usually do not care about issues on the collision mesh that are very high; thus, we whitelist any hole that is found above the upper half of the mesh. The second rule that we use to whitelist is when holes are very big. Our collision mesh contains barriers along the track that have big boundaries, which are all by design; the intent of the second rule is to whitelist those barriers. Whitelisting based on a large hole size has proven to be safe; of course, we could have a giant hole in the track that is indeed a bug, but those are easily and quickly found by playing the build normally. Moreover, the user can also remove the whitelisting and let all holes appear and give a quick inspection by flying above the track.

3.3.4   Detecting Bad Normals

As mentioned in Section 3.2.2, there are two kinds of bad normals: flipped normals and skewed normals. Flipped normals (see Figure 3.3) are straightforward to detect. We loop through all the normals of the collision mesh and mark as flipped any normal that satisfies the following equation:

$$\mathbf{n} \cdot \hat{\mathbf{y}} < \mathbf{0},$$

where $\hat{\mathbf{y}}$ is the unit Y-up vector. Skewed normals are more complicated because we can have those kind of normals by design; see Figure 3.7. However, the ones that are actual bugs come from defects in the crafted mesh, usually very small triangles. The first approach we have tried to identify those is to simply flag triangles with small areas. This did not work well because a normal is influenced by the entire one-ring neighborhood of a vertex and looking locally at only one triangle produced too many incorrect results.

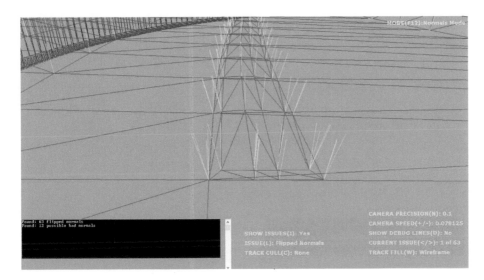

Figure 3.7. By-design skewed normals to simulate the effect of bumpy surfaces on the tires.

Later we arrived on a heuristic that works quite well for our meshes to detect those bad skewed normal. Our normals are exported with a 64-bit precision, and in the tool we recalculate the normal with the following non-weighted formula:

$$\text{normalize}\left(\sum_{i=0}^{k} n_i\right),$$

where k is the number of faces in the one-ring neighborhood of a vertex and n_i is the face normal of each triangle. We calculate this formula with 32-bit precision. After this, we have two set of normals: the original one with 64-bit precision and the calculated one with 32-bit precision. We then compare the two normals of each set; if their directions differ more than a specific threshold, it is highly likely that there are bad skewed normals in that area of the mesh and we flag it. This was done to simulate the behavior of the exporter in order to make a meaningful comparison and catch less false positives.

This method has proven to be a good heuristic; however, it can still cause false positives sometimes. When looking at those issues, we ask the testers to pay attention to the area around the flagged vertex and to see if all normals are following a well-behaved pattern. The threshold for comparing the two sets of normals is predefined for the user, but it can be modified at runtime in case some weird physics behavior is still happening in the area and the tool is not flagging anything. As the threshold gets smaller, there will be more false positives flagged.

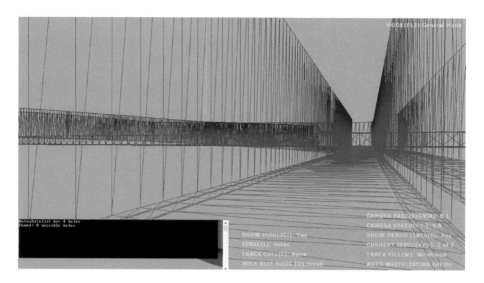

Figure 3.8. For the same small hole from Figure 3.2, the user can easily find it with the help of the green lines.

3.3.5 Detecting Malformed Triangles

Malformed triangles are simple to detect. When traversing the mesh to fill the half-edge data structure, we look at the triangle data and see if any triangles have vertices set in the same coordinates or if the three vertices are collinear. Those issues are flagged by the tool.

3.4 Visualization

Our visualization scheme has proven to be simple and effective. Usually the users of the tool are not very technical, and when designing the tool, we took into consideration that visualizing the issues should be very straightforward. The tool has basically two modes. The *general mode* is used to display holes and malformed triangles, and the *normal mode* is used to display flipped and skewed normals. In each mode, the user selects the type of issue that he wants to visualize (i.e., holes) and all of them are highlighted. The user can then loop through them by using the keyboard arrows, and while he is looping, a set of green lines that goes from each of the highlighted vertices to very high up in the Y-axis appears. Those green lines are extremely useful to actually find where in the mesh the issue appears; see Figure 3.8.

3.5 Navigation

As mentioned in the previous section, the users of the tool are not very technical, and our navigation system should be as easy as possible for a first-time user to learn. For multiscale environments, 3D content creation packages usually use some sort of an arc-ball camera scheme to navigate in the scene. Although artists are usually pretty comfortable with such schemes, regular users may find it hard and nonintuitive at the beginning. The ideal navigation scheme for the testers would be a first-person shooter style, which they would find very familiar. The biggest problem for such a scheme in a multiscale environment is the velocity of the camera; sometimes the user wants it to be very fast to traverse a long distance, and other times one may need it to be very slow to take a closer look at a very small hole. To solve this velocity issue, we tried automated approaches similar to [Trindade et. al 11], where a dynamic cubemap is generated to calculate the distance between the camera and surrounding objects and to automatically adjust the speed based on the distance. This approach worked to some extent, but there were still very bad cases where the camera was going too slow or too fast, which caused frustration to the user.

After testing some possible navigation approaches, we found one that was the best cost benefit in terms of usability and learning curve for our environment. The camera starts at a default speed and the user can increase its speed linearly with subtle moves on the mouse wheel. Yet, quicker moves in the wheel will make it increase exponentially (doubling each time), and a threshold controls the lower and upper speed limit. We also have a shortcut bound to a hotkey for snapping directly to a particular selected issue. Although this is not a scheme used in first-person shooter games, we found that after a few sessions the user can use this scheme quickly and precisely.

3.6 Workflow

The workflow in the studio begins with the artist crafting content source files, then the track will be built with its collision mesh and every other piece of content into binaries that are ready to be read by the game at runtime. After the build finishes, the tracks sits on an escrow folder waiting to be promoted by a test pass; if every test criteria passes, the track is promoted and others in the studio will see it in the build. At the beginning we had a separate export process for the collision mesh from the 3D content creation package to a format that our tool would read. However, this caused too many synchronization-related issues. Sometimes the export process would fail and new collision files would not be created, and testers would do an entire test pass in an old mesh. Moreover, the export script had to always be updated if artists try to use different source files for the collision mesh; if the export process did not get an update, testers would also be testing a wrong collision mesh. To solve this problem, we got rid of the export process and made the tool read the same binary file that is read by the physics engine at runtime.

The tool also has a couple of nice features that improve testers' and artists' workflows when filing and fixing bugs. Whenever an issue is highlighted, the user can press a hotkey to output the coordinates of the issue in the 3D content creation package space. Thus, when fixing the bug, the artist knows the exact coordinates where the hole is. Also, every time the tester presses "print screen" while in the tool, a screenshot will automatically be saved in a user folder with the type and the number of the issue, which makes it easier for the tester to navigate to the tool, take screenshots with the coordinates of every bug, and later file them all.

3.7   Conclusion

This chapter presented a 3D visualization tool for detecting collision mesh issues. This tool was used in production, and we were able to save hundreds of manual testing hours during development by using it. Our goal is not only to provide a solution to this particular problem but also to hopefully inspire the readers to use computer graphics techniques to solve problems in other domains, as it was shown with our testing problem.

3.8   Acknowledgments

Thanks to Zach Hooper for constantly providing feedback in the development of this tool and to Daniel Adent for the support on publishing this. Special thanks to my wife and family for all their help and to my friend F. F. Marmot.

Bibliography

[Botsch et al. 10] Mario Botsch, Leif Kobbelt, Mark Pauly, Pierre Alliez, and Bruno Levy. *Polygon Mesh Processing.* Natick, MA: A K Peters/CRC Press, 2010.

[Kettner 99] Lutz Kettner. "Using Generic Programming for Designing a Data Structure for Polyhedral Surfaces." *Computational Geometry* 13.1 (1999), 65–90.

[Mäntylä 88] Martti Mäntylä. *An Introduction to Solid Modeling.* New York: W. H. Freeman, 1988.

[McGuire 00] Max McGuire. "The Half-Edge Data Structure." http://www. flipcode.com/articles/articlehalfedgepf.shtml, 2000.

[Trindade et al. 11] Daniel R.Trindade and Alberto B. Raposo. "Improving 3D Navigation in Multiscale Environments Using Cubemap-Based Techniques." In *Proceedings of the 2011 ACM Symposium on Applied Computing*, pp. 1215–1221. New York: ACM, 2011.

Semi-static Load Balancing for Low-Latency Ray Tracing on Heterogeneous Multiple GPUs
Takahiro Harada

4.1 Introduction

Ray tracing is used to render a realistic image but the drawback is its high computational cost. Although there are studies accelerating ray tracing using the GPU, even with the latest GPU, we cannot get a satisfactory rendering speed. An obvious way to accelerate it further is to use more than one GPU. To exploit the computational power of multiple GPUs, the work has to be distributed in a way so that it minimizes the idle time of GPUs. There are studies on load balancing CPUs, but they are not directly applicable to multiple GPUs because of the difference of the architectures, as discussed in Section 4.2.

If we could restrict the target platform as GPUs with the same compute capability, the problem is simpler. However, there are more and more PCs with multiple GPUs with different compute capabilities (e.g., a PC with an integrated GPU on a CPU and a discrete GPU). Also, when we build a PC with multiple discrete GPUs, it is easier to get different-generation GPUs than GPUs with the same specification, or the same compute capability. Therefore, if we develop a ray tracing system that works well on multiple GPUs with nonuniform compute capabilities, there are more PCs that benefit from the method comparing to a ray tracing system developed only for GPUs with a uniform compute capability.

If we restrict ourselves to a system with multiple GPUs of the same specification, we could use alternate frame rendering [Advanced Micro Devices, Inc. 16]. However, an issue of the method is latency; it does not improve the latency to render a single frame. There are many applications that prefer a low-latency rendering. They include games and other interactive applications. Also, the rise of the head-mounted display is another strong push of a low-latency rendering.

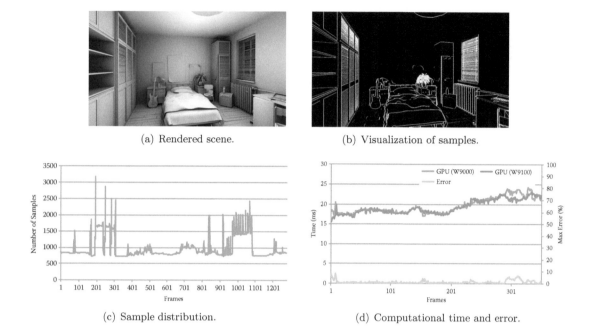

(a) Rendered scene.   (b) Visualization of samples.

(c) Sample distribution.   (d) Computational time and error.

Figure 4.1. (a) Ray traced scene on AMD FirePro W9000 and W9100 GPUs. (b) Visualization of the number of samples per pixel (black = 1, white = 5). The depth buffer of the scene is first rendered using OpenGL. Then, an edge detection algorithm computes this image, which is an input for a primary ray generation kernel generating more samples at pixels containing geometry edges. (c) Histogram of the number of samples of (b) for each vertical scanline. (d) Computational time on two GPUs and maximum deviation of computational time under a camera motion. Average error is 1.2%.

The goal of this chapter is to develop a low-latency ray tracing system for multiple GPUs with nonuniform compute powers. To realize this goal, we propose a semi-static load balancing method that uses rendering statistics of the previous frame to compute work distribution for the next frame. The proposed method does not assume uniform sampling density on the framebuffer, thus it is applicable for a problem with an irregular sampling pattern as shown in Figure 4.1. The method is not only applicable for the multi-GPU environment, but it can be used to distribute compute work load on GPUs and a CPU as we show in Section 4.4.

4.2   Load Balancing Methods

4.2.1   Frame Distribution

Frame distribution, also known as alternate frame rendering, is often used to utilize multiple GPUs for a raster graphics for interactive application [Advanced

Micro Devices, Inc. 16]. Although it performs well when all the GPUs in a system have the same compute capability, it results in underutilization of GPUs unless we use the same GPUs. When n GPUs are used, a GPU should spend $n \times t$ for computation of a single frame to have zero idle time where t is the time to display a single frame. Therefore, the latency of interaction is high; it takes time to propagate a user input to all the GPUs. Thus, alternate frame rendering is not suited for many GPUs with different compute capabilities.

4.2.2 Work Distribution

Data distribution, also known as sort last rendering, splits input geometry into small chunks each of which is processed on a node (when GPUs are used, a node is a GPU). Although it reduces the rendering time for each GPU, it is not straightforward to use for global illumination in which rays bounce. Moreover, the computation time is view dependent, thus it is difficult to get a uniform computation time for all the nodes. It also requires transferring screen-sized images with depth, which results in large network traffic. Therefore, it is not suited for rendering running at an interactive speed.

Pixel distribution, also known as sort first rendering, splits the screen into cells, and rendering a cell is distributed on nodes as work. If the works are distributed proportional to the compute capability of the nodes, all the nodes remain active and therefore we maximize the computation power of all nodes. This is often the choice to distribute work on multiple CPUs [Heirich and Arvo 98]. We also employ pixel distribution for work distribution, although the preferable work size is different for GPUs than for CPUs.

4.2.3 Work Size

CPUs prefer small work size for pixel distribution because it allows the system to adjust the workload on each node, which results in a uniform computation time on all nodes. However, when GPUs are used for computation, we also need to take the architectural difference into consideration. A GPU prefers a large or wide computation because of its architecture optimized for very wide computation. If a work size is small, it cannot fill the entire GPU, which results in underutilization of the GPU. Thus, we want to make the work as large as possible when GPUs are used as compute nodes. However, load balancing becomes more difficult if we make the work size larger and the number of works smaller, as it easily causes starvation of a GPU. The optimal strategy for our case is to generate m works for m GPUs and to adjust the work size so that computation times on GPUs are exactly the same. This is challenging for ray tracing in which the computation time for a pixel is not uniform. We realize this by collecting GPU performance statistics and adjust the work size for each GPU over the frames.

Cosenza et al. studied a load balancing method utilizing frame coherency, but they assume the same compute capability for processors [Cosenza et al. 08]. The method only splits or merges a work, thus it cannot perform precise load balancing unless using small leaves. Therefore, it is not well suited as a load balancing strategy for multiple compute devices. Another similar work to ours is work by Moloney et al., who studied load balancing on multiple GPUs for volume rendering [Moloney et al. 07]. However, they assume uniform compute capabilities and uniform distribution of samples. They also assume that the computational cost for each ray can be estimated. As none of those applies to ray tracing, their method cannot be used for our purpose.

4.3 Semi-static Load Balancing

A frame rendering starts with a master thread splitting the framebuffer into m areas using the algorithm described below, where m is the number of GPUs. Once the framebuffer assignment is sent to slaves, parallel rendering starts. Each GPU executes the following steps:

1. Generate samples (primary rays) for the assigned area.

2. Ray trace at sample location to compute radiance.

3. Send the framebuffer and work statistics to the master.

Note that master-slave communication is done only twice (send jobs, receive results) in a frame computation.

At the first frame, we do not have any knowledge about workload nor compute capabilities of the GPUs. Thus, an even split is used for the frame. After rendering frame t, compute device i reports the area of processed framebuffer s_i^t, the number of samples processed n_i^t, and the computation time for the work t_i^t. That information is used to compute the optimal framebuffer split for frame $t+1$.

The algorithm first estimates processing speed $p_i^t = n_i^t/t_i^t$ (number of processed samples per second) for each compute device. Then, it computes the ideal time $T = N^t/\sum p_i^t$ to finish the work with the perfect load balancing, where $N^t = \sum n_i^t$ is the total number of samples processed at t. With these values, we can estimate the number of samples we need to assign for compute device i at frame $t+1$ as $n_i'^{t+1} = Tp_i^t$.

If the sample distribution is uniform on the screen, we could assign area $s_i'^{t+1} = Sn_i'^{t+1}/N$ for compute device i, where $S = \sum s_i^t$. However, as we do not assume the uniform distribution over the frame, we need to compute the area of the framebuffer that contains $n_i'^{t+1}$ samples for compute device i. The procedure to compute area s_i^{t+1} is illustrated in Figure 4.2 in which we assume that there are four GPUs. GPU i processed the assigned area s_i^t at frame t and reported that there are n_i^t samples in the area (Figure 4.2(a)). A histogram of sample

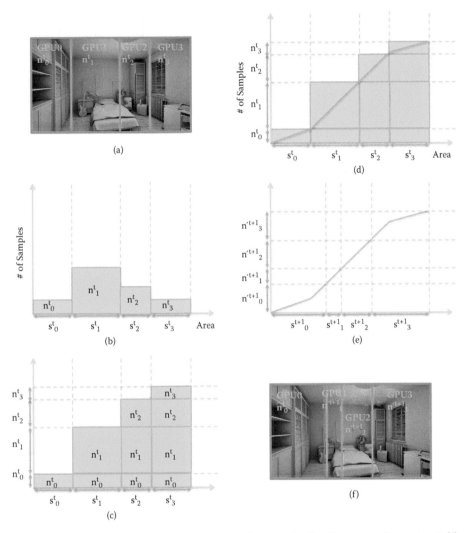

Figure 4.2. Illustration of computation steps for sample distribution at frame $t + 1$ (f) using the information reported at frame t (a).

distribution at frame t is built from these values (Figure 4.2(b)). Samples n_i^t are stacked up, as shown in Figure 4.2(c), to draw lines as shown in Figure 4.2(d). These lines are built to look up the number of samples at a given area. For example, we can find that there are n_0^t samples at s_0^t, and $n_0^t + n_1^t$ samples at $s_0^t + s_1^t$. When building the lines, we ignored the distribution of samples in s_i^t and assumed the uniform distribution. After building them, we search for s_i^{t+1} corresponding to $n_i'^{t+1}$ by the binary search.

Since we linearize the sample distribution at area processed at each GPU, there is no guarantee that the computed work distribution is perfect. Therefore, we gradually move the distribution to the computed distribution by interpolating the split of t and $t+1$ as $n_i''^{t+1} = (1-\alpha)n_i^t + \alpha n_i'^{t+1}$, where α is the only parameter for the proposed method. We set $\alpha = 0.4$ for computation of Figures 4.1 and 4.3 and $\alpha = 0.2$ for Figure 4.4, which has a higher variation in the sample density.

4.4 Results and Discussion

The proposed method is implemented in a OpenCL ray tracer. Experiments are performed using three combinations of compute devices: AMD FirePro W9000 GPU + AMD FirePro W9100 GPU, Intel Core i7-2760QM CPU + AMD Radeon HD 6760m GPU, and four AMD FirePro W9000 GPUs. The framebuffer is split vertically for all the test cases. The method can be used with rendering pipelines with any sampling strategies, but here we show example usages of it with two rendering pipelines.

The first test rendering pipeline is similar to [Mitchell 87] but implemented as a hybrid of rasterization and ray tracing. It first fills the depth buffer using OpenGL, and it is used to compute a sample density map, as shown in Figure 4.1(b). The primary ray generation kernel for ray tracing reads the map and decides the number of samples per pixel. In our test case, we generate five samples for a pixel containing edges of geometry to reduce geometric aliasing, and one for the other pixels. Ambient occlusion is progressively calculated at 1280×720 resolution with two shadow rays per sample per frame. This is a challenging case for the proposed method because it has high variation in the number of samples in the direction of the split axis, as shown in Figure 4.1(b). We interactively control the camera for all the test cases to evaluate the robustness of the method for a dynamic environment. Sample distribution changes as the camera moves. This is the reason why the computational times and work distribution reported in Figures 4.1 and 4.3 have ups and downs. We can see that the method successfully keeps the computational time on different compute devices almost the same. Figures 4.3(d) and (e) show that the analysis of the work load distribution on the framebuffer is good. The same number of pixels would have been assigned for GPUs if we ignored the sample distribution. It however splits the framebuffer into works with different framebuffer area to achieve load balancing. The averages of the maximum deviations of computational time are 1.4, 0.9, 1.8, 2.9, and 2.1% for Figures 4.3(a), (b), (c), (d), and (e), respectively.

The other test rendering pipeline uses a foveated sampling pattern [Guenter et al. 12]. The sampling pattern we prepared in advance has higher sampling density at the center of the screen, and density decreases as the distance of the pixel from the center increases (Figure 4.4(a)). Sample density is less than one per pixel for sparse area. Primary rays are generated according to the pattern,

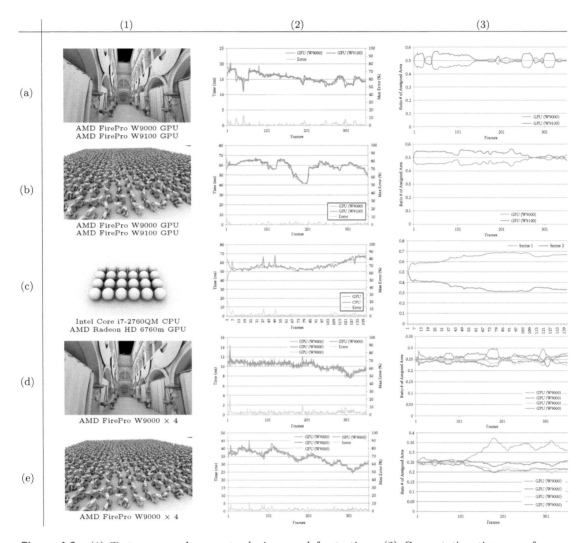

Figure 4.3. (1) Test scene and compute devices used for testing. (2) Computation time over frames. (3) Ratio of the number of processed pixels.

and direct illumination is computed. We can see that the method keeps the computation time on four GPUs almost the same (Figure 4.4).

The method is also applicable to load balancing on multiple machines. In the example shown in Figure 4.5, the framebuffer is split into three areas each of which are processed by each machine, and each machine split the area further to distribute the computation on installed GPUs.

(a) Sample pattern.

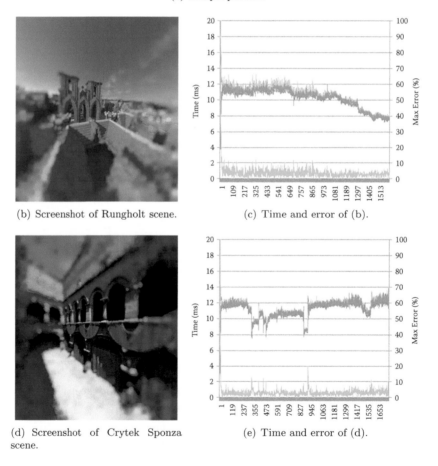

(b) Screenshot of Rungholt scene.   (c) Time and error of (b).

(d) Screenshot of Crytek Sponza   (e) Time and error of (d).
scene.

Figure 4.4. Foveated rendering on four AMD FirePro W900 GPUs. Samples are only created at white pixels in (a).

Figure 4.5. Bedroom scene rendered using three machines connected via 10-Gb Ethernet. The frame is split horizontally to distribute the work for machines. In each machine, the frame is split vertically on GPUs. We used 4 × AMD Radeon HD 7970, 2 × AMD Radeon HD 6970, and 1 × AMD Radeon HD 6850.

4.5 Acknowledgments

We thank Syoyo Fujita for help in implementing the foveated rendering. We thank David Vacek and David Tousek for Bedroom, Frank Meinl and Crytek for Crytek Sponza, Stanford for Dragon, and kescha for Rungholt.

Bibliography

[Advanced Micro Devices, Inc. 16] Advanced Micro Devices, Inc. "AMD Radeon Dual Graphics." http://www.amd.com/en-us/innovations/software-technologies/dual-graphics, 2016.

[Cosenza et al. 08] Biagio Cosenza, Gennaro Cordasco, Rosario De Chiara, Ugo Erra, and Vittorio Scarano. "On Estimating the Effectiveness of Temporal and Spatial Coherence in Parallel Ray Tracing." In *Eurographics Italian Chapter Conference*, pp. 97–104. Aire-la-Ville, Switzerland: Eurographics Association, 2008.

[Guenter et al. 12] Brian Guenter, Mark Finch, Steven Drucker, Desney Tan, and John Snyder. "Foveated 3D Graphics." *ACM Trans. Graph.* 31:6 (2012), 164:1–164:10.

[Heirich and Arvo 98] Alan Heirich and James Arvo. "A Competitive Analysis of Load Balancing Strategies for Parallel Ray Tracing." *J. Supercomput.* 12:1-2 (1998), 57–68.

[Mitchell 87] Don P. Mitchell. "Generating Antialiased Images at Low Sampling Densities." *SIGGRAPH Comput. Graph.* 21:4 (1987), 65–72.

[Moloney et al. 07] Brendan Moloney, Daniel Weiskopf, Torsten Möller, and Magnus Strengert. "Scalable Sort-First Parallel Direct Volume Rendering with Dynamic Load Balancing." In *Proceedings of the 7th Eurographics Conference on Parallel Graphics and Visualization*, pp. 45–52. Aire-la-Ville, Switzerland: Eurographics Association, 2007.

VI Compute

This section covers techniques that are made possible with the usage of compute GPU interfaces.

The first chapter, "Octree Mapping from a Depth Camera," shows how to render artificial objects with consistent shading from arbitrary perspectives in a real-world scene. This chapter uses CUDA to reconstruct 3D scenes from depth cameras at near real-time speeds. The scene is represented by a sparse voxel octree (SVO) structure that scales to large volumes.

The second chapter, "Interactive Sparse Eulerian Fluid," describes a method for computing and rendering smoke-like fluid in real time on the GPU using DirectX 11+ with a key focus on the advantages of simulating and storing these simulations in a sparse domain. This technique was used with impressive results in the NVIDIA *Mech Ti* demo.

—Wolfgang Engel

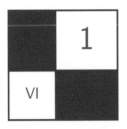

1

Octree Mapping
from a Depth Camera
Dave Kotfis and Patrick Cozzi

1.1 Overview

To render artificial objects with consistent shading from arbitrary perspectives, a 3D scene needs to be constructed from the camera frames. Data parallel GPU computing allows for real-time 3D mapping of scenes from depth cameras such as the Kinect sensor. Noise in the camera's depth measurements can be filtered over multiple image frames by representing the scene as a voxel-based map rather than as a collection of raw point clouds. However, a dense voxel grid representation is not suitable for large scenes or live rendering for use in games.

In this chapter, we present our method that uses CUDA to reconstruct 3D scenes from depth cameras at near real-time speeds. A scene is represented by a *sparse voxel octree* (SVO) structure that scales to large volumes. We render these scenes with CUDA and OpenGL using methods that eliminate the slow process of generating meshes from point clouds or voxel grids. We will describe an SVO

Figure 1.1. Augmented reality: A kitchen scene rendered with voxel cone tracing (left); rendering a textured Stanford Bunny sitting behind a stool in the kitchen (center); and the augmented scene rendered from an alternative view (right).

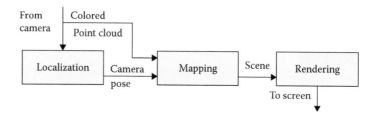

Figure 1.2. Top-level system view of an augmented reality system that simultaneously maps and renders a scene.

representation of a scene and data parallel methods to update and expand from incrementally received colored point clouds. While real-time 3D mapping has a variety of applications ranging from robotics to medical imaging, this chapter will focus on applications to augmented reality. (See Figure 1.1.)

1.1.1 Augmented Reality

In recent years, low-cost depth cameras using structured light or time of flight methods have become commonplace. These *RGB-D* (color + depth) cameras directly measure additional 3D information that previously could only be generated through sophisticated computer vision algorithms in software. These cameras are useful for creating models for 3D printing, computer vision for robotics, and creating immersive and interactive video game experiences.

Augmented reality (AR) is a field that lives on the boundary between computer graphics and vision to create experiences that blend artificial graphics with the real world. AR systems today typically render virtual objects in front of a raw depth camera frame. Future AR systems will seamlessly render virtual graphics blended with a live camera scene. Real scenes could be viewed with artificial lighting conditions and with virtual objects that cast shadows. (See Figure 1.2.)

There are many AR applications where raw color and depth data provides sufficient 3D data. This is generally the case where the application does not need to make use of information that is outside of the current physical camera view. A few example applications of mapping include object collisions with occluded surfaces and casting shadows from objects outside of view. Multiple nearby cameras could interact with the same AR application, by registering and merging their maps to establish a cohesive operating picture. Even without mapping, some AR applications may need at least a localized estimate of the camera's motion. This is required for a moving camera to maintain fixed virtual object locations. Many current AR systems use inertial sensing available on smartphones to track orientation changes. With this sensing, the absolute positioning will drift over time, but a more robust visual motion estimate can improve performance.

1.1.2 Localization

To reconstruct a scene, the movement of the camera between each frame must be determined so the points in each frame can be spatially correlated. GPU computing enables dense camera pose tracking techniques that match every pixel in 640 × 480 frames at 30 frames per second to track the motion of the camera without the need for a motion capture system. Previously, sparse techniques required detection of a smaller set of invariant features to track, which are not always available [Dryanovski et al. 13].

RGB-D cameras provide enough information to generate 3D positions and surface normals. The *iterative closest point* (ICP) algorithm attempts to align one frame to the previous by iteratively reducing the error between the points of each frame and the surfaces of the scene. Visual odometry with depth is a similar process that minimizes a photometric (color) error term rather than a geometric one [Steinbrucker et al. 11]. In different scenes, either geometric or photometric detail may be more prominent, so recent approaches use a combined error function that mixes the two [Whelan et al. 12].

The hard part is computing the error gradient fast enough to keep up with the camera's motion for the solution to converge. If that rate cannot be maintained and frames are skipped, the space of possible transformations that must be searched to align the frames grows. This increases the computational burden, slowing the computation down even further and creating a vicious cycle that makes the process fail. GPU computing that exploits the parallelism of the computation is critical to achieve the speeds required to avoid this downward spiral.

The methods presented in this chapter focus on mapping and rendering techniques. However, a localization method for tracking a camera's motion is a necessary part of any mapping application involving a moving camera. The ICP techniques described above offer real-time localization solutions using camera data, though alternative methods exist. An alternate approach requires the use of an external motion capture system, and many commercial *virtual reality* (VR) systems use this method for localization of a user's head pose.

1.1.3 Mapping

Reconstructing a scene requires a map representation to incrementally update and store data from each camera frame. There are many possible representations to do this, the simplest of which would be to concatenate each new point cloud by transforming all points according to the pose of the camera, assuming it is known. However, the size of this map would grow linearly with time, even when observing the same part of the scene, so it is not a suitable candidate for concurrent rendering. A standard RGB-D camera can generate several GB of raw data within only a minute. This data explosion could easily be avoided by fixing the map size to a maximum set of frames, though this can create undesirable effects when parts of the map become forgotten over time.

We will focus our discussion on mapping methods that accumulate information over the full life of a program rather than a fixed history of frames. If the camera used for mapping remains in a finite volume of space, the map size will be finite as long as spatially redundant information is never duplicated in the representation. To do this, 3D bins at a maximum resolution can be used to identify and filter duplicate points. However, this will result in loss of detail, and the map will contain any noise produced by the camera data. While the binning of the points is trivially data parallel, the removal of point duplicates requires parallel sorting and reduction.

1.2   Previous Work and Limitations

1.2.1   KinectFusion

KinectFusion is a 3D reconstruction technique that attempts to filter the noise of incoming depth data by representing the map as a 3D voxel grid with a truncated signed distance function (TSDF) data payload storing the distance from a surface [Newcombe et al. 11]. The values are truncated to avoid unnecessary computations in free space as well as reduce the amount of data required for surface representation. Building this grid is far more maintainable than storing a raw point cloud for each frame, as the redundancy enables the sensor noise to be smoothed. It also avoids storing significant amounts of duplicate data and is highly data parallel for GPU acceleration.

However, the memory footprint of a voxel grid approach scales poorly to large volumes. The dense representation requires voxel cells allocated in memory for the large amount of free space that will almost always be prominent in scenes. Also, while the voxel grid and TSDF are an appropriate representation for the surface function, it is inefficient for any color data. The rendering process either requires ray marching to directly render the grid, or a slow surface extraction and remeshing process, neither suitable for concurrent real-time rendering.

1.2.2   OctoMap

OctoMap is a probabilistic framework where the log-odds of occupancy are stored in an octree data structure [Hornung et al. 13]. Log-odds is a quantity directly related to the probability, though it is in a form that provides the convenience of an update rule that uses addition and subtraction to incorporate information from new observations. The sparse octree structure overcomes the scalability limitations of a dense voxel grid by leaving free space unallocated in memory. OctoMap also filters sensor noise by assigning probabilities of hit and miss that represent the noise of the sensor. Nodes in the tree are updated by logging each point from a point cloud as a hit. All points along the ray from the camera position to the end point are logged as a miss. This process takes place serially on a CPU, looping over each point in each frame.

The OctoMap is rendered by iterating through the leaves of the tree and extracting cells that have a probability greater than 0.5 of being occupied. These voxels are rendered as cubes with edge length determined by the depth of the corresponding node in the octree. This framework is most commonly used with LIDAR sensors, which have only a few points per scan, which has little benefit from parallelization. An RGB-D sensor would provide millions of points per frame that could be parallelized. However, the pointer-based octree structure used by OctoMap is less suitable for GPU parallelization than a stackless linear octree.

1.3 Octree Scene Representation

1.3.1 Data Format

We developed a sparse octree representation of a scene on a GPU, along with methods to efficiently update and expand it from incrementally received colored point clouds. The GPU data structure is based on the work of GigaVoxels [Crassin et al. 09] that uses a node pool in linear memory and a brick pool in texture memory. The nodes are composed of two 32-bit words. The first word has two 1-bit flags and 30 bits for the index of the first child node. The second word holds either an RGBA value or the location in the brick pool to be used when interpolating values within the node.

Although the sparse octree does not allocate every node of the tree in memory, we use Morton codes as keys for unique identification of voxels. Here is an example key: 1 001 010 111. The key starts with a leading 1 to identify the length of the code, and thus the depth in the tree. After that, the key is made up of a series of 3-bit tuples that indicate a high or low value on the binary split of the x-, y-, and z-dimensions, respectively.

Using a 32-bit integer, this can represent 10 levels of depth in the tree. However, this is insufficient for mapping with a Kinect camera. The Kinect has a range of 0.3–5.0 meters in depth resolution, and doing a back-of-the-envelope calculation for the horizontal resolution (480 pixels, 5-m range, 43 degree field of view) shows that the camera will typically provide sub-centimeter resolution. A 10-meter edge volume can only achieve 1-cm resolution using 10 levels of depth. Therefore, we have transitioned to representing these keys with long integers (64 bit), which could represent more than kilometers of volume at millimeter precision, if needed. Figure 1.3 and Listing 1.1 provide descriptions of our data format.

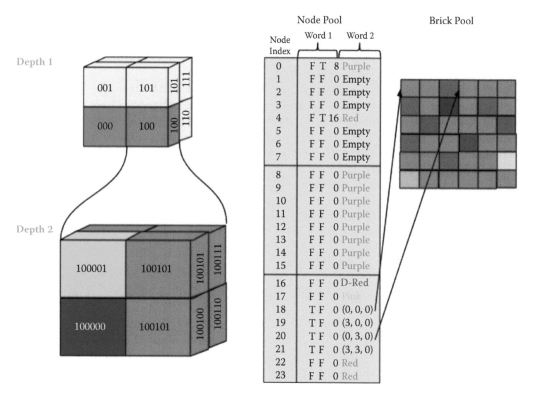

Figure 1.3. Sparse voxel octree data structure in linear GPU memory. It uses keys based on Morton codes to uniquely index nodes. The compact structure uses 64 bits per node. For hardware interpolation of values within the tree, node values can be backed by a brick in texture memory.

1.3.2   Updating the Map

Because our data structure is sparse, each new point cloud frame may contain points in parts of space that were previously unallocated in memory. For this reason, updating the map requires two steps: resizing the octree structure into newly observed space, and updating the color values within the tree with the new observations. Figure 1.4 shows the program flow for updating the map in more detail.

Update octree structure To expand our scene into unallocated space, we first must determine which new points correspond to unallocated nodes. We do this by computing the key for each point to determine its location in the octree. Fortunately, we can do this with only the constant octree parameters, its size and center location, without the need for any data within the octree. This makes the calculation completely data parallel over the incoming point cloud positions. The process of computing keys is in Listing 1.2.

```
struct char4 {
  char x, y, z, w;
};

struct Octree {
//The node data in GPU memory.
//Each node is 2 unsigned int's long.
unsigned int* node_pool;
//The number of nodes allocated in the node pool.
int size;
//The half length of each edge of the root node of the octree.
float edge_length;
//The 3D position of the center of the root node of the octree.
glm::vec3 center;
//The brick pool data in CUDA texture memory.
//Note: Our examples are limited to use of the node pool only.
cudaArray* brick_pool;
};

struct PointCloud {
//The 3D position of each point in the point cloud.
glm::vec3* positions;
//The corresponding RGBA color of each corresponding point.
char4* colors;
//The number of points in the cloud.
int size;
};
```

Listing 1.1. Data structures representing a sparse linear octree and colored point cloud data in GPU memory.

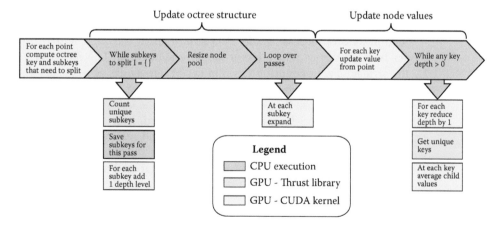

Figure 1.4. Program flow for updating the sparse octree from a point cloud frame. The process of updating the octree map from each incoming point cloud starts by counting how many new octree nodes must be created and resizing the node pool. Then, we can filter the updated color values through the tree.

```
typedef long long int octkey;

__device__ octkey computeKey(const glm::vec3& point,
  glm::vec3 center, const int tree_depth,
  float edge_length) {
  //Initialize the output value with a leading 1
  //to specify the depth.
  octkey key = 1;

  for (int i = 0; i < tree_depth; i++) {
    key = key << 3;

    //Determine in which octant the point lies.
    uint8_t x = point.x > center.x ? 1 : 0;
    uint8_t y = point.y > center.y ? 1 : 0;
    uint8_t z = point.z > center.z ? 1 : 0;

    //Update the code.
    key += (x + 2*y + 4*z);

    //Update the edge length.
    edge_length /= 2.0f;

    //Update the center.
    center.x += edge_length * (x ? 1 : -1);
    center.y += edge_length * (y ? 1 : -1);
    center.z += edge_length * (z ? 1 : -1);
  }
  return key;
}
```

Listing 1.2. CUDA device function to compute a key for a point. A kernel that parallelizes over points should call this.

The process of increasing the SVO size requires copying the data from GPU device to GPU device into a larger memory allocation. The SVO is represented by linear memory, so counting the number of new nodes is necessary to allocate sufficient continuous memory. Once we have the keys for all nodes that need to be accessed, we can use these keys to determine the subset that are not currently allocated in memory. This prepass loops through every tree depth, each time truncating all of the keys at the current depth and removing duplicate keys. We check the node for each key to determine whether its child nodes are allocated in memory. In each stage, keys that need to be allocated are stored in a list, and the length of this list $\times 8$ is the number of new nodes that need to be allocated, one for each child node.

With the set of unallocated keys in hand, we allocate a new set of continuous memory large enough for the new nodes, and we copy the old octree into this new location. Now, for each depth we parallelize over the keys in our collected set to initialize the new nodes. If GPU memory is available, it is advantageous to preallocate a large volume of memory to avoid this costly resizing process.

Update node values We use the same model as OctoMap, giving the probability that leaf node n is occupied given a series of sensor measurements $z_{1:t}$:

$$P(n|z_{1:t}) = \left[1 + \frac{1 - P(n|z_t)}{P(n|z_t)} \frac{1 - P(n|z_{1:t-1})}{P(n|z_{1:t-1})} \frac{P(n)}{1 - P(n)}\right]^{-1}.$$

This model conveniently reduces to addition of individual measurements when stored as a log-odds value. For convenience, we choose to use symmetric probability models where the probabilities of hit and miss are both equivalent. This reduces our log-odds calculation into simply keeping a running count of hits and misses.

To update the node values, we use the alpha channel of RGBA to encode a pseudo-log-odds of occupancy for each cell. When allocated, we initialize our cells to alpha = 127, which we interpret as probability 0.5 because it is the midpoint for an 8-bit unsigned integer. For a Kinect sensor, we use a probability of hit such that each observation adds 2 to the alpha value. This is for convenience since alpha is stored as an unsigned integer, and it seems to work well for the Kinect sensor model, saturating after 64 consistent hits or misses. The more often a point is observed within a portion of space, the more confident we are that the node is occupied. This helps to filter sensor noise in depth measurements by ensuring that we consistently receive point returns from a location before considering it to be occupied.

We also filter the color values received by the camera by using a running average, using the alpha channel as a weight function. Listing 1.3 shows the update and filtering process for each node. After the values are updated in the leaves of the octree, we can trickle them into the inner limbs of the tree by having each parent assume a value that averages their children.

1.3.3 Dynamic Scenes

When building a scene where all objects are static, it would be sufficient to update the map in only an additive fashion as discussed earlier. However, when objects are moving, it becomes necessary to have an update process that can remove parts of the map when they are observed to be unoccupied. Similar to OctoMap, we do this by processing the free space between the camera origin and each point in our point cloud. In each update, these nodes are observed to be free. Rather than adding an additional registered hit to these nodes, we register them as misses. With enough misses, these nodes will eventually return to being unoccupied.

Once these nodes are completely unoccupied, the memory for them is released. Rather than the expensive process of shifting all of the data in memory to fill in these holes, maintaining a list of free memory slots allows future tree expansions to fill data into them first.

```
__device__ int getFirstValueAndShiftDown(octkey& key) {
  int depth = depthFromKey(key);
  int value = getValueFromKey(key, depth-1);
  key -= ((8 + value) << 3 * (depth - 1));
  key += (1 << 3 * (depth - 1));
  return value;
}

__global__ void fillNodes(const octkey* keys, int numKeys,
  const char4* values, unsigned int* octree_data) {

  int index = blockIdx.x * blockDim.x + threadIdx.x;

  //Don't do anything if out of bounds.
  if (index >= numKeys) {
    return;
  }

  //Get the key for this thread.
  octkey key = keys[index];

  //Check for invalid key.
  if (key == 1) {
    return;
  }

  int node_idx = 0;
  int child_idx = 0;
  while (key != 1) {
    //Get the child number from the first three bits of the
    //Morton code.
    node_idx = child_idx + getFirstValueAndShiftDown(key);

    if (!octree_data[2 * node_idx] & 0x40000000) {
      return;
    }

    //The lowest 30 bits are the address of the child nodes.
    child_idx = octree_data[2 * node_idx] & 0x3FFFFFFF;
  }

  char4 new_value = values[index];
  unsigned int current_value = octree_data[2 * node_idx + 1];

  char4 current;
  short current_alpha = current_value >> 24;
  current.r = current_value & 0xFF;
  current.g = (current_value >> 8) & 0xFF;
  current.b = (current_value >> 16) & 0xFF;

  //Implement a pseudo low-pass filter with Laplace smoothing.
  float f1 = (1 - ((float)current_alpha/256.0f));
  float f2 = (float)current_alpha / 256.0f;
  new_value.r = new_value.r * f1 + current.r * f2;
  new_value.g = new_value.g * f1 + current.g * f2;
  new_value.b = new_value.b * f1 + current.b * f2;
  octree_data[2 * node_idx + 1] = ((int)new_value.r) +
    ((int)new_value.g << 8) + ((int)new_value.b << 16) +
    (min(255, current_alpha + 2) << 24);
}
```

Listing 1.3. CUDA kernel for updating values stored in octree nodes based on newly observed colors.

1.3.4 Managing Memory

The sparse octree used to represent a reconstructed 3D map will quickly grow too large to fit entirely in GPU memory. Reconstructing a typical office room at 1 cm resolution will often take as much as 6–8 GB. Use of a GPU with more memory will allow for larger scenes at higher resolutions, but there will always be applications where a physical memory increase is not practical to meet the requirements.

To handle this, we developed an out-of-core memory management framework for the octree. At first glance, this framework is a standard stack-based octree on the CPU. However, each node in the tree has an additional boolean flag indicating whether the node is at the root of a subtree that is located in linear GPU memory. It also holds a pointer to its location on the GPU as well as its size.

Next, these nodes can push/pull the data to and from the GPU. The push method uses recursion to convert the stack-based data into a linear array in CPU memory, then copies the memory to the GPU. It avoids the need to over-allocate or reallocate the size of the linear memory by first recursing through the node's children to determine the size of the subtree. The pull method copies the linear memory back to the CPU, then uses it to recursively generate it as a stack-based structure.

We use a *least recently used* (LRU) approach where all methods operating on the tree must provide an associated bounding box of the area that they will affect. First, this allows us to make sure that the entire affected volume is currently on the GPU before attempting to perform the operation. The octree will also keep a history of the N most recently used bounding boxes. When space needs to be freed, it will take the union of these stored bounding boxes and pull data that lies outside of this region back to the CPU.

1.4 Rendering Techniques

1.4.1 Extracting and Instancing Voxel Cubes

The brute-force method for rendering the SVO map is to extract the color values and 3D positions of each occupied leaf node. With these values, we can render a cube at each center position with a scale based on the depth in the SVO. (See Figure 1.5.)

Extracting the voxels requires two steps. First, in a prepass where each CUDA thread is assigned a Morton code, each voxel traverses into the SVO to determine whether the node with the corresponding code is occupied. We start with a set of keys at the minimum depth, iteratively create the 8 child keys for the occupied nodes, and remove the unoccupied node keys. Once we have determined the valid keys, we allocate space for our resulting data and extract it from the SVO into the buffer. We decode the Morton codes back into the 3D positions for each voxel.

Figure 1.5. Octree scene constructed from a live Kinect camera stream using CUDA. (a) The original raw camera image. (b) Voxel extraction and instanced rendering of an SVO map. (c) Voxel cone tracing of an SVO map. (d) Voxel cone tracing from a virtual camera view that does not match the physical view.

Once we have the position and color for each occupied voxel, we map it to an OpenGL *texture buffer object* (TBO), which is used by our vertex shader that instances a colored cube to represent the voxels (Listing 1.4).

1.4.2 Voxel Cone Tracing

Voxel cone tracing (VCT) is a physically based rendering technique similar to ray tracing [Crassin et al. 11]. It exploits the SVO data structure to avoid Monte Carlo integration of multiple rays to approximate the integral of the rendering equation. Instead, it approximates a cone by sampling values at higher levels of the SVO as the cone becomes wider. If all of the needed lighting information is incorporated into the octree, mip-mapping the values into the inner tree branches and texture interpolation performs the integration step inherently. (See Figure 1.6.)

We used voxel cone tracing to render our scene with CUDA. For each pixel, a CUDA thread traverses along a ray and samples a value from the SVO. The

```
#version 420

uniform mat4 u_mvpMatrix;
uniform mat3 u_normMatrix;
uniform float u_scale;

out vec3 fs_position;
out vec3 fs_normal;
out vec3 fs_color;

layout (location = 0) in vec4 vox_cent;
layout (location = 1) in vec4 vox_color;

layout (binding = 0) uniform samplerBuffer voxel_centers;
layout (binding = 1) uniform samplerBuffer voxel_colors;

const vec3 cube_vert[8] = vec3[8](
    vec3(-1.0, -1.0,  1.0),
    vec3( 1.0, -1.0,  1.0),
    vec3( 1.0,  1.0,  1.0),
    vec3(-1.0,  1.0,  1.0),
    vec3(-1.0, -1.0, -1.0),
    vec3( 1.0, -1.0, -1.0),
    vec3( 1.0,  1.0, -1.0),
    vec3(-1.0,  1.0, -1.0)
);

const int cube_ind[36] = int[36] (
    0, 1, 2, 2, 3, 0,
    3, 2, 6, 6, 7, 3,
    7, 6, 5, 5, 4, 7,
    4, 0, 3, 3, 7, 4,
    0, 1, 5, 5, 4, 0,
    1, 5, 6, 6, 2, 1
);

void main (void){
    gl_Position = u_mvpMatrix *
        vec4(cube_vert[cube_ind[gl_VertexID]]*u_scale +
        vec3(texelFetch(voxel_centers, gl_InstanceID)), 1.0);
    fs_position = gl_Position.xyz;
    fs_normal = u_normMatrix *
        normalize(cube_vert[cube_ind[gl_VertexID]]);
    fs_color = vec3(texelFetch(voxel_colors, gl_InstanceID));
}
```

Listing 1.4. GLSL vertex shader for instancing of colored voxel cubes using a TBO bound from CUDA.

octree depth sampled, d, for a distance, r, along the ray with a camera field of view, θ, the number of pixels in the camera image, n, and with an octree root node size, o, is given by

$$d = \left\lceil \log_2 \frac{o * n}{r \tan \theta} \right\rceil. \tag{1.1}$$

Each pixel continues to integrate its total color value using the alpha channel until it reaches its maximum of 255, or until the ray reaches a maximum length (usually 10 m).

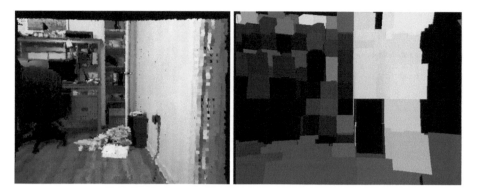

Figure 1.6. Multiple renders of the same scene, both with voxel cone tracing. On the left, the maximum resolution is 1 cm, while on the right, it is capped at 16 cm.

1.5   Results

We tested the time required to expand, update, and filter an SVO scene with an updated point cloud frame from a Kinect sensor. We found that the time increased logarithmically with the number of allocated nodes in the SVO (Figure 1.7). The kernels that update the SVO execute serially in tree depth, but parallel over the nodes in each depth. The octree structure divides the nodes

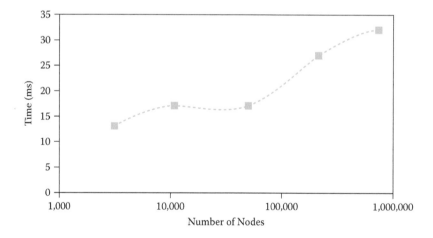

Figure 1.7. Evaluation of updating the SVO scene from a Kinect camera using an NVIDIA GTX 770 with 2 GB memory. The same scene is updated with multiple maximum depths. The edge length of the full SVO is 1.96 meters. We evaluate the update time and compare it with the change in the number of allocated nodes in the octree.

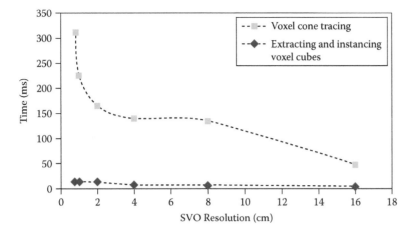

Figure 1.8. The SVO scene rendered with both voxel extraction and instancing and cone tracing (same scene as Figure 1.7). Voxel extraction and instancing achieves real-time performance at every resolution tested, but cone tracing slows down below real-time resolutions higher than 16 cm.

so that we can expect the depth to increase logarithmically with the number of nodes.

We compare the rendering time between both the voxel instancing and voxel cone tracing approaches with an identical scene at multiple levels of resolution. We found that the voxel instancing approach has steady real-time performance at all resolutions tested. Even at the lowest resolution, the voxel cone tracing technique was not real time. The runtime for VCT grows exponentially as the resolution increases (Figure 1.8).

1.6 Conclusion and Future Work

We have found that use of an SVO map allows for memory-efficient mapping. Camera noise is quickly filtered out within a few frames to create stable scenes. For debug views, voxel extraction and instanced rendering is useful for rendering values of the map at different levels of resolution. However, voxel cone tracing requires minimal additional computational cost and can render the scene at different views with similar quality to that of the original. (See Figure 1.9.)

There are similar mapping techniques implemented using conventional CPU computing, and we would like to benchmark the performance of our GPU mapping method against them on common data sets. We will also evaluate performance of complete AR pipelines (localization, mapping, rendering) with various hardware (GPUs, cameras) to determine the conditions where our techniques work best.

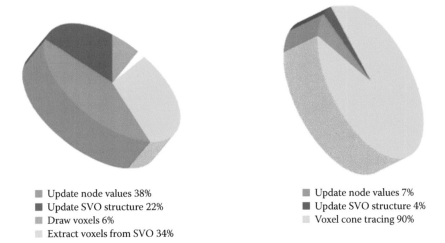

Update node values 38%
Update SVO structure 22%
Draw voxels 6%
Extract voxels from SVO 34%

Update node values 7%
Update SVO structure 4%
Voxel cone tracing 90%

Figure 1.9. Using NVIDIA GeForce GTX 770 with 2 GB RAM, we measure the relative runtimes of mapping and rendering stages. In both cases, we map and render a $4 \times 4 \times 4$ meter volume at 2 cm resolution: Mapping and rendering with voxel instancing takes 32 ms (left) and with voxel cone tracing requires 184 ms (right).

We would like to explore use of intrinsic images in preprocessing the color values before adding them to the map. This would allow us to re-cast an artificial light into the scene without the rendering artifacts that we expect from improper shading. Rendering with a virtual light source would also blend virtual objects into the scene by casting shadows.

Also, today we are only able to add static virtual objects to our constructed scenes. It would be useful for dynamic virtual objects to move efficiently within the SVO.

1.7   Acknowledgment

We would like to thank Nick Armstrong-Crews for his valuable feedback in reviewing this chapter.

Bibliography

[Crassin et al. 09] Cyril Crassin, Fabrice Neyret, Sylvain Lefebvre, and Elmar Eisermann. "GigaVoxels: Ray-Guided Streaming for Efficient and Detailed Voxel Rendering." In *Proceedings of the 2009 Symposium on Interactive 3D Graphics and Games*, pp. 15–22. New York: ACM, 2009.

[Crassin et al. 11] Cyril Crassin, Fabrice Neyret, Miguel Sainz, Simon Green, and Elmar Eisemann. "Interactive Indirect Illumination Using Voxel Cone Tracing." *Computer Graphics Forum* 30:7 (2011), 1921–1930.

[Dryanovski et al. 13] Ivan Dryanovski, Roberto G. Valenti, and Jizhong Xiao. "Fast Visual Odometry and Mapping from RGB-D Data." In *IEEE International Conference on Robotics and Automation (ICRA)*, pp. 2305–2310. Washington, DC: IEEE Press, 2013.

[Hornung et al. 13] Armin Hornung, Kai M. Wurm, Maren Bennewitz, Cyril Stachniss, and Wolfram Burgard. "OctoMap: An Efficient Probabilistic 3D Mapping Framework Based on Octrees." *Autonomous Robots* 34:3 (2013), 189–206.

[Newcombe et al. 11] R.A. Newcombe, S. Izadi, O. Hilliges, D. Molyneaux, D. Kim, A. J. Davison, P. Kohli, J. Shotton, S. Hodges, and A. Fitzgibbon. "KinectFusion: Real-Time Dense Surface Mapping and Tracking." In *IEEE International Symposium on Mixed and Augmented Reality (ISMAR)*, pp. 127–136. Washington, DC: IEEE Press, 2011.

[Steinbrucker et al. 11] F. Steinbrucker, J. Sturm, and D. Cremers. "Real-Time Visual Odometry from Dense RGB-D Images." Paper presented at ICCV Workshop on Live Dense Reconstruction with Moving Cameras, Barcelona, Spain, November 12, 2011.

[Whelan et al. 12] T. Whelan, J. McDonald, M. Fallon M. Kaess, H. Johannsson, and J. Leonard. "Kintinuous: Spatially Extended KinectFusion." Paper presented at RSS Workshop on RGB-D: Advanced Reasoning with Depth Cameras, Sydney, Australia, July 9–13, 2012.

2

VI

Interactive Sparse Eulerian Fluid
Alex Dunn

2.1 Overview

Real-time simulation of fluid dynamics has been around for a while now, but it has not made its way into many games because of its performance characteristics, which have never been at a level acceptable enough to be deemed "game-ready." In game development, there is this imaginary scale used to determine whether or not a piece of visual effects (VFX) will make it into a game: on one end of this scale is ultra-high visual quality—which is used to describe the purest of physically based effects—and at the other end is low-quality/performance. All real-time VFX are subject to this scale, and all lie somewhere around the middle of the two extremes; this can be thought of as the *performance/quality tradeoff*. When it is desirable to take an effect from the physically based perfection side over to the performance (game-ready) side, then some work has to be done in order to significantly reduce the cost of that effect while still maintaining as much quality as possible.

This chapter describes a method for computing and rendering smoke-like fluid in real time on the GPU using DirectX 11+ with a key focus on the advantages of simulating and storing these simulations in a sparse domain. Simulation is only half the battle; in order to view fluid in its full glory, advancement in rendering is also required. This chapter also presents an extension of common volume rendering techniques that dramatically reduces the cost associated with rendering volumetric fluid simulations.

2.2 Introduction

Fluid emulation in games is quite common—e.g., things like smoke and fire effects—and typically these effects are implemented as particle systems using a relatively simple equation of motion—compared to its real-world counterparts. It is these equations of motion that ultimately dictate how the overall effect looks. Real-time fluid simulation offers a physically based alternative to particle kinematics, where these effects can move and interact with the world in a much more realistic manner. Simulation of this complexity does not come without a cost, but using the technique outlined in this chapter, we can reduce this cost to the absolute minimum—a step up on other real-time techniques for simulating fluid.

The type of fluid simulation in question is the *Eulerian* simulation; this is a grid-based simulation in which quantitative fluid data such as velocity and pressure are calculated at fixed cell intervals across a Cartesian grid. On the GPU, it is fairly typical to represent this grid using volume textures.

The Eulerian method for simulating fluid is not to be confused with *Lagrangian* fluid simulation, like SPH (smoothed particle hydrodynamics) [Müller et al. 03], which does not use the fixed cell model, but instead uses free-moving particles to calculate this data.

Current Eulerian simulation implementations in use today tend to perform a simulation across the entire grid. This is not only computationally expensive, but it consumes a lot of memory in 3D—amongst other things. This chapter will be addressing these issues by proposing a method for simulating and storing these grids sparsely.

2.3 GPU Eulerian Fluid Simulation

A simplified motion of fluid can be expressed by the inviscid Euler equation for incompressible flow [Landau and Lifschitz 82, p. 3]:

$$\frac{\partial u}{\partial t} + u \cdot \Delta u = -\frac{\Delta P}{\rho}.$$

(The incompressibility constraint dictates that the volume of the fluid does not change over time, a perceptually subtle modification that allows for a significant reduction in mathematics.) Using this, we can fairly accurately approximate the motion of fluid.

Solving the above equation on the GPU requires us to break it down into smaller pieces and compute each piece individually, one after the other [Harris 04]. Breaking the equation down in this manner exploits the parallel nature of the GPU, in order to achieve the most optimal speed possible. Each equation section can be implemented using compute shaders in DirectX 11. (See Figure 2.1.)

Figure 2.1. Simulation flow diagram, with time traversal between the various stages of simulation.

```
Texture3D<float4> g_VelocityRO  : register(t0);
RWTexture3D<float4> g_VelocityRW : register(u0);

[numthreads(8, 4, 4)]
void main(uint3 idx : SV_DispatchThreadID)
{
    float3 uvw = idx * g_invGridSize.xyz + g_halfVoxel.xyz;
    float3 relativePos = uvw - g_emitter.Position.xyz;

    // A simple falloff function.
    float invSqrMag = saturate(1 - dot(relativePos, relativePos) /
                      (g_emitter.Radius*g_emitter.Radius)); // [0-1]

    float strength = invSqrMag * invSqrMag * invSqrMag
                     * g_emitter.Force;

    float4 velocity = g_VelocityRO[idx];

    velocity.xyz += g_emitter.Direction.xyz * strength;

    g_VelocityRW[idx] = velocity;
}
```

Listing 2.1. A compute shader emitting fluid into the system using a sphere primitive. It is worth noting that this has been simplified to only update the velocity textures—in practise it will likely be favorable to also update the density/opacity textures.

2.4 Simulation Stages

2.4.1 Inject

The *inject* stage is not strictly speaking part of the equation, but it is a necessary step in the simulation process. It is here that fluid is "injected" into the simulation domain through various user-defined emitters; such emitters can be based on primitive shapes, like spheres or cubes (see Listing 2.1), or they can be more complex, such as emitting from a texture or mesh.

2.4.2 Advect

During the *advect* stage, fluid quantities (such as opacity—for rendering—or velocity) are moved through the grid with respect to velocity. The advection technique used in this chapter is backward advection, which is a first-order scheme and as such is subject to a degree of numerical diffusion due to interpolation artifacts between the fixed grid cell locations. See Listing 2.2.

2.4.3 Pressure

The *pressure* term of the equation must be solved, and for that there are many options; for simplicity's sake, this chapter will focus on the Jacobi method for

```
Texture3D<float4> g_VelocityRO : register(t0);
RWTexture3D<float4> g_VelocityRW : register(u0);

[numthreads(8, 4, 4)]
void main(uint3 idx: SV_DispatchThreadID)
{
    float3 velocity = g_VelocityRO[idx].xyz;

    float3 uvw = idx * g_invGridSize.xyz + g_halfVoxel.xyz;
    float3 sample = uvw - velocity;

    float3 newVelocity = g_VelocityRO.Sample(BilinearBorder, sample);

    g_VelocityRW[idx] = float4(newVelocity, 0);
}
```

Listing 2.2. A compute shader advection kernel—first-order backward advection is implemented. This shader has been simplified to only show the velocity advection—but other fluid quantities such as density/opacity should also be updated.

computing pressure in a localized system. The Jacobi method is an iterative solver, and though this method can yield very accurate results, the number of iterations required for satisfactory convergence is quite high. It can be too high, in fact, for real-time simulation. For this reason when using the Jacobi solver in real-time simulations, more often than not a small number of iterations is used—which leads to reduced quality—or a different method for calculating pressure is used—such as the multi-grid method [Chentanez and Müller 11], which converges much faster. For simplicities sake we are using a Jacobi solver with a reasonable number of iterations. See Listing 2.3.

```
Texture3D<float2> g_PressureRO : register(t0);
RWTexture3D<float2> g_PressureRW : register(u0);

[numthreads(8, 4, 4)]
void main(uint3 idx: SV_DispatchThreadID)
{
    float2 C = g_PressureRO[idx];

    float U = g_PressureRO[idx + int3(0, 1, 0)].x;
    float D = g_PressureRO[idx - int3(0, 1, 0)].x;
    float L = g_PressureRO[idx - int3(1, 0, 0)].x;
    float R = g_PressureRO[idx + int3(1, 0, 0)].x;
    float F = g_PressureRO[idx + int3(0, 0, 1)].x;
    float B = g_PressureRO[idx - int3(0, 0, 1)].x;

    float divergence = C.y;
    float pressure = (U + D + L + R + F + B - divergence) / 6;

    g_PressureRW[idx] = float2(pressure, divergence);
}
```

Listing 2.3. A compute shader that calculates pressure using the Jacobi method. This shader should be run for several iterations in order to achieve accurate results.

```
Texture3D<float4> g_VelocityRO : register(t0);
RWTexture3D<float4> g_VorticityRW : register(u0);

[numthreads(8, 4, 4)]
void main(uint3 idx : SV_DispatchThreadID)
{
    float3 U = g_VelocityRO[idx + int3(0, 1, 0)].xyz;
    float3 D = g_VelocityRO[idx - int3(0, 1, 0)].xyz;
    float3 L = g_VelocityRO[idx - int3(1, 0, 0)].xyz;
    float3 R = g_VelocityRO[idx + int3(1, 0, 0)].xyz;
    float3 F = g_VelocityRO[idx + int3(0, 0, 1)].xyz;
    float3 B = g_VelocityRO[idx - int3(0, 0, 1)].xyz;

    float3 dX = R - L;
    float3 dY = U - D;
    float3 dZ = F - B;

    float3 vorticity = float3((dY.z - dZ.y), (dZ.x - dX.z),
                              (dX.y - dY.x));
    g_VorticityRW[idx] = float4(length(vorticity), vorticity);
}
```

Listing 2.4. A compute shader calculating the curl gradient of the velocity field and storing that vector, along with its magnitude, in a separate vorticity field.

2.4.4 Vorticity Confinement

Vortices in fluid dynamics best describe the swirling or rotational motion of turbulent flow. Due to dissipation of fluid details caused by first-order advection schemes, it can be desirable to detect these vortices and increase motion around their center of rotation. Doing so in a GPU solver is a two-step process first introduced in [Fedkiw et al. 01] and is known as *vorticity confinement*.

First, vortices are determined by calculating the tangential gradient of the velocity grid and storing the magnitude along with the vector in a vorticity grid. See Listing 2.4. The vorticity grid is later used to apply a rotational force in the evolve stage, which adds the swirling motion back in.

2.4.5 Evolve

The *evolve* stage quantifies all forces in the system and ticks the simulation. See Listing 2.5. It is here that the vorticity force described in the pervious section is applied, but it is also what is typically referred to as the *project stage*—where the force coming from pressure is applied.

```
Texture3D<float4> g_VelocityRO : register(t0);
Texture3D<float4> g_PressureRO : register(t1);
Texture3D<float4> g_VorticityRO : register(t2);

RWTexture3D<float4> g_VelocityRW : register(u0);

[numthreads(8, 4, 4)]
void main(uint3 idx : SV_DispatchThreadID)
{
    float4 FC = g_VelocityRO[idx];

  // Apply the density force.
    {
        float U = g_PressureRO[idx + int3(0, 1, 0)].x;
        float D = g_PressureRO[idx - int3(0, 1, 0)].x;
        float L = g_PressureRO[idx - int3(1, 0, 0)].x;
        float R = g_PressureRO[idx + int3(1, 0, 0)].x;
        float F = g_PressureRO[idx + int3(0, 0, 1)].x;
        float B = g_PressureRO[idx - int3(0, 0, 1)].x;

        float dX = R - L;
        float dY = U - D;
        float dZ = F - B;

        FC.xyz -= float3(dX, dY, dZ) * 0.5f;
    }

  // Apply the vorticity force.
    {
        float4 C = g_VorticityRO[idx];

        float3 uvw = idx * g_invGridSize.xyz + g_halfVoxel.xyz;
        float U = g_VorticityRO.Sample(PointClamp, uvw + g_invSize.wyw).x;

        float D = g_VorticityRO.Sample(PointClamp, uvw - g_invSize.wyw).x;

        float R = g_VorticityRO.Sample(PointClamp, uvw - g_invSize.xww).x;

        float L = g_VorticityRO.Sample(PointClamp, uvw + g_invSize.xww).x;

        float F = g_VorticityRO.Sample(PointClamp, uvw + g_invSize.wwz).x;

        float B = g_VorticityRO.Sample(PointClamp, uvw - g_invSize.wwz).x;

        float dX = R - L;
        float dY = U - D;
        float dZ = F - B;

        float3 force = float3(dX, dY, dZ);

        // Do not normalize(0).
        if (dot(force, force) > 0.0f)
        {
        float3 vorticityForce = cross(normalize(force), C.yzw);
        FC.xyz += vorticityForce * g_VorticityForce;
      }
  }

  g_VelocityRW[idx] = FC;
}
```

Listing 2.5. A compute shader that sums up all the forces acting on the fluid and advances the simulation to the next frame.

Simulation (256³)

☐ Inject   ☐ Advect   ☐ Vorticity   ☐ Pressure   ■ Evolve

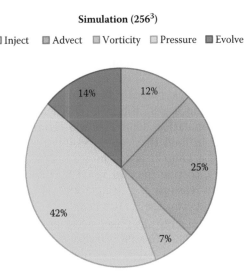

Figure 2.2. A chart showing the GPU cycle distribution of simulation stages across a number of modern GPUs.

2.5 Problems

2.5.1 Performance

Using the code above, a simple test application was devised. This test was run on a number of GPUs, and the chart in Figure 2.2 shows the average distribution of simulation work among the various stages of the simulation.

The top two hitters in terms of performance are the pressure and advect stages—and for similar reasons. Using GPU profiling, we can see that the amount of data the GPU is required to read is incredibly large. Doing some back-of-the-envelope calculations, we can see that the pressure stage (with 10 iterations on a 256^3 grid) reads around 2.5 GB per simulation cycle. Given that an NVIDIA GTX980 has a memory bandwidth of 224 GB/sec [NVIDIA n.d.], that would allow a speed-of-light FPS of 90—for the pressure stage alone. The advect stage suffers from a similar problem. Note how the advect stage accounts for 25% of the total simulation time (slightly more than half of that of pressure), but the amount of data read per simulation cycle (using the same conditions as we did for pressure) is only around 864 MB (around three times less than pressure). The additional problem with the advect stage is the relatively low cache hit rate caused by sampling voxels in a seemingly random sampled pattern—this is because we read from locations in the volume relative to the velocity at each cell.

2.5.2 Features

As well as the main performance concerns discussed above, there are some other flaws with this type of fluid simulation that we would like to address in the solution.

Fluid is not naturally box shaped! The Eulerian fluid simulation attempts to encapsulate fluid within a grid volume. This leads to one of two common problems: either the simulation domain is too tightly discretised around the flowing-fluid—resulting in fluid that can be visibly seen leaving the simulation space—or the simulation domain is too large—and there is a vast amount of empty simulation space, costing the user in GPU cycles and memory. Both are undesirable for separate reasons, and dealing with these issues consumes much time in authoring—time better spent elsewhere.

In a game scenario, it is more than likely that more than one fluid simulation volume will be required. (How often do you just see a single particle system in a game?) Doing this with current fluid simulation implementations would require placing and configuring many small simulation volumes around the game scene, or placing one large volume in some cases. The problem with this ("many volumes") approach is that each simulation is separate. Forgetting the fact that this means lots of time must be spent in authoring having to place all these volumes, try to reduce clipping/wastage, etc. But perhaps most importantly, *these simulation volumes are individual*; in other words, there is no volume-to-volume interaction. Sure, it is possible to implement such a thing, but it is nontrivial; would it not be better if this "just worked"?

The ideal approach would be to create a single large volume that would encompass the entire game scene, avoiding all the above mentioned problems. In order to maintain satisfactory visual fidelity for such a simulation volume, an extremely high grid density would be required—Figure 2.3 shows the memory consumed by a single volume texture across a range of grid densities.

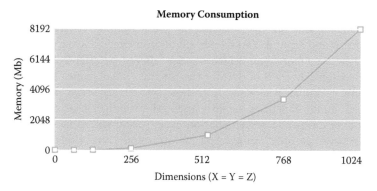

Figure 2.3. Graph showing the memory consumption of a 4-channel, 16-bit floating point volume texture across a variety of resolutions.

Figure 2.4. The brick discretization of the simulation domain.

Considering that (at the time of writing this chapter) the largest memory capacity on any consumer GPU is 12 GB—and that this graph only shows memory consumption for a single texture—running a simulation at higher than 256^3 resolution in a real game scenario is not practical yet. This is where the idea of sparse simulation comes in, which decouples (mostly) the cost of simulation—in terms of memory and computational complexity—from the grid resolution, which makes it possible to create highly detailed simulations that cover a large space (such as an entire game scene).

2.5.3 Sparse Simulation

Going back to a point touched on earlier, *wastage* is a problem born from creating largely empty simulation volumes in an attempt to encapsulate the entire fluid simulation within its bounded domain. It is quite likely that wastage occurs—to some degree—in every fluid volume. That is to say, there is likely a percentage of the volume that contains data that does not affect the result of the simulation— this is an assumption based on the likelihood that fluid is not necessarily box shaped. The first optimization presented here attempts to address this by calculating a sparse domain for a simulation to run within.

Bricking is not a new concept in computer graphics; in the context of fluid simulation, it is the process of dividing up the simulation volume at regular intervals of voxels, and each grouping of voxels is now furthermore known as a *brick*. (See Figure 2.4.) The idea is that each brick can be simulated independently of the others, making it possible to disable bricks that do not affect the simulation.

By creating an additional volume texture, it is possible to track which bricks are of interest to the simulation. This volume texture is called a *brick map* and should have dimensions equal to the number of bricks contained within the simulation on each axis. Storing either a 1 or a 0 in each voxel of the brick map— depending on whether the brick requires simulation, or if it should be ignored—is an effective method for tracking active simulation bricks.

Using an entire voxel to store either a 1 or 0 may seem wasteful; however, it does not require atomics unlike other methods [Gruen 15], which keeps it nice and fast. Constraining the algorithm to only allow for setting either the entire brick map to 0 at once (e.g., the clear at the start of the simulation frame) or

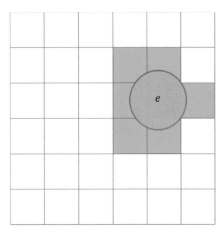

Figure 2.5. A 2D representation of a simulation grid—note the primitive emitter e and the overlapping simulation bricks denoted in red.

a particular voxel to 1 based on some condition, avoids the need for atomics without introducing any race conditions.

When the simulation first starts, a way of identifying which bricks should initially be part of the simulation domain is essential. Emitters specify where fluid gets injected into the simulation. This makes it possible to determine which bricks the emitter(s) occupy and to use this information to kick the simulation off. (See Figure 2.5.) It is also worth doing this calculation throughout the life of the simulation if the emitter moves from frame to frame so that any bricks it is overlapping continue to be part of the simulation domain.

Once the actual simulation is underway, a way of identifying which bricks should or should not continue to be part of the simulation is required. For this two new terms are introduced—*expansion* and *reduction*—and both are handled during the old evolve stage.

Expansion occurs when fluid moves from one brick to another; this can be calculated by checking if the axial velocity in a simulation cell is large enough to transverse the brick boundary. If so, the neighboring brick must be included in the next simulation frame.

Reduction, which is the opposite of expansion, occurs when fluid dissipates or completely moves out of a brick. In this algorithm, this is taken care of by clearing the brick map at the beginning of every simulation step and letting expansion do its work.

Figure 2.6 shows how the sparse simulation looks. Note the addition of the new steps (in blue) that were not in the basic algorithm initially put forward in Figure 2.1. The first is a *clear* step that sets all bricks to an "ignore" state in the brick map. This is done before each simulation frame. After the usual

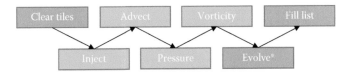

Figure 2.6. A chronological flow diagram showing the various stages of sparse simulation. Note the addition of new stages in blue—compare to Figure 2.1.

```
Texture3D<uint> g_BrickMapRO : register(t0);
AppendStructredBuffer<uint4> g_ListRW : register(u0);

[numthreads(8, 4, 4)]
void main(uint3 idx : SV_DispatchThreadID)
{
    if(g_BrickMapRO[idx] != 0)
    {
        g_ListRW.Append(idx);
    }
}
```

Listing 2.6. A compute shader to create a linear list of bricks to be included in the sparse simulation domain.

simulation steps, inject, advect, pressure, and vorticity—which have not changed significantly—the check for expansion is inserted in the evolve stage after the velocity of each cell has been calculated in preparation for the next frame. Lastly, in order to feed the following simulation frame, a list of bricks that are part of the next frame simulation needs to be populated. This is done using a compute shader, run at a granularity of one thread per brick; see Listing 2.6.

When using a list of brick indices like this, a subtle modification to the previous code listings for the various simulation stages is required, allowing the algorithm to handle the sparse simulation—that is, to dispatch enough thread groups (number of bricks × number of thread groups per brick)—and to check the index of the current brick from the list. See Listing 2.7.

```
StructredBuffer<uint4> g_ListRO : register(t0);

[numthreads(8, 4, 4)]
void main(uint3 threadIdx: SV_DispatchThreadID)
{
    uint3 idx = g_Sparse ? g_ListRO[GetBrickIdx(threadIdx)].xyz :
    threadIdx;
    ...
}
```

Listing 2.7. A code snippet demonstrating how to determine the current location of a simulation cell when simulating sparsely compared to non-sparsely. The variable g_Sparse should be set accordingly.

Physical memory

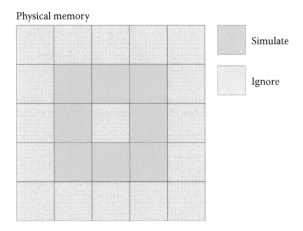

Simulate

Ignore

Figure 2.7. A 2D representation of the memory usage in a typical simulation. All memory is allocated but only regions pertinent to simulation are used.

All of this allows for sparsely simulating fluid but so far does not offer up anything in terms of memory savings. (See Figure 2.7.)

By only sparsely computing a fluid simulation in the above manner, there has not actually been a reduction in any memory used. This method for storing simulations is called *uncompressed storage*. Recalling back, part of the problem with using fluid simulations in games is the awful memory consumption. So, what are the options?

One solution is to use compressed storage. (See Figure 2.8.) A volume texture is used to store offsets for each brick into what can conceptually be thought of as a list of bricks (`vector<brick>`). This results in good memory consumption as it is only required to allocate memory for bricks that are pertinent to the simulation. The downside to this approach is that in order to reap the memory saving benefits, the list resource must be dynamically resized on the fly. The better the memory savings, the more aggressive the resizing strategy has to be; and resizing is not free! Along with the resizing issue, another problem here is that all cell lookups now require an indirection. This is called *software translation*, and it is particularly bad in the case of a bilinear filtering operation that happens to straddle a brick corner. In this case, each of the eight lookups that are part of the filtering kernel may end up reading from regions of memory very distant from one another, affecting cache performance. One option to mitigate this issue is to pad each brick with one extra cell on each side and to copy neighboring data into these padding cells before simulation.

As a representative example, take a four-cubed brick and add the padding cells, as in Figure 2.9. The number of cells per brick will more than triple in this example. Still an option, the memory savings on the whole might outweigh the extra cells required for padding; however, it is not ideal.

Indirection table

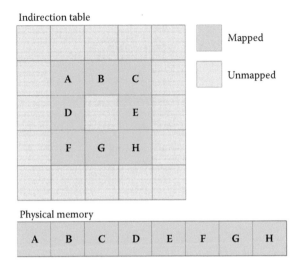

Physical memory

Figure 2.8. A diagram showing the memory usage pattern in a compressed simulation. Physical memory can be seen along the bottom while the 2D indirection table showing regions of simulation space mapped and unmapped above.

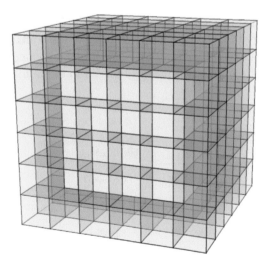

Figure 2.9. A simulation brick padded to include neighboring values. In this case the number of cells in the original brick is 64, and a further 152 cells are required for padding.

```
ID3D11Device3* pDevice3 = nullptr;
pDevice->QueryInterface(&pDevice3);

D3D11_FEATURE_DATA_D3D11_OPTIONS2 support;
pDevice3->CheckFeatureSupport(D3D11_FEATURE_D3D11_OPTIONS2,
                              &support,
                              sizeof(support));

m_UseVTR = support.TiledResourcesTier ==
D3D11_TILED_RESOURCES_TIER_3;
```

Listing 2.8. A snippet of C++ code demonstrating how to query the driver for volume tiled resources support in DirectX 11.3.

2.5.4   Enter DirectX 11.3 . . .

Tiled resources are not new; support for 2D tiled resources has been around since DirectX 11.2. In DirectX 11.3 it is now possible to extend this functionality into the third dimension, allowing for tiled resource operations on volume textures—this feature is called *Volume Tiled Resources* (VTRs).

With DirectX 11.3 cvomes the return of the `caps` system used in DirectX 9—in other words, it is once again no longer safe to assume as a developer that all GPUs that support DirectX 11.3 can support all its features; and one of those features is VTRs. Querying the device for VTR support is demonstrated in the code example in Listing 2.8. This means that as a developer a fall-back technique should be considered for the case where VTRs are not available.

Similar to DirectX 11.2 tiled resources, each tile must be 64 KB in size. With respect to volume resources, this means that tiles are limited to the dimensions shown in Table 2.1.

BPP	Tile Dimensions
8	64×32×32
16	32×32×32
32	32×32×16
64	32×16×16
128	16×16×16

Table 2.1. The various tile dimensions with respect to the number of bytes per voxel.

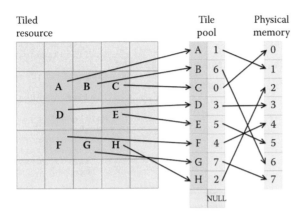

Figure 2.10. A 2D representation of a simulation grid using tiled resources.

Using tiled resources, it is possible to get the best features of the two previously mentioned memory storage techniques: compressed and uncompressed. This is partly because tiled resources appear and behave like regular volume resources (a trait from uncompressed storage) and partly because, in terms of physical memory, only a minimal set of tiles necessary to compute the simulation are allocated.

Tiled resources are a high-level abstraction of the paged memory model used in modern GPUs. Physical memory is allocated in pages, and virtual address tables (pointers in C++ terms) allow indexing of the hardware pages. Most modern memory architectures work in this fashion.

In the context of fluid simulation, tiled resources can be used to sparsely allocate the simulation grid (one brick per tile), and the virtual address table can be manipulated to represent our indirection volume. (See Figure 2.10.) This becomes a powerful tool because, like compressed storage, simulation memory is only allocated for select bricks and the indirect cell lookup can be handled in hardware—and becomes as simple as any paged memory read (which is any read on any resource on modern GPUs). All the tricky corner cases exposed by compressed storage are handled at the hardware level, which means speed-of-light memory access—something that is of high value in bandwidth-bound regimes.

Of course, there is a downside to using tiled resources, and that is that tile mappings must be updated from the CPU—the DirectX API does not allow for any other method at this present time.

Updating the tile mappings from the CPU is done using the DirectX API call `UpdateTileMappings`—which has not changed since DirectX 11.2. (See Listing 2.9.)

It is highly recommended when using this API that tile mapping deltas are calculated and used within the API—mappings can be one of three states: mapped, unchanged, and unmapped. Using the unchanged state to define which tiles have

```
HRESULT ID3D11DeviceContext2 :: UpdateTileMappings (
    ID3D11Resource                          *pTiledResource ,
    UINT                                     NumTiledResourceRegions ,
    const D3D11_TILED_RESOURCE_COORDINATE
                              *pTiledResourceRegionStartCoordinates ,
    const D3D11_TILE_REGION_SIZE
                                   *pTiledResourceRegionSizes ,

    ID3D11Buffer                            *pTilePool ,
    UINT                                     NumRanges ,
    const UINT                              *pRangeFlags ,
    const UINT                              *pTilePoolStartOffsets ,
    UINT                                    *pRangeTileCounts ,
    UINT                                     Flags );
```

Listing 2.9. The function prototype for the `UpdateTiledMappings` method in C++ DirectX.

not changed since the last simulation frame has significant performance benefits. This can be done using the `pRangeFlags` parameter:

Mapped	$\rightarrow$	`D3D11_TILE_RANGE_REUSE_SINGLE_TILE`
Unchanged	$\rightarrow$	`D3D11_TILE_RANGE_SKIP`
Unmapped	$\rightarrow$	`D3D11_TILE_RANGE_NULL`

It is worth reiterating the importance of the `D3D11_TILE_RANGE_SKIP` flag; without it the driver would not know which tiles can safely be skipped when updating paged memory access tables, and the performance of the `UpdateTileMappings` function would suffer *significantly* as a result.

What use is a CPU API that controls the domain bounds of a GPU simulation? Fortunately, this is a restriction that can be worked around using the (somewhat) predictable nature of fluids.

2.6   Latency Resistant Sparse Fluid Simulation

For a long time it has been possible to get data back from the GPU to the CPU, although the feature is something of a taboo in real-time graphics. The reason for which is the inherent risk of causing a CPU-GPU synchronization point. The CPU and GPU run out of sync with one another as they are two completely separate systems. The GPU is fed with commands from the CPU using the producer/consumer model of parallel systems—and reading the contents of GPU resident memory forces a synchronization of that process. The only efficient way of fetching data back from the GPU is to allow for two frames of latency in reading that data back—this ensures that the data requested has finished being processed by the GPU. (See Figure 2.11.)

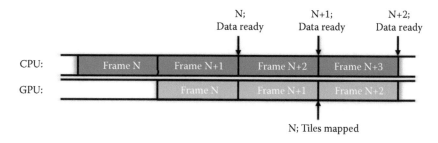

Figure 2.11. Accessing GPU resident data from the CPU without causing a synchronization point.

Reading the list of simulation bricks back on the CPU two frames after they have been calculated to feed information about which bricks should be resident in memory for the current frame would create artifacts because the resident memory would be two frames behind.

In the case of fluid simulation, this can be handled by predicting the course simulation ahead of time using simple Eulerian integration. A maximum velocity for each brick is calculated at the time of simulation, and this value is read back as part of the brick information contained within the simulation brick list. This maximum velocity is used for dead reckoning logic on the CPU, which determines the next two frames of *probable* simulation bricks and adds them to the list of *definite* bricks obtained from the GPU. This process is called the *prediction engine* in Figure 2.12.

In Figure 2.12 the flow of the overall algorithm can be seen. Again, the new stages discussed in this section are shown in blue (and, for simplicities sake, the previously covered stages for *sparse Eulerian simulation* have been combined into a single green block). Note how the simulation flow begins with a branch on the CPU. Is read-back data ready? This is a necessary step in dealing with the latency introduced by the CPU read-back. For the first two frames of the simulation or if any fluid emitter has changed, there would not be any (meaningful) data available for read-back. So, the algorithm must have a fall-back—which is to use the bricks overlapping any emitter.

2.7   Performance

A deterministic performance testing scene was constructed; a spherical emitter spins around the bottom of a simulation volume. The test was run for several minutes and the results were averaged during that time. The test was performed on a NVIDIA GTX980 using Windows 10. See the results in Table 2.2.

Clearly, the sparse grid simulation provides a significant speedup over the full grid method—however, admittedly, this amount will vary wildly on a case-by-case

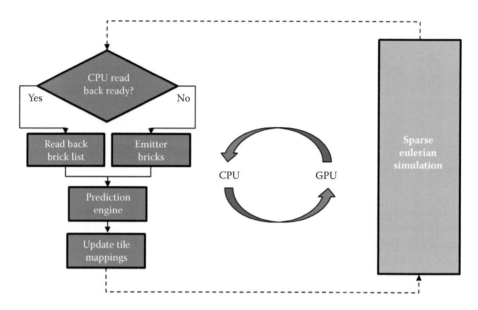

Figure 2.12. The flow diagram for latency-resistant fluid simulation. On the left (in blue) you can see the various CPU components, while on the right is the previous sparse fluid simulation algorithm presented in Figure 2.6.

		Grid Resolution			
	128^3	256^3	384^3	512^3	$1,024^3$
			Full Grid		
Num. Bricks	256	2048	6,912	16,384	131,072
Memory (MB)	80	640	2,160	5,120	40,960
Simulation	2.29 ms	19.04 ms	64.71 ms	NA	NA
			Sparse Grid		
Num. Bricks	36	146	183	266	443
Memory (MB)	11.25	45.63	57.19	83.13	138.44
Simulation	0.41 ms	1.78 ms	2.67 ms	2.94 ms	5.99 ms
Scaling Sim.	78.14%	76.46%	75.01%	NA	NA

Table 2.2. The performance statistics of the sparse simulation versus the regular simulation across a variety of grid resolutions. Note the significant reduction in time taken for the simulation. This is mostly down to the fact that the simulation volume contained lots of empty space. The "Num. Bricks" line shows how many bricks were actively involved in the simulation.

basis. The same can be said about memory consumption. Note how the 4-GB frame buffer of the GTX980 cannot run full grid simulations at a resolution of 512 or higher. This is because the simulation would not fit in memory at around 5 GB.

2.8 Sparse Volume Rendering

2.8.1 Introduction

Volumetric rendering is traditionally performed by blending a collection of samples taken from a data set at a fixed step along each screen pixel's view ray. This is usually done in real-time graphics by using a method called a ray marching [Pawasauskas 97]. The problem with the traditional approach to volume rendering with respect to fluid simulation is that many of the samples collected when traversing a screen pixels view ray would not contribute to the final color of the pixel, due to them coming from areas of the volume not containing any data—in other words, empty regions of memory. Using the information gathered from the simulation, it is possible to implement a mechanism to skip over the empty regions while performing the volume rendering, significantly reducing the number of samples collected and making the whole process faster.

2.8.2 Preprocess

Being with the list of simulation bricks calculated during simulation—this list of bricks should be available on the CPU (see Section 2.6). This list of bricks next needs to be sorted in front-to-back order before being ready for rendering.

An index/vertex buffer is constructed at start-up time. The contents will be a number of unit cubes placed at the origin, one cube for each brick—so that there are enough to cover the maximum expected number of bricks. With the number of bricks for rendering at hand, it is time to `DrawIndexed` on that index/vertex buffer, ensuring to set the correct parameters so that there is one unit cube rendered for each brick in the sorted simulation brick list.

2.8.3 Vertex Shading

During the vertex shader execution, a lookup into the simulation brick list is performed to determine the offset of the brick currently being rendered (there are a number of ways to do this, e.g., using the `SV_VertexID` semantic to index the buffer). Listing 2.10 is an example vertex shader; note how, rather than passing the texture space position `posTS` down to the pixel shader, a ray direction is calculated instead. This is to avoid any triangle order sorting artifacts that might occur during rendering. A direction is not order dependant because it has a lack of positional identity. In the pixel shader, `posTS` is recalculated for the front and back faces using a ray-box intersection test.

```
// List of brick indices to render.
StructuredBuffer<uint4> g_OccupiedTileListRO;

// Vertex shader.
v2f vsMain(float4 Pos : POSITION, uint idx : SV_VertexID)
{
  v2f o;

  // Div num verts in cube to get idx.
  uint brickIdx = idx / 8;

  // Get currently rendering brick UVW offset.
  float3 cellOffset = g_OccupiedTileListRO[ brickIdx ].xyz
                    * g_invGridSize;

  // Calculate brick size (actually uniform across grid).
  float3 brickSize = BRICK_SIZE_XYZ * g_invGridSize;

  // Bounding box for brick.
  o.boxmin = cellOffset;
  o.boxmax = cellOffset + brickSize;

  // NOTE: VB consists of a unit cube.
  float3 posTS = lerp(o.boxmin, o.boxmax, Pos.xyz);
  float3 posWS = mul(g_fluidToWorldMatrix, float4(posTS, 1)).xyz;

  o.posPS = mul(g_worldToProjectionMatrix, float4(posWS, 1));

  // Calculate ray direction in texture space.
  float3 relPosTS = posTS     g_eyePositionTS;
  o.rayDirTS = relPosTS / dot(relPosTS, g_eyeForwardTS);

  return o;
}
```

Listing 2.10. A vertex shader demonstrating how to calculate the necessary components for ray marching. A brick map index is determined from the vertex index, which is used to determine the brick offset in the simulation.

2.8.4   Pixel Shading

For each desired brick, ray marching is performed through its bounding box just as would be done for the bounding box of a regular (non-sparse) volume; this is done using a pixel shader. As ray direction is calculated and passed from the vertex shader, ray intersections must be calculated during the pixel shader stage. The code in Listing 2.11 efficiently calculates ray intersections with a box defined by its minimum and maximum bounds [Green 05].

With the pixel–view-ray intersection information, it is now possible to ray-march through each brick. Sampling from the volume tiled resource is exactly the same as sampling from a regular volume texture in HLSL. The only difference is on the memory transaction code happening behind the scenes in the driver and hardware, as discussed earlier.

```
float2 IntersectBox(Ray r, float3 boxmin, float3 boxmax)
{
    // Compute intersection of ray with all six bounding box planes.
    float3 invR = 1.0 / r.d;
    float3 tbot = invR * (boxmin.xyz - r.o);
    float3 ttop = invR * (boxmax.xyz - r.o);

    // Reorder intersections to find smallest and largest on
    // each axis.
    float3 tmin = min (ttop, tbot);
    float3 tmax = max (ttop, tbot);

    // Find the largest tmin and the smallest tmax.
    float2 t0 = max (tmin.xx, tmin.yz);
    tnear = max (t0.x, t0.y);
    t0 = min (tmax.xx, tmax.yz);

    tfar = min (t0.x, t0.y);

    return float2(tnear, tfar);
}
```

Listing 2.11. A vertex shader demonstrating how to calculate the necessary components for ray marching. A brick map index is determined from the vertex index, which is used to determine the brick offset in the simulation.

2.8.5 Bucketed Opacity Thresholding

Sparse volume rendering may provide a considerable performance boost over non-sparse techniques when rendering fluid, but the algorithm prevents handy rendering optimization typically used in regular volume rendering: early ray termination. This is because each brick is being ray-marched separately; early ray termination can (and should) be performed within the brick but cannot be extended to cover the whole volume because of this.

An alternative to early ray termination is to use *bucketed opacity thresholding* [Dunn and Bavoil 14]. Here, the depth testing hardware is repurposed to terminate rays early if their full opacity has been reached—in other words, if following samples would not contribute to the final outcome of the rendering. To do this, bricks must be presorted in a front-to-back order, and the under blend operator must be used. This is because the under blend operator stores alpha in the render target, a quantity which is required to be known. The following are the under blend mode equations for the color and alpha channel modes:

$$C_{\text{dst}} = A_{\text{dst}} \left(A_{\text{src}} C_{\text{src}} \right) + C_{\text{dst}},$$
$$A_{\text{dst}} = 0 + (1 - A_{\text{src}}) A_{\text{dst}}.$$

Bricks are grouped into view-Z buckets, each rendered in separate draw calls. Immediately following each bucket's draw call, a full screen pass must be run that checks every pixel in the render target used to render the bucket and determines

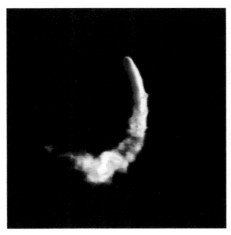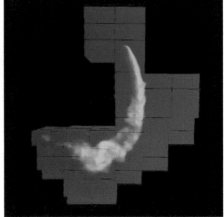

Figure 2.13. Sparse fluid simulation and rendering in action: a still of the test scene described in Section 2.5.1 (left) and an overlay of the bricking structure for the same image (right).

if there are any for which further blending operations (under operator) would have no effect. This is done by checking the alpha channel of each pixel (which holds the transmittance value when using under blending), and if it is 0 (or close to it), then this pixel can safely be discarded from all other operations.

Once these pixels have been determined, a 0 (or min-Z) value is written to the depth buffer at these locations—and with depth testing enabled when rendering the fluid volumes, this effectively implements early ray termination using the depth testing hardware present on GPUs. The stencil buffer could also have been used to perform this kind of thing; however, during testing, it became apparent that use of the depth buffer was far more performant across a wide range of hardware.

2.9   Results

Figures 2.13, 2.14, and 2.15 show the algorithm in action.

2.10   Conclusion

This chapter has described an effective method for computing and rendering smoke-based, Eulerian fluid simulations, in real-time, on the GPU using the DirectX 11+ APIs by leveraging the sparse nature of fluid, allowing the GPU to skip over areas of simulation that would not contribute to the final result. Several sparse simulation methods have been discussed—each with their own benefits and each applicable for use in modern games.

Figure 2.14. A still from the NVIDIA Mech Ti demo—using the sparse fluid simulation and rendering presented in this chapter.

Figure 2.15. A high-resolution still from the test scene mentioned in Section 2.5.1.

The recommended solution for computing fluid is described in Section 2.6; however, if platform-specific constraints prevent the use of VTRs, then a suitable fall-back can be found in Section 2.5.3. Using one of the memory storage solutions presented there—although they may yield slightly worse performance—the "uncompressed storage" method has worse memory consumption and the "compressed storage" method consumes more GPU cycles. When using one of these fall-back methods, quality reduction should be considered in order to make up for the benefits lost with VTRs.

A method for rendering the sparse grid information produced by the simulation has been demonstrated in Section 2.8. Using the list of simulation bricks from the simulation, it is possible to construct a rendering primitive to represent the sparse domain, which can then be used for volume rendering. By using this method, empty space within the simulation can be removed from the rendering process—significantly speeding up the technique.

Bibliography

[Chentanez and Müller 11] Nuttapong Chentanez and Matthias Müller. "Real-Time Eulerian Water Simulation Using a Restricted Tall Cell Grid." In *ACM SIGGRAPH 2011 Papers*, article no. 82. New York: ACM, 2011.

[Dunn and Bavoil 14] Alex Dunn and Louis Bavoil. "Transparency (or Translucency) Rendering." https://developer.nvidia.com/content/transparency-or-translucency-rendering, 2014.

[Fedkiw et al. 01] R. Fedkix, J. Stam, and H. W. Jensen. "Visual Simulation of Smoke." In *SIGGRAPH '01: Proceedings of the 28th Annual Conference on Computer Graphics and Interactive Techniques*, pp. 15–22. New York: ACM, 2001.

[Green 05] Simon Green. "Volume Rendering for Games." http://http.download.nvidia.com/developer/presentations/2005/GDC/Sponsored_Day/GDC_2005_VolumeRenderingForGames.pdf/, 2005.

[Gruen 15] Holger Gruen. "Block-Wise Linear Binary Grids for Fast Ray-Casting Operations." In *GPU Pro 6: Advanced Rendering Techniques*, edited by Wolfgang Engel, pp. 489–504. Boca Raton, FL: A K Peters/CRC Press, 2015.

[Harris 04] Mark Harris. "Fast Fluid Dynamics Simulation on the GPU." In *GPU Gems*, edited by Randima Fernando, pp. 637–665. Upper Saddle River, NJ: Addison-Wesley, 2004.

[Landau and Lifschitz 82] L. D. Landau and E. M. Lifschitz. *Fluid Mechanics*, Second Edition. Oxford, UK: Pergamon Press, 1982.

[Müller et al. 03] Matthias Müller, David Charypar, and Markus Gross. "Particle-Based Fluid Simulation for Interactive Applications." In *Proceedings of the 2003 ACM SIGGRAPH/Eurographics Symposium on Computer Animation*, pp. 154–159. Aire-la-Ville, Switzerland: Eurographics Association, 2003.

[NVIDIA n.d.] NVIDIA. "GeForce GTX 980 Specifications." http://www.geforce.co.uk/hardware/desktop-gpus/geforce-gtx-980/specifications, no date.

[Pawasauskas 97] John Pawasauskas. "Volume Visualization with Ray Casting." Course notes for CS563 Advanced Topics in Computer Graphics, http://web.cs.wpi.edu/~matt/courses/cs563/talks/powwie/p1/ray-cast.htm, 1997.

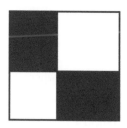

About the Editors

Marius Bjørge is a Graphics Research Engineer at ARM's office in Trondheim, Norway. Prior to ARM he worked in the games industry as part of Funcom's core engine team. He has presented research at SIGGRAPH, HPG, and GDC and is keenly interested in anything graphics-related. He's currently looking at new ways of enabling advanced real-time graphics on current and future mobile GPU technology.

Wessam Bahnassi is a software engineer and an architect (that is, for buildings not software). This combination drives Wessam's passion for 3D engine design. He has written and optimized a variety of engines throughout a decade of game development. Together with his brother Homam, they recently shipped their own company's first game, *Hyper Void*, which is a live showcase of shaders and GPU techniques (some of which are featured in previous *GPU Pro* volumes and in this volume). The game runs on PlaystationVR at natively rendered 120 FPS at 1440p.

Carsten Dachsbacher is a full professor at the Karlsruhe Institute of Technology. His research focuses on real-time computer graphics, global illumination, scientific visualization, and perceptual rendering, on which he published articles at various conferences and journals including SIGGRAPH, IEEE VIS, EG, and EGSR. He has been a tutorial speaker at SIGGRAPH, Eurographics, and the Game Developers Conference.

Wolfgang Engel is the CEO of Confetti (www.conffx.com), a think tank for advanced real-time graphics for the game and movie industry. Previously he worked for more than four years in Rockstar's core technology group as the lead graphics programmer. His game credits can be found at http://www.mobygames.com/developer/sheet/view/developerId,158706/. He is the editor of the *ShaderX* and *GPU Pro* book series, the author of many articles, and a regular speaker at computer graphics conferences worldwide. He is also a DirectX MVP (since 2006), teaches at UCSD, and is active in several advisory boards throughout the industry. You can find him on twitter at @wolfgangengel.

Christopher Oat is the Technical Director at Rockstar New England where he works on real-time rendering techniques and low-level optimizations for many of Rockstar's latest games. Previously, he was the Demo Team Lead for AMD's Game Computing Applications Group. Christopher has published his work in various books and journals and has presented at graphics and game developer conferences worldwide. Many of the projects that he has worked on can be found on his website: www.chrisoat.com.

Michal Valient leads the technology team at Guerrilla in Amsterdam. He spends his time working on the core engine technology powering the highly acclaimed *Killzone* games on PS3 and PS4 as well as some yet unannounced projects. Previously he worked as a programmer and a lead at Caligari where he developed the shader-based real-time rendering engine for Caligari trueSpace7. His interests include many aspects of light transfer, shadows, and parallel processing in general. He believes in sharing the knowledge, and he gave talks at GDC and SIGGRAPH and wrote graphics papers published in *ShaderX* books and conference journals.

About the Contributors

Homam Bahnassi is a lead technical artist with over a decade of computer graphics experience supported by a strong and wide multi-disciplined engineering background (i.e., software, robotics, and civil engineering). He has developed and published new techniques for accomplishing challenging visual effects on game consoles—some of which were embraced by the industry, like Mega Particles. For many years, he has designed and developed workflows and tools in different game engines such as Frostbite, Unreal, and Dead Space Engine, including the engine that he developed with his brother Wessam. His experience was effective in optimizing production pipelines of several AAA projects.

Sylwester Bala is an ARM software graphics engineer. In his childhood, he enjoyed building his own bikes when it was sunny and getting familiar with BASIC programming language on C64 when it was raining. As luck would have it, he lived in a rainy land. He worked in the TV broadcast industry for eight years programming real-time graphics engines. Since 2012 he has been part of ARM, and he is responsible for leading development of GPU demonstration software that incorporates the latest mobile technology with highly optimized graphics techniques on the market.

Wade Brainerd is a principal technical director at Activision, where he enjoys all kinds of graphics programming and performance optimization. He lives in Portland, Maine, with his wife and two children.

Ka Chen started his career as a 3D programmer at Ubisoft Shanghai in 1998. In 2006 he moved to Ubisoft Montreal and continued his game developing effort, focusing on graphics rendering. He has helped develop multiple games such as *F1 Championship 2000*, *Splinter Cell: Pandora Tomorrow*, *Splint Cell: Double Agent*, *Rainbow Six: Vegas*, and *Ghost Recon*. From 2011 to 2015, he took a new role as central technique architect and focused on identifying and researching advanced rendering technologies for his company. His work includes Adaptive Virtual Texturing in *Far Cry 4* and Temporal Re-Projection Rendering in *Rainbow Six: Siege*. He is currently working at EA Motive.

Patrick Cozzi is coauthor of *3D Engine Design for Virtual Globes* (2011), coeditor of *OpenGL Insights* (2012), and editor of *WebGL Insights* (2015). At Analytical Graphics, Inc., he leads the graphics development of Cesium, an open source WebGL virtual globe. He teaches "GPU Programming and Architecture" at the University of Pennsylvania, where he received a masters degree in computer science.

Jürgen Döllner is a full professor at the Hasso Plattner Institute at the University of Potsdam, where he is leading the computer graphics and visualization department. He studied mathematics and computer science at the University of Siegen, Germany and got his PhD in computer science from the University of Münster, Germany, in 1996. He also received there his habilitation degree in 2001. His major research areas are in information visualization, software visual analytics, and geospatial visual analytics. In particular, his research is focused on concepts, tools, and techniques for complex software systems and graphics-based systems. He is an author of more than 200 papers in computer graphics and visualization (for an overview of publications, see http://www.hpi3d.de). He serves as a reviewer to a number of international and national journals, conferences, and workshops.

Alex Dunn, as a developer technology engineer for NVIDIA, spends his days passionately working toward advancing real-time visual effects in games. A former graduate of Abertay University's Games Technology Course, Alex got his first taste of graphics programming on the consoles. Now working for NVIDIA, his time is spent working on developing cutting-edge programming techniques to ensure the highest quality and best player experience possible is achieved.

Mathieu Einig has a BSc in computer graphics science and is the technical lead of the PowerVR demo team at Imagination Technologies. He has a passion for generating pretty pixels in real time and has strong interests in real-time raytracing, computer vision, and augmented reality.

Takahiro Harada is a researcher and the architect of a GPU global illumination renderer called Firerender at AMD. He developed Forward+ and the GPU rigid body simulation solver that is used as a base of Bullet 3.0. Before joining AMD, he engaged in research and development on real-time physics simulation on PC and game consoles at Havok. Before coming to the industry, he was in academia as an assistant professor at the University of Tokyo, where he also earned his PhD in engineering.

Tomasz Janczak is a principal engineer working at the Intel Corporation site located in Gdansk, Poland. His professional work focuses on analyzing and modeling new 3D rendering features for the upcoming processor graphics products, covering both software and hardware aspects. He received his PhD in 2004 and has authored a number of technical papers, as well as several patent applications. In his private life, he enjoys traveling around the world with his family and visiting places of diverse cultures and climates.

Dave Kotfis is a software engineer and is pursuing a master's degree in robotics at the University of Pennsylvania. He also competes in the DARPA Robotics Challenge. His research interests include augmented reality, artificial intelligence, and virtual worlds. He has a passion for tackling hard research problems.

Daniel Limberger is a PhD student at the Hasso Plattner Institute at the University of Potsdam. His research interests include interactive image processing and stylization, rendering system design and architecture, and visualization of massive, multi-dimensional data in real time. He has been involved as a graphics engineer in the industry for over ten years and lately manages the development of various open-source graphics libraries, applications, and services (https://github.com/cginternals).

Johannes Linke received his BA in IT systems engineering in 2014 at the Hasso Plattner Institute in Potsdam, Germany. After interning at the rendering department of Unity Technologies, he joined the Master program at said institute, specializing in real-time rendering and GPU computing.

Roberto Lopez Mendez is an ARM software graphics engineer. He studied nuclear physics at university, but after a decade working in physics research, he discovered his real passion and since 1995 has been working in 3D graphics for a variety of companies. In 2012 Roberto joined the ARM Demo Team. Since then he has been developing optimized rendering techniques for mobile devices, creating demos that show the capabilities of the latest ARM Mali GPUs. He also regularly delivers workshops at different universities and presents at game-related events.

Anton Kai Michels, while studying computer science at Concordia University, entered a game design competition with fellow students Zoe Briscoe, Kirsty Beaton, Joel Daignault, and Nicolas Cattanéo. Their game *Panopticon* earned them all internships at Ubisoft Montreal, after which Anton was hired fulltime as a graphics programmer on *Rainbow Six: Siege*. He later left Ubisoft to join a talented research-and-development team at Eidos Montreal, where he devised novel rendering techniques for *Tomb Raider*, *Deus Ex*, and *Hitman*. He is now the rendering lead at DICE LA.

Morten S. Mikkelsen has had graphics as his hobby for more than a quarter of a century and has been an industry professional for 16 years. He was with IO-Interactive for seven years and with the ICE team at Naughty Dog for almost five years. More recently, he was the lead/principal graphics programmer on *Rise of the Tomb Raider*. He has a double major in mathematics and computer science from the University of Copenhagen and a master's in computer science. Today he is a director of graphics at Unity Technologies Lab in San Francisco.

Krzysztof Narkowicz worked for more than 10 years as an engine programmer with a very strong focus on graphics. Currently he is the Lead Engine Programmer at Flying Wild Hog. He loves working with artists, coding graphics, and coding "close to metal."

Gustavo Bastos Nunes is a graphics engineer in the Engine team at Microsoft Turn 10 Studios. He received his BSc in computer engineering and MSc in computer graphics from Pontifícia Universidade Católica do Rio de Janeiro, Brazil. He has several articles published in the computer graphics field. He is passionate about everything real-time graphics related. Gustavo was part of the teams that shipped Microsoft Office 2013, Xbox One, *Forza Motorsport 5*, *Forza Horizon 2*, and *Forza Motorsport 6*.

Kevin Örtegren is a junior graphics programmer in the core technology team at Guerrilla Games, where he works on the rendering engine that brings the world of *Horizon: Zero Dawn* to life on the Playstation 4. Kevin started out his graphics programming career by pursuing a master's degree in games and software development at Blekinge Institute of Technology, where he wrote his master's thesis at Avalanche Studios.

Emil Persson is the Head of Research at Avalanche Studios, where he is conducting forward-looking research, with the aim to be relevant and practical for game development, as well as setting the future direction for the Avalanche Engine. Previously, he was an ISV Engineer in the Developer Relations team at ATI/AMD. He assisted tier-one game developers with the latest rendering techniques, identifying performance problems and applying optimizations. He also made major contributions to SDK samples and technical documentation.

Rahul P. Sathe works as a senior software engineer at Intel Corporation. His current role involves defining and prototyping the next-generation technologies in Intel Graphics Performance Analyzer. Prior to this role, he worked in various capacities in research and product groups at Intel. He is passionate about all aspects of 3D graphics and its hardware underpinnings. He holds several patents in rendering and game physics. Prior to joining Intel, he studied at Clemson University and University of Mumbai. While not working on the rendering-related things, he likes running and enjoying good food with his family and friends.

Christoph Schied is a scientific researcher at the computer graphics group at Karlsruhe Institute of Technology (KIT), working on his PhD. He received his diploma with honors from Ulm University in 2013. His research interests include real-time rendering pipelines, antialiasing, and global illumination.

Andrew Schneider is the Principal FX Artist at Guerrilla Games in Amsterdam. In addition to developing effects solutions, his focus is developing the real-time volumetric cloud system for *Horizon: Zero Dawn*. He has presented this work at SIGGRAPH 2015 as part of the "Advances in Real-Time Rendering" course. Previously, he was a Senior FX Technical Director at Blue Sky animation studios in Greenwich, Connecticut, where his focus was developing the volumetrics pipeline, SmogVox, for use with rendering fluid effects, billion+ fine particle renders, and clouds. This work was presented as production talks at SIGGRAPH 2011, 2012, and 2013. He completed his bachelor's degree in computer art and visual effects at the Savannah College of Art and Design in 2005.

Peter Sikachev graduated from Lomonosov Moscow State University in 2009, majoring in applied mathematics and computer science. He started his career game development in 2011 at Mail.Ru Games as a graphics programmer. He contributed to a range of rendering features of the *Skyforge* next-generation MMORPG. In 2013 he joined Eidos Montreal as a research-and-development graphics programmer. He helped ship *Thief* and *Rise of the Tomb Raider* and contributed to *Deus Ex: Universe*. Peter has been an author of multiple entries in the *GPU Pro* series and a speaker at ACM SIGGRAPH courses. He now holds a senior graphics programmer position at Rockstar Toronto.

Ashley Vaughan Smith is a leading applications engineer at Imagination Technologies and works on creating graphical and compute demos showcasing PowerVR. With a BSc in computer games programming and having worked in the games industry, he enjoys investigating up-coming technologies and graphical techniques, currently including Vulkan and ray tracing.

Karsten Tausche is a student at the Hasso Plattner Institute, enrolled in the Master program of IT systems engineering, focusing on visualization techniques and GPU computing.

T - #0756 - 101024 - C320 - 235/191/14 [16] - CB - 9781498742535 - Gloss Lamination